# Grieve Not For Wrightsie

# Grieve Not For Wrightsie

by

**Nancy M. (Harkins) Brunson**

with

**Commander W.A. Brunson,**
USN (Retired)

**LOGOS INTERNATIONAL**
**Plainfield, New Jersey**

In a few instances names have been changed and/or specific identities omitted in order to protect individual privacy.

## DEDICATION

This book is dedicated with love to my daughter Beth.

Her deep love for her brother, her quiet courage and strong Christian faith have blessed my heart and soul.

# CONTENTS

# Acknowledgments

Throughout my life the Lord has sent many wonderful people to minister to me. This was particularly true during the period that began with my son's illness and ended with the publication of this book. I wish to acknowledge the loving care of these people.

First, I want to thank my dear husband, Wright, for his love and perseverance, and for understanding my urgency to share our story. I also wish to thank our families for their love, prayers, deep concern and understanding.

Next, I want to express my sincerest appreciation to our many neighbors, friends—military and civilian—and my son's and daughter's teachers and schoolmates for their great help and gentle understanding. And I offer a particular thanks to all those involved with the Boy Scouts of America, especially Wrightsie's den mother, Shirley Pylant.

I also owe a great debt of gratitude to those in the medical profession and the clergy who attended to my family and me. In those rare instances where an unfortunate incident occurred, I can only attribute it to the pressures of the situation, and to the human frustrations experienced by compassionate people working in demanding professions.

As for the book itself, I owe particular thanks also to Jackie Casey, Karen Cartier, and Tracy Brunson. Jackie's prayers and constant encouragement were an ever present source of strength; Karen's typing skills were exceeded only by her sound advice and warm friendship; and Tracy's enthusiasm and sincere concern was instrumental in bringing our book to publication. I wish also to thank Dan and Viola Malachuk and Lloyd Hildebrand at Logos International Fellowship, Inc., for their gentle patience, perception, and expertise. I also offer my deepest thanks and appreciation to our families and friends who have so graciously shared their thoughts, their feelings and their experiences as written within the pages of this book.

Above all else, I prayerfully thank God for His very special gift of children. How often His little ones touch our hearts and bring us to Jesus Christ.

"O give thanks unto the Lord; for he is good: because his mercy endureth forever" (Ps. 118:1).

# Preface

As I look back, I'm amazed at the events that have led to the writing of this book. It began when Floss, my husband's mother, came down to Texas to help us during Wrightsie's illness. Floss had kept a journal for most of her life. Each night before bedtime, I noticed she wrote down the day's events. I remember thinking, "I should keep a journal too." Then with a heavy heart I told myself, "No, I won't want to remember these days."

However, one evening Floss read to me from her journal about a heartwarming breakthrough Wrightsie had had the previous week. I was disappointed when I discovered I'd already forgotten the incident. And I thought, "I do want to remember." With that thought my journal keeping began.

Much later, using my journal as an outline, I wrote my story in narrative form for my own comfort. About the same time, my husband, Wright, our daughter, Beth, and I participated in a number of Faith Alive Weekends at various Episcopal churches in Texas. Often after I'd told my story, I was approached by someone saying something like, "Oh, you should write a book about your experiences. I know a woman whose child is seriously ill, and she needs to know what Jesus has done in your life."

This encouragement, along with an urgent desire to help those who have gone, are going, or will go through the experience my family and I survived, led me to write the book.

Then, as the Lord would have it, Logos International Fellowship, Inc., sponsored a Christian writing seminar at Christ for the Nations in Dallas. My husband and I attended the intensive writing course. Subsequently, using my journal and narrative story for reference, my husband and I began to write in earnest. The months slipped into years and many, many prayers later, we completed our task.

It is now my sincerest prayer that all who read this book will, in their hours of need, experience—as my family and I did—the supernatural love and mercy of Jesus Christ. And further, I pray that they will be most assured that they and their loved ones both in heaven and on earth are eternally provided for by our precious Savior Jesus Christ.

In His love,

*Nancy M. Harkins Brunson*

Nancy M. (Harkins) Brunson

# Grieve Not For Wrightsie

# 1

## I Wanted Him to Be Perfect

"Mom, should I sign my birthday thank-you note to Mary, 'Love, Wrightsie,' or just, 'Your friend, Wrightsie'?" my eight-year-old son asked, looking up from the kitchen table.

"For Mary you can use, 'Love,' " I answered with an approving smile.

"Okay," he said, as a little shy, embarrassed grin spread across his face.

And again, for the second or third time that morning, I noticed something unusual about his smile, but I couldn't pinpoint the difference. Then I realized what was wrong: only the right side of his face crinkled into his familiar broad, sunny grin. The left side was expressionless.

"You know, Wrightsie, you're getting into a funny little habit there," I cautioned.

"I'm not doing anything, mom," he answered in a quick, defensive manner. "And besides my head feels kinda numb." And he rubbed the left side of his forehead.

Our conversation had caught my husband, Wright's, attention. "Wrightsie," he said, as he lowered the Sunday paper to the kitchen table, "give me a big grin."

Wrightsie tried to force a big smile but the left side of his face did not respond.

My husband got up from his chair and pulled a table fork from the kitchen drawer. He knelt before Wrightsie and explained, "Son, I'm going to touch each side of your forehead with this fork. Let me know if you feel any difference."

He touched the tines to Wrightsie's forehead, first on one side, then the other. "Any difference?" he asked.

"I feel it more on this side," Wrightsie replied, touching the right side of his forehead.

My husband repeated the test several times with the same results. Then he said, "Wrightsie, you told mom your head was numb. Show me where."

Wrightsie's forefinger traced out an area from over his left eyebrow to halfway down and around his left cheek. Then, my husband startled Wrightsie by snapping his thumb and finger directly in front of his son's nose. Wrightsie's right eye blinked closed, but his left eye remained open.

My husband stood up, turned to me and shook his head with a worried look. Then I was really frightened. I hurried to the kitchen wall phone announcing, "I want a doctor to see him; I'm going to call Carswell." I quickly dialed the number for the hospital at Carswell Air Force Base in nearby Fort Worth, Texas.

Immediately I asked if a doctor could see Wrightsie that day. They assured me that the physician-on-duty would be able to see him and I felt greatly relieved.

It didn't take our daughter, Beth, Wrightsie, my husband and me long to get into the car. When we arrived at the hospital—after a twenty-five-minute drive—my husband saw us to the waiting room and then hurried over to the admissions desk.

After giving the clerk the necessary information, Wright joined us in the waiting room. It wasn't long before we heard our name announced over the loudspeaker. Beth decided to stay in the waiting room and the rest of us walked into the emergency room. The medic met us and took us to a small, canvas-enclosed examination room.

A few minutes later, the doctor came in and we introduced ourselves. Then he turned to Wrightsie and said, "And what's your name, young man?"

Wrightsie, sitting on the examining table, squared his shoulders and announced, "Wright Abel Brunson."

"Well, Wright Abel, let's have a look at you. What seems to be the trouble?"

My husband and I explained the circumstances as the doctor started the familiar physical routine: blood pressure, ears, throat, reflexes and so on. He nodded approval after each test and I began to relax a little. But when he looked puzzled as he checked Wrightsie's face and forehead, my fear and worry returned.

"I'd like to take some skull x-rays," the doctor said, turning to Wright and me. "You can stay here. I'll have the medic take him down to x-ray. We'll develop the pictures right away and take a look."

They returned in about thirty minutes. Wright lifted Wrightsie to the examining table and I helped him dress. Meanwhile, the doctor placed the x-rays on a fluorescent screen and began to study the film. Wrightsie chuckled when he saw the outline of his skull.

"Well, it looks like Bell's palsy to me," the doctor said as he flipped off the fluorescent light. "I didn't see anything on the x-rays, but then I really didn't expect to. This sort of condition is caused by an infection behind the ear—in Wright Abel's case, the left ear. Swelling caused by the infection has pinched the nerve serving the left side of his face. But it should clear up in four to six weeks."

I breathed a sigh of relief. "Is there anything we can do?"

"No," the doctor replied. "But since there's nerve involvement I would like a neurologist to see him—tomorrow if possible."

Wright and I nodded our approval.

"Fine," the doctor said. "I'll set you up with a nine o'clock appointment."

We thanked the doctor, picked up Beth in the waiting room and left the hospital. There wasn't much conversation on the way home to Arlington. Wright concentrated on his driving, Beth and Wrightsie read some books they'd brought along, and I tried to unwind. I was relieved and I was sure the visit to the neurologist on Monday would be routine.

The next day my husband took off from work. On active duty with the U.S. Navy, Wright was assigned to the Naval Plant Representative Office in Dallas. After we saw Beth off to school, Wright, Wrightsie and I drove back to Carswell. We found the neurologist's office on the fifth floor of the hospital, waited our turn, and before long Wrightsie was seen by the doctor.

He gave Wrightsie a very thorough examination. Then he said, "Yes, it's Bell's palsy. We don't see this in a child very often, but it can happen. He's picked up an infection somewhere. Do you have a window air conditioner?"

"No," I answered.

"Well, anyway," the doctor continued, "sometimes this happens when a person sleeps too close to an air conditioner or is exposed to a cold draft."

Then recalling what the doctor had said the day before, I asked, "How long before he'll recover from this, doctor?"

"I'd say around four to five weeks; in ninety-five percent of the cases it lasts that long," the doctor replied.

"What about the other five percent, doctor?" Wright asked.

"Well, there have been a few cases where the affected nerves and muscles never fully recovered. And that results in a slight drooping at the corner of the mouth. But only a neurologist or someone familiar with the problem would recognize it," he answered.

"But, doctor," I exclaimed, "I wanted him to be perfect!"

"Don't worry, Mrs. Brunson, he is perfect," the neurologist said in a convincing voice.

Next the doctor scribbled a note on a prescription pad and said, "If you'll take this down to the pharmacy, they'll give you an eye patch. Since the blinking reflex isn't working in his left eye, I want it protected. Have him wear it when he's playing outdoors."

I took the prescription and glanced over at Wrightsie to see his reaction; I just knew he'd be thinking about playing pirate with his eye patch. Sure enough, the anticipation was written all over his face.

The doctor continued, "And I'd like to see him next Monday, just to check his progress."

"Fine," I replied.

The doctor saw us to the door and said, "Now don't worry, Mrs. Brunson, and I'll see you at 9:00 A.M. a week from today. Goodbye."

"Goodbye, doctor, and thank you very much," I replied.

The doctor's reassuring words and manner had dispelled most of my fears. But still I had a lingering sense of uneasiness.

# 2
## I'll Get the Troops Together

I took Wrightsie back to Carswell the next Monday as scheduled, and there was no change in his condition. But then one evening a few days later, Wright noticed Wrightsie cocking his head to one side while he watched TV.

"Wrightsie," he asked, "why are you holding your head like that?"

Wrightsie seemed somewhat confused by this question. Wondering if his son's hearing was impaired, Wright tested both ears twice. Both times Wrightsie reported he was unable to hear with his left ear.

The next morning I called the neurologist at Carswell. He didn't seem alarmed by Wrightsie's hearing loss, but he did refer us to an ear, nose and throat specialist who gave us an appointment that afternoon. Before leaving for Carswell I ran next door to see my neighbor, Evelyn Fox. She agreed to check on Beth after school.

After the ENT specialist at Carswell examined Wrightsie, he sent him to physiotherapy for the first of what was to be an everyday facial muscle test. Then we went to the pharmacy to fill a prescription the doctor had ordered.

When we returned to Arlington, I dropped Wrightsie off at his Cub Scout meeting, drove to the house and walked next door to tell Evelyn I was home.

"Hi, Nan," she greeted me. "How 'bout a cup of coffee? What'd the doctor say?"

"Sure," I answered. "I've got a few minutes before I have to start supper. Oh, he didn't think the hearing loss was unusual in the case of Bell's palsy. But Wrightsie has to have a daily facial check for the next week or so."

"Are you worried, Nan?"

"No, not really," I answered. "You know, Evelyn, ever since Wrightsie came down with this, I've heard about a lot of people who've had Bell's palsy, and in every case, they've had a complete recovery."

"Yes," Evelyn answered. "In fact I know a little girl up the street—I'm sure she goes to Hill School with Wrightsie—who had the same thing about a year ago. Her folks took her to a neurologist in Dallas. She's fine now."

"Well, I guess that's why I'm not worried," I said. "Also, the other night, Wright and I called a husband-and-wife doctor team we knew when we were stationed in Japan. Didn't I tell you about Marie-Louise and Kenneth Johnson?"

"No," Evelyn shook her head.

"They both worked at the Atomic Bomb Casualty Commission Hospital in Hiroshima; Doctor Ken was chief of medicine and Doctor Marie-Louise was the dermatologist.

"You see, we found out Beth had a dermatology problem just before we left for Japan," I explained. "And a stateside doctor recommended we look up Marie-Louise when we arrived in Japan.

"We did. And she treated Beth while we were over there. Then we all left Japan about the same time. The Johnsons returned to New York City and we went to Virginia. But Marie-Louise wanted to keep track of Beth, so whenever we visited my folks in Danbury, Connecticut, near New York, we always stopped to see Marie-Louise.

7

"She thinks the world of Beth, so we decided to call and tell them about her brother."

"Did they seem concerned?" Evelyn asked.

"Oh, yes," I answered. "But not worried. They do want us to keep in touch with them. But they're going back to Japan for a visit, so they gave us the name of a friend who is a doctor at Johns Hopkins in Baltimore. We're to call him if we need any advice while they're in Japan. So you see, Evelyn, we've got help if we need it."

"Oh, good," she answered.

"Hey, Evelyn, it's getting late," I said, noticing the time on her wall clock. "I've got to get supper ready. See ya later."

"Listen, Nan," she said, "let me know if I can help you in any way at all."

"Thanks, Evelyn," I answered. "I will."

During supper I told Wright about the day's events, including my talk with Evelyn. In the course of our conversation, he mentioned that he had called Commander Carl Wilgus in Washington, his friend from graduate school.

Wright wasn't sure why he called Carl, but he told his friend about Wrightsie's problem and when he had finished Carl said, "I'll get the troops together and we'll pray for his healing."

Wright continued, "Carl asked me to call him back when Wrightsie's okay. Get that? When Wrightsie's okay."

Wrightsie turned to me and with a smile nodded his approval of Carl's optimism.

# 3

## *It's a Rotten Ball Game!*

But Wrightsie didn't improve. If anything, his condition worsened. Finally on Friday morning, November 12, almost four weeks since we'd first taken Wrightsie to the Air Force doctor, my patience ended. I wanted a second opinion.

Remembering Evelyn's recommendation of a neurologist in Dallas, I got the doctor's name and called him. After I explained the situation, he said, "If you can get your son here by 10:00 A.M., I'll see him."

Because of the distance between Arlington and Dallas, it was impossible to get there by that time. I asked the doctor if Wrightsie could have an afternoon appointment instead. He explained that he had to meet his sister-in-law at the airport during the afternoon so he would be off for the rest of the day.

Although I was very disappointed, I settled for a Monday morning appointment. Later I was to discover the doctor's reason for being off that afternoon.

Wright and I had planned to attend a Dallas Cowboys-Philadelphia Eagles football game on Sunday. The officers at Wright's office had planned the outing weeks before. I decided I'd stay home with Beth who had a sore throat. Everything worked out for the best. Wrightsie got to go to his first pro football game with his dad, and Beth and I had a fun time at home.

"How'd it go?" I asked when they returned late in the afternoon.

"Great, just great!" my husband replied. "We had a wonderful time. Didn't we, Wrightsie?"

"Yeah, mom! And the Cowboys won, too!" Wrightsie responded enthusiastically. "Dad bought us two Cowboy flags and two boxes of popcorn."

"Naturally," I laughed. They both loved popcorn.

"Yes, and I guess I loaded us up too much before we got to the stadium," my husband explained. "Wrightsie had trouble with the escalator. He had one arm wrapped around this big box of popcorn, and he held his Cowboy pennant in the other hand. When we got to the escalator he couldn't judge when to step on. So, we climbed the stairs instead. It was a long climb; our seats were way up over the end zone. And Wrightsie said he felt dizzy a couple of times during the game."

"How do you feel now, Wrightsie?" I asked.

"Oh, fine, mom," he replied.

"Nan, I think it's the eye patch," Wright assured me. "His depth perception isn't too good with one eye covered. That caused the problems on the escalator. And our seats were so high up I almost felt dizzy myself."

"How's Bethy?" Wrightsie asked.

"Would you believe she's fine now," I answered. "After you left for the game I called Carswell and they wanted to see her. So, we drove out and then on the way home her sore throat cleared up—completely. She's perfect now."

Wrightsie ran into the den to see his sister and Wright walked over and put his arm around my shoulders, "Nan, thanks for giving up your ticket. We really had a good time."

"Oh, come on," I replied. "I wouldn't have gone anyway what with Beth not feeling well. And besides I think you were supposed to go with Wrightsie."

We planned to start out early for Carswell the next morning to pick up Wrightsie's medical records to take to Dallas with us. Wright and I were still asleep when our bedroom door banged open. Wright, startled awake by the noise, raised up on one elbow and saw Wrightsie weaving his way to our bed.

Just as he asked Wrightsie what his problem was, he stumbled and fell hard on the carpeting, face first. Before we could get to him, he picked himself up and struggled to the bed.

"I don't feel good," he cried in a pleading voice. "My stomach hurts and I'm dizzy."

I put my arms around him. "Oh, Wrightsie, you're going to be all right. We're going to see another doctor today." I tried to sound reassuring, but I didn't believe what I was saying. It'd been almost four weeks since his first symptoms and now he was worse than ever. And I was more than worried. I was scared. I tucked Wrightsie into our bed and said, "Try to get a little more sleep, Wrightsie—before we go to the doctor's."

For some reason we got a late start. We were rushing around the various clinics picking up Wrightsie's records, when, quite unexpectedly, we ran into the Air Force neurologist. The doctor asked how Wrightsie was doing and we told him about the early morning fall. The doctor took us into a nearby waiting room and gave Wrightsie a hurried examination. He encouraged us to admit Wrightsie to the hospital.

"But, doctor," my husband explained, "we're on our way to Dallas. We'd like a neurologist there to see him."

"All right. But I'd admit him right now," the doctor repeated.

It was after 9:00 A.M. before we rounded up all the records and it was a good forty-five-minute drive to Dallas. We literally ran to the car and headed for the Dallas-Fort Worth Turnpike. We exited from the turnpike and then Wright turned off into a downtown Dallas area. We were lost!

I pleaded with him to ask for directions. What a nightmare! It was already past ten o'clock and we were driving all over with no idea of how to get to the doctor's office. Finally, Wright pulled into a gas station. He asked the attendant for directions and within minutes we pulled up to the medical building. While Wright looked for a parking place, Wrightsie and I hurried down the hallway. I found the neurologist's office and introduced myself to his receptionist.

Wrightsie and I sat down, and in a few minutes Wright walked into the waiting room carrying Wrightsie's records and x-rays. After a brief wait, the neurologist came in, wearing a fresh white lab coat.

He asked us to take Wrightsie into the examining room. We then introduced ourselves and the familiar neurological examination began.

When he'd finished, the doctor looked up, and without any preliminaries he said, "He should be admitted." Wright and I both nodded our acceptance, and the doctor directed Wright to go to the admissions office at a nearby hospital while his secretary made arrangements for a bed. It all seemed so sudden. Yet I felt a sense of relief. "Now they'll find out what's wrong with Wrightsie," I thought to myself.

Wrightsie's hospital room was bright and cheerful, and decorated to please the eye of a child. By the time my husband returned from the admissions office I'd tucked Wrightsie into bed, and the TV set was on. Wright and I were still trying to collect our thoughts when the doctor walked into the room.

"Everything all right?" he asked.

"Yes, fine," I replied.

"I've scheduled your son for a brain scan tomorrow morning," the doctor said as he walked over to the bed. Then, softening his professional tone, he looked down at Wrightsie and said, "You look comfortable, son. Just rest and I'm sure you'll feel better." Wrightsie acknowledged with a weak smile.

Turning to me the doctor said, "Mrs. Brunson, you can stay with your son if you like. That chair," he motioned to a brown leather chair next to the window, "makes down into a single bed."

"Oh, thank you, doctor," I answered. "I do want to stay with him."

"Fine," the doctor replied. "I'll see you tomorrow. I plan to meet you for the brain scan."

After the doctor left, I gave my husband a list of the things we would need. Then, as Wright was leaving for Arlington he said, "Nan, I'm going to tell the head nurse you're a registered nurse."

"Oh, Wright, I wish you wouldn't. It's been so long since I've worked. They might expect—"

"That doesn't make any difference," Wright interrupted. "If they know you're an R.N. I'm sure they'll let you help with Wrightsie."

I agreed with some reluctance, and Wright seemed pleased. He told me that he would ask for the morning off so he could be with us for the brain scan.

Wrightsie and I watched TV awhile, then he dropped off to sleep. I sat in a comfortable chair in the room and alternately planned and worried. I hadn't realized I was so tired and before I knew it I'd dozed off.

When we had entered the hospital, Wrightsie had noticed a doctor's bag in the window of the gift shop. He startled me awake by asking if we could go to the shop.

The head nurse gave us a wheelchair to use. I got Wrightsie situated and we went down to the first floor. I surprised him by buying the doctor's bag.

Wrightsie asked me to push him slowly around the small shop because he wanted to buy something for Beth. He decided to get her a package of colored felt-tip pens, some gum and a roll of candy. He told me he would pay for them. I picked out the items, and, at the counter, I noticed Wrightsie was having difficulty holding his head up.

"You okay?" I asked.

He tried to nod his head, but couldn't. I took hold of him, and with one hand I held him in a sitting position, and with the other I pushed the wheelchair back to the elevator. When we returned to the room, I tucked him into bed and soon he was asleep.

He awakened in time for supper and then about 6:00 P.M. Wright walked in the room. "There," he said, placing a suitcase on the floor. "I think I brought everything you'll need."

"I should hope so," I answered with a smile when I saw he'd brought my largest blue suitcase. Then I asked, "Where's Beth?"

Wright explained that the receptionist had informed him of the hospital's rule that visitors under the age of twelve were not permitted to see a patient. Since Beth was only eleven, she had to wait in the lobby.

Next, he walked over to the bed and said, "Wrightsie, this is for you." And he flipped Wrightsie's favorite stuffed animal from behind his back.

"Tigeree!" Wrightsie exclaimed, as he wrapped his arm around the little tiger's well-worn neck. Tigeree had shared Wrightsie's triumphs and trials through the years. He even had an old Band-Aid on one paw. I'd stuck it there many months before to correspond with the bandage Wrightsie had had on his big toe after accidently dropping a manhole cover on his foot.

Wright suggested that we go down to the lobby to see Beth, and Wrightsie responded to the idea with enthusiasm. Beth was delighted to see her brother and as she put down her school work she asked Wrightsie if he would like to play some of the games she brought along.

14

They played for ten or fifteen minutes while Wright and I chatted. Then I heard Wrightsie tell his sister that he was tired. He turned to me and asked if he could go back to his room. Once we returned to the room, Wrightsie fell asleep before we even had time to say prayers.

"I'm worried about how tired he gets," I said to Wright.

"Oh, he always has been able to fall asleep fast," Wright answered.

"I know, but this isn't right."

"Well, he's had a busy day and I'm tired too, and I imagine you are. We all need a good night's rest."

"You're right," I agreed.

"Well, I'd better get Beth home. We'll be up here around nine o'clock tomorrow morning."

"I'm glad Beth will be here," I said. "Since she's had a brain scan at Bethesda Naval Hospital she might make Wrightsie feel better."

"Yes," Wright agreed. "It's a good idea."

"Well, see you early tomorrow. Good night, hon."

The next morning, Wright, Beth and I accompanied Wrightsie. As we waited our turn in a crowded hallway, Beth said, "Wrightsie, don't worry 'bout a thing. I remember my brain scan at Bethesda. They'll give you a little shot, then you'll lay on a table and they'll lower a big machine over your head. It'll start to hum, and in a little minute it's all over. Don't worry."

"I won't, Bethy," Wrightsie said in a thankful tone of voice.

We waited an hour before it was Wrightsie's turn. The neurologist arrived to observe the test. He let Beth sit beside Wrightsie during the procedure. The doctor scooted his chair up beside Beth's, put his arm around her shoulder and spoke a few words of encouragement.

After the brain scan, Beth stayed in the lobby while Wright and I waited with Wrightsie in his room for the results of his test. I suppose it was an hour before the neurologist came to the room. As he motioned for us to step into the hallway, I searched his face, but his expression revealed nothing. I asked the doctor the results of the test and he said they were inconclusive. He then told us that he had scheduled a pneumo-encephalogram for the next day.

Then, almost as if someone else were speaking I exclaimed in a professional tone of voice, "Doctor! You're not looking for a brain tumor, are you?"

"Yes, I am," he replied reluctantly.

Suddenly, I was utterly and completely broken.

"I wouldn't have told you unless you'd asked," the neurologist continued in an apologetic voice. "You see, I know how you feel; we're comrades of a sort. That's why I couldn't see your son last Friday; my sister-in-law flew down here to help me care for my wife. She is critically ill."

Then with a look of compassionate despair he said, "It's a rotten ball game!"

I stood in stunned silence as he turned and retreated quickly down the corridor.

# 4
## *Oh, Tom Terrific!*

I still couldn't believe I'd asked the question, much less heard the answer. A feeling of numbness and isolation came over me. This was followed by the thought, "There is hope. The doctor hasn't found a brain tumor. He's only looking for one."

But I wasn't encouraged by my thought. Then I felt Wright's hand on my shoulder, gently urging me back into the hospital room. Wrightsie was watching TV, and Wright walked over to the set and turned up the volume so he couldn't overhear our conversation.

"One thing I'm sure of," I said, "we won't tell Wrightsie."

Wright nodded his head in agreement.

"And let's not say anything to Beth," I suggested. "At least not now."

Again Wright nodded.

Then he said, "Nan, I'd better go to the office and check out on emergency leave. I'll be back as soon as I can."

"What about Beth?" I asked.

"Oh, that's right," he answered. "Well, I think I'll take her back to Arlington, see if Evelyn Fox will look after her, then I'll go to the office. Okay?"

"Yes," I answered. "And tell Beth I'll call her later at the Foxes'."

Wright walked over to the bed, "See ya later, best buddy. Take care of mom 'til I get back."

Wrightsie answered with his little lopsided smile.

Wright and I walked into the hall together, and tears began to flood my eyes. I looked up at Wright and said, "What are we going to do?"

"I don't know, Nan," he answered, shaking his head. "I don't know."

I noticed tears in his eyes too. Then he turned and started for the waiting room to pick up Beth.

Later that afternoon, the neurologist came back to the room. He examined Wrightsie and then motioned for me to follow him out of the room. He told me again about the test he had scheduled for the next day. He explained the procedure in detail and told me, "If there is a tumor, we should be able to see it on x-ray." When he finished his explanation I nodded my understanding. A shudder ran through me from the realization that the test was difficult and dangerous.

Later, about five o'clock, Wright returned to the hospital. He told me that the captain gave him a leave of two weeks or longer if necessary. I had called Evelyn Fox earlier and I was able to tell Wright that she had agreed to look after Beth.

Then I learned that Wright had made some calls. He had called Saint Alban's Episcopal Church in Arlington to ask the priest to visit us. And I was surprised to learn that he had also called Carl Wilgus again.

"What did Carl say?" I asked.

"His first reaction was, 'Oh, no!', but after that he talked to me a long time about religion and healing," Wright explained. "He finally ended with a prayer for you and Beth and me, and then he asked the Lord to heal Wrightsie."

"Well, isn't it funny you'd call him again," I commented.

"Oh, and he said something else. He knew of a man in Dallas who's a member of the local chapter of the Full Gospel

Business Men's something or other. He couldn't recall the man's name, but he said he'd find out and have the man come over to the hospital to see us.

"I hope you don't mind?" Wright asked.

"No," I replied, "it certainly won't hurt us."

"Carl also said he's going to mail us a couple of books. He said the books explain some things he'd like to have said to me back in Washington. But he didn't feel my mind was open then. He was gentle with me and I appreciated his concern," Wright explained.

"He must be a wonderful man," I said.

"Well," Wright continued, "I don't know if I agree with his form of Christianity but he's a fine, fine person."

After checking his watch, Wright suggested that I call my folks in Danbury, Connecticut. I walked down the hall to a pay phone so Wrightsie couldn't hear my conversation. I placed the call to Connecticut and in a moment my mother answered. Concerned about her chronic heart condition, I asked her to sit down.

Then when I heard my father pick up the extension, I said, "Well, I've got something to tell you—brace yourselves. I'm calling from a hospital in Dallas. Wrightsie's been admitted and the doctor thinks he may have a brain tumor."

"Nan! You don't mean it!" mother exclaimed.

"Oh! No!" dad responded.

"Yes, I'm afraid so," and I heard my voice waver. Then I explained the whole situation.

"We'll fly down tomorrow morning," dad said.

We talked this over a minute and then I agreed. "Okay, Wright will meet you at Love Field. Call us back later and tell us what flight you'll be on. Oh, and please call Tom and tell him."

The plans were made and then dad asked, "How are you doing, Nan?"

"I don't know—oh, I guess I'm all right," I answered. "I just can't believe this horrible thing is happening."

With that we said our goodbyes and I went back to Wrightsie's room.

Wright and I said our usual bedtime prayer with Wrightsie. "Now I lay me down to sleep. . . ." Wrightsie dropped off to sleep quickly. And then in a hushed voice I began to tell Wright about the conversation with my folks. I heard a soft knock on the door. The floor nurse stuck her head around the door and said, "Mrs. Brunson, there's a long distance call from Huntington, Long Island, for you at the nurses' station."

It was my brother, Tom. He had just talked with mom and dad, and they'd all decided it would be best if he came to Dallas instead of them. I agreed. How grateful I was for my big brother.

Next, I called my younger sister, Kathy, in San Francisco where she worked as a registered nurse. She was shocked by the news and towards the end of our conversation she offered to seek medical advice from the doctors she knew.

About noon the next day, Tom walked into the room. "Hi, everybody. Hi, Wrightsie," he said, walking over to the bed. His enthusiasm and optimism filled the room.

"Oh, Tom Terrific!" Wrightsie beamed, using his favorite term for his uncle. "I'm so glad you're here."

"Nan, you look good," he said, giving me a big hug. Then he shook hands with Wright. I felt refreshed and relieved. Tom's good-natured confidence was a tonic. I think we all needed him.

And then, too soon, Wrightsie was wheeled out of the room for his test. Tom, Wright and I waited in the room. For the next two hours Wright paced the floor while Tom and I nervously talked a mile-a-minute about anything and everything.

The doctor finally came to let us know that Wrightsie was in the recovery room. Then anticipating my question, the doctor said, "We didn't find anything." I didn't know how to feel about the information. But I did know there'd be more tests so I asked him what would happen next.

The doctor explained that there would be another series of x-rays the next day. If nothing showed up from them, an arteriogram would be necessary. He explained the purpose and procedures involved with such a test. Again, I shuddered as I realized the dangers.

The doctor tried to give us a realistic understanding of Wrightsie's condition. He encouraged us not to be extremely pessimistic or optimistic, realizing that something was causing the problem. He was very determined to discover the cause.

They wheeled Wrightsie back to the room about three-thirty that afternoon. Tigeree was accompanying him on the stretcher. I helped as the nurses put Wrightsie into his bed. I noticed he wore a Band-Aid low on the middle of his back and I thought, "Oh, they must have taken a spinal tap."

Then, when I placed Tigeree beside Wrightsie, I noticed he also had a new Band-Aid on his back. A thoughtful nurse must have put it there after the procedure.

While Wrightsie rested, Tom, Wright and I talked in low voices. Finally, I suggested, "Why don't you both go home and get some rest—it's been a hard day. Get a good night's sleep and I'll see you late tomorrow morning."

Tom and Wright agreed and I walked to the door with them. Keeping his voice low, my brother Tom turned to me and said, "Please don't worry, Nan. You heard the doctor; they haven't found a thing. And I'm sure they won't find a tumor tomorrow. They'll find some other reason for this whole problem and Wrightsie will be good as new in a few weeks."

Tom's optimism was still very apparent, but I didn't share it with him.

"I hope you're right, Tom," I said a little sadly. "I hope you're right."

# 5
## We'll Have to Operate

Shortly after Wright and Tom left for Arlington, I heard a quiet knock at the door. A well-dressed man came into the room and introduced himself as Sherwin McCurdy. Behind him was a younger man on crutches who was introduced as Captain Kris Mineau. Mr. McCurdy was the man Carl Wilgus said he would ask to visit us from the local chapter of the Full Gospel Business Men's Fellowship.

As we talked I could sense both men had great compassion and empathy for Wrightsie, for me and for the whole situation. Kris said he was an Air Force pilot, and then he told me about his miraculous escape from a crippled jet fighter and his resulting hospitalization. He was in Dallas to address a meeting of the fellowship.

"Of course I was broken up pretty good when I ejected," he explained. "But I'll be off these crutches soon." Then with sincere and quiet conviction he said, "The Lord got me out of the airplane and I know He'll fix these legs."

I'd never met a man like Kris before. He was completely honest and had the deepest faith I'd ever seen. I was thankful he and Mr. McCurdy had come to see Wrightsie.

I stood back as they talked with Wrightsie. He was quiet and slowly nodded his head in response to their questions. Then, as they started to pray, Wrightsie closed his eyes and folded his hands on his chest.

Out of the corner of my eye I saw the door to the room open. Turning, I recognized our parish priest from Saint Alban's. He hesitated for a moment—I nodded hello—and he walked into the room and stood beside me.

Mr. McCurdy ended the time of prayer by saying, with great respect and conviction, "Heavenly Father, in the name of our precious Saviour Jesus Christ, I ask that this child be healed." Kris and Mr. McCurdy gently squeezed Wrightsie's hand and said goodbye. Then I introduced them to our priest. After a polite exchange, Kris and Mr. McCurdy left the room.

As soon as they were out the door the priest asked if Mr. McCurdy was a minister. I explained to him about my husband's call to Carl Wilgus and how he had asked Mr. McCurdy to visit us from the Full Gospel Business Men.

"And that younger man, he's had an encounter with the Lord," the priest stated, referring to Kris.

"Why, yes," I answered. "He told me the Lord had given him a startling revelation when he was recovering from his injuries. How did you know?"

"I can tell by his face," the priest answered, with a faraway tone in his voice.

He was silent for a moment, then he walked slowly over to the bed. He chatted with Wrightsie a few minutes, said a prayer, then he too left the room. Much later I found out that Kris Mineau and Sherwin McCurdy had made a lasting impression on our parish priest. As a result, the lives of some members of Saint Alban's Episcopal Church would be changed.

The next morning I accompanied Wrightsie while an aid wheeled him down to the x-ray room. Before the x-rays were taken a technician lifted Wrightsie from the stretcher and began to rotate him upside down, around—and all over. I hurried over to help and then Wrightsie's stomach rebelled against the acrobatics and he vomited.

I tried to wipe his mouth. Oh, how I wanted to help Wrightsie—to comfort him. But then I saw I was just in the way and I backed away. Tears of frustration and remorse filled my eyes and I turned away from the scene. Then, as if from nowhere, Mr. McCurdy appeared in the doorway leading from the x-ray room. Without a moment's hesitation, I ran into his arms. After a few seconds he led me to an adjoining room. He tried to reassure me—to comfort me—but it didn't help much. All I could think about was my son as I listened to the sounds coming from the x-ray room.

Eventually the doctor joined us with the x-rays in hand. "We didn't find anything," he said.

I think I detected a note of perplexity or frustration in his voice.

Then he said, "They're taking him back to the room now. If you want to go with him I'll talk to you later."

"Oh, yes, yes," I answered.

I turned to say goodbye to Mr. McCurdy, but he'd slipped out of the room, unnoticed. I hurried out the door and caught up with the stretcher. When we returned to the room I made Wrightsie as comfortable as possible, then I sat down in the chair beside the bed. I felt a little weary.

Later that morning Wright and Tom returned to the hospital. I told them of the morning's events. Tom must have detected my weariness for when I'd finished my story he asked, "Nan, when were you home last?"

"Four days ago—Monday," I answered.

"That's too long," he said with mock sternness. "I'm going to take you home; you need some rest. Then tonight, I'm going to take you and Beth out for supper."

"No, Tom. I can't leave Wrightsie. I won't—"

My protest was interrupted by the doctor's arrival. He informed us that he had rechecked all the tests and found nothing conclusive. The arteriogram was scheduled for twelve-thirty the next afternoon at a nearby hospital because the necessary equipment was located there. He told us that he was going to call in another specialist.

After the doctor left, Wright remembered Tom's earlier suggestion and urged me to go home for a rest.

"I'll stay here with my 'best buddy,' and when he drops off to sleep it'll give me a chance to read these," he said holding up two paperback books.

The books aroused my curiosity and when I questioned Wright he explained that Carl Wilgus had sent them, but he hadn't had time to read them.

"Let's see," he said, and he read the titles out loud. "This one is *I Believe in Miracles* by Kathryn Kuhlman, and this one is *Episcopalians and the Baptism in the Holy Spirit*. I wonder what that means. Well, anyway, there's plenty to read."

When I was ready to leave, Tom picked up the big blue suitcase and I walked over to say goodbye to Wrightsie.

I leaned over the guard rail of the bed and kissed his fat little cheeks. "Love you," I said.

"Love you, mom," he answered. "Bye."

When Tom drove into our driveway in Arlington, it seemed like I'd been away for ages. Beth spotted our car, ran to meet us and gave me a big hug.

Later that afternoon after washing a few clothes, I took a long, hot shower. Brother Tom had been correct; I needed the break. Tom, Beth and I had a relaxing meal, yet towards the end of the evening, I wanted to get back to Wrightsie. We took Beth to the Foxes' and Tom drove me back to Dallas.

When we walked into the hospital room, Wrightsie was asleep and Wright was sitting in the chair reading.

"How'd it go?" I asked after checking Wrightsie.

"Fine," Wright answered. "I had a good time with Wrightsie. And Kris Mineau and Sherwin McCurdy dropped in for a visit early this evening. Boy, are they two fine people!"

Later, I found out that as a result of meeting and talking with Kris, Wright made the most important decision in his life. It was a decision that affected all our lives.

We talked for a few moments and then we all said goodbye and I made the chair bed up and turned in for the night. But I couldn't sleep. I worried all night about Wrightsie's arteriogram.

When Wright and Tom returned to the hospital that Friday morning, Tom was carrying his suitcase. He had made reservations to return to New York for the weekend and, depending on the outcome of Wrightsie's test, he planned to come back the first part of the week.

We tired to comfort Wrightsie as best we could while we were waiting to go to the nearby hospital. He was extremely thirsty but we were unable to give him a drink until after the test. From time to time I would moisten his lips with a wet washcloth.

When the aid came to tell us it was time to go, we decided that Wright would carry Wrightsie downstairs. I would ride in the station wagon with our son while Wright and Tom would follow us in our car.

We were met at the hospital by an orderly with a stretcher. And then Wrightsie was wheeled to a hallway just outside the special procedures room. In a few minutes Tom and Wright joined us.

We waited and waited for the nurse to give Wrightsie his pre-operative injection. Wrightsie was so uncomfortable and thirsty. Finally, the nurse walked up and gave Wrightsie his shot.

"Now, we should wait about another hour," I said to Wright and Tom.

Then, before I knew it, Wrightsie was wheeled into the special procedures room.

"This isn't right," I exclaimed. "They haven't waited long enough for the shot to take effect!"

The door closed and in a minute we heard Wrightsie plead faintly, "Oooooh, Ooooh."

I clenched my fist, and angry tears spilled down my cheeks. But there was nothing I could do. Wright and Tom led me into a cold, sterile-looking eating area. Four or five metal tables were precisely lined up side by side in the center of the room. And numerous food and drink vending machines stood at attention around the room. Tom sat with me at a table and Wright said, "I'll get us some coffee."

He dropped coins into one of the vending machines and it clicked, hummed and poured out a bitter, black instant coffee. We sipped a few drops of the liquid, then Wright said, "We'd better go up to the waiting room."

As before, Tom and I sat down and did a great deal of talking while Wright paced the floor outside the waiting room. An eternity passed, then Wright announced, "Here they come!"

Tom and I joined Wright in the hall. The neurologist, the specialist and two or three other doctors marched towards us in almost military fashion. As they approached us the neurologist tried to put on a reassuring smile.

"We could not find anything," he said.

For a moment I felt a glimmer of hope stir in my heart.

But it was instantly shattered when the specialist said, "We'll have to operate."

"But, doctor," I protested, "I didn't think you'd operate unless you found a tumor."

"I'm sorry," he replied. "There's something wrong back there and we have to see what it is. Also, we have the lab report from the spinal tap we took Wednesday; they found some abnormal-looking cells."

"When will you operate?" I asked in a defeated voice.

"Next Tuesday morning," the specialist answered.

There was nothing more I could say or ask. The medical team waited a few seconds, then regrouped, performed an about-face and marched back the way they'd come. Then, I couldn't control my tears any longer.

The head nurse saw my dilemma and gently led me to her office. Wright followed me while Tom waited for us in the waiting room. "Please stay here as long as you like," the nurse said with empathy as she gently closed the door.

Wright waited for me to regain my composure, then he said, "I don't understand. Why can't they find something?"

I shook my head and said, "I don't know. I don't know."

We were silent a moment, then I said, "Oh, Wright, I can't bear to think of Wrightsie having brain surgery. Why? Why? Why?"

Wright didn't answer.

Finally, I resigned myself to the fact and said hopelessly, "But there's nothing else we can do."

Again, Wright didn't answer.

"At least we have good doctors," I said after another period of silence.

"Yes," Wright agreed. "I suppose we should be thankful for that."

We talked a few minutes longer, each trying to point out some positive aspects to our situation. Then we remembered Tom had a plane to catch, so we rejoined him in the waiting room. His earlier optimism had vanished; disappointment was written all over his face and his voice sounded weary. He offered to remain with us, but we assured him we'd be all right.

We made our way down to the hospital entrance, said our goodbyes and then Tom climbed into a waiting taxi cab. Wright and I waved, then watched in silence, as the yellow car wound its way down the long hospital driveway. As it disappeared from view, I felt my hopes go with it.

"How I wish you and Beth and Wrightsie and I were going with Tom to spend the weekend on Long Island," I said to Wright.

"Yes," Wright answered slowly. "Yes, so do I."

# 6
## Let's Go to Boston!

Wright and I stayed in the waiting room until Wrightsie was ready to be driven by ambulance back to his hospital. I accompanied him and Wright followed in our car. The road was clogged with the evening rush hour traffic. The ambulance driver turned on his flashing red light and siren, crossed over the highway divider and headed south in the northbound lane.

Wrightsie was conscious and I said, "They've got the siren on just for you." Even with all he'd been through he couldn't help but reply with a weak grin.

It took Wright a little while to make his way back. By the time he arrived, the nurses and I had Wrightsie settled into bed. The doctor came to the room within the hour to examine Wrightsie and check his progress. "You should check his right leg for warmth throughout the night. He could throw a blood clot. I've left orders for the nurses to check his pulse and blood pressure every thirty minutes. If his right leg gets cold or his pulse unsteady I want to be called immediately. I'll look in on him during the weekend," the doctor said as he left the room.

"Thank you, doctor," I replied. "Good night."

Wrightsie did well. I was amazed with his recuperative ability. Later in the evening he dropped off to sleep. Wright had gone home, and I decided to call Evelyn from the phone booth down the hall.

I gave her a quick report of the day's events, but she questioned our decision to go ahead with neurosurgery. Her father, Bopo, a huge bombastic man with a giant personality, and a heart to match, had taken a great liking to our family—especially Wrightsie. Bopo had a friend who was a brain surgeon and he wanted us to call this doctor for his opinion. I told Evelyn I'd talk it over with Wright.

After my talk with Evelyn, I ran back to the room to check Wrightsie. He was still sleeping, his leg was warm and his pulse steady. He was fine so I decided to slip out again and call my mom and dad in Danbury.

Mom answered the phone and dad picked up the extension. I told them about Tom's great support to us; then I went on to describe everything that had happened. My voice broke when I told them about the scheduled surgery, and dad insisted that I get a second opinion. I assured him that I would talk it over with Wright and call them back. Their loving concern helped me greatly even though I was confused about the decision we had made.

After the call, I again hurried back to the room to check Wrightsie. Moments later, a nurse came to the door and told me I had a long distance call from San Francisco. I was sure it was my sister Kathy, and I took the call at the nurses' station.

It was Kathy. She had called the Boston hospital where she had once worked as a nurse. Her friend who was a doctor there told her about a Doctor Andrew Shaw at Boston's Children's Hospital, and Kathy strongly recommended that I contact him. I agreed with Kathy that it would not hurt to call him and told her that I'd inform her of our decision. I said goodbye and returned to the room.

I spent a restless night; I couldn't wait to talk this all over with Wright in the morning. When he came into the room, we immediately began to discuss our plans. We decided that

Wright would call Bopo's doctor friend. We also decided that for the sake of privacy, he would make the call from his office. Saying a quick hello and goodbye to Wrightsie, he hurried off to make his call.

Wright called me about 11:30 A.M. "Nan, I talked with Bopo's friend for at least an hour. What a wonderful gentleman."

"What did he say?" I asked impatiently.

"He said he was sure the doctors in Dallas were as capable as any we could find," Wright explained. "And then I told him we were from the east and what your sister Kathy said."

"What'd he say then?" I asked.

"He said the most important consideration was for us to have confidence that we were doing the very best for Wrightsie. And then he said if we would feel more confident taking him back east then we should go."

"Did he recommend a hospital or a doctor?" I asked getting more excited by the minute.

"Well, not really," Wright replied, "but he did say that if we decided to go back east we couldn't find a better hospital than Boston's Children's.

"What do you think?" I asked Wright.

"Nan, you may think I'm stupid," Wright answered, "but I don't want to offend the doctors in Dallas."

"I know, I know," I replied, "but if these doctors are as competent and professional as we think they are they won't be offended. Let's go to Boston!"

"Okay," Wright agreed. "Let's go to Boston! I'll try to get a call through to Dr. Shaw. I'll call you back."

I knew we had made the right decision. We'd just have to hope the Dallas doctors would understand.

Wright called back within the hour. He was excited. "Nan!" he shouted, "I talked with Dr. Shaw. He'll take Wrightsie!"

"Wonderful! Wonderful!" I answered.

"Then I called the dispensary at the Naval Air Station. They've set up a medical evacuation flight aboard an Air Force hospital airplane—a DC-9. And you and I will accompany Wrightsie. What do you think of that?" Wright asked.

"I can't believe it," I replied.

"Listen, hon," Wright continued, "everything's set now. I'm coming back to the hospital."

"Wait!" I said. "What about Beth?"

"Well, I thought we'd call your brother Tom and see if he and Hilda would keep her for a while. Or, she could stay here with the Foxes," Wright said.

"I think she should go to Long Island," I answered. "I'm sure Tom and Hilda would love to have her. And Beth will enjoy being with Susan, Tommy and David. Also, more important than anything else, she'll be able to visit Wrightsie in Boston."

"Okay," Wright agreed. "Why don't you call Tom? I want to get up there to tell Wrightsie the surprise."

"All right," I answered.

I was thrilled! I called Tom and told him our plans. He asked me to let Beth stay with them. Things seemed to be fitting together well. For the first time in over a week I felt my hopes soaring. I knew everything would be all right when we got to Boston. I felt my prayers were being answered.

# 7

## I Wish You Luck in Boston

"Hi, best buddy," Wright said to his son when he walked into the room. "Have I got a surpise for you."

"What is it, dad?" Wrightsie asked, sensing the excitement in his father's voice.

"We're going to take you to Boston to see another doctor. Next Tuesday an Air Force hospital airplane is going to land at the Naval Air Station to pick you up—just like G.I. Joe," Wright explained. "And mom and dad are going with you."

"You mean it, dad?" Wrightsie exclaimed.

"I sure do."

"Oh, boy!" Wrightsie responded. "Can Bethy go too?"

"No," Wright answered. "I'm sorry, Wrightsie. She's going to fly to New York and stay with Uncle Tom and Aunt Hilda on Long Island. But maybe she'll be able to visit you in Boston."

Wrightsie turned to me, "Mom, can I call Bethy and tell her?"

"Sure, go ahead," I answered.

Wrightsie talked with Beth on the phone, and Wright and I started to make plans for the trip. Later in the evening, with our plans pretty well settled, Wright said good night to his son.

Late the next morning, I drove home to see Beth. She spotted me from Evelyn's house as I pulled in our driveway.

She came running over to the car and I explained our decision to her.

Beth understood the reasons why she could not accompany us to Boston, and she seemed satisfied that she would stay on Long Island. After a snack and a long talk about our plans and arrangements, we began to pack. We finished the packing, loaded the suitcases in the car, then I took Beth back to Evelyn's house.

Evelyn poured me a cup of coffee and we had a pleasant chat. She had a gift for Wrightsie—a small cassette recording. "All the kids recorded this last night," she explained. "Kathy, Carrie and Connie sang, and played the piano and organ—Beth sang one solo—and Nicky played the drums and narrated, too."

"Evelyn, thanks," I said. "Wrightsie will love it."

"They had a great time recording it," Evelyn said. "The first part is the kids with Christmas songs. Then Nicky filled in the second side by recording some of Wrightsie's favorite country-western songs."

"You're kidding, Evelyn," I said. "I didn't know Wrightsie liked country-western."

"Yes," Evelyn replied. "Many a day he's sat in Nicky's room playing his favorite country-western records. In fact, one day—I'll never forget it—I walked in Nicky's room to put some clothes away and Wrightsie was listening to 'Country Roads.' I noticed he had tears in his eyes and I said, 'What's the matter, Wrightsie?' He looked up and said, 'This song reminds me of Virginia and all my friends up there.'"

"Evelyn, that chokes me up," I replied. "He loves Virginia. And he'll never forget his friends up there."

"I know," Evelyn answered. "He's told me quite a bit about it. He even mentioned his school—wasn't it called Fairfax Christian School?"

"Yes," I answered. His birth date was one day too late for him to enter public school, so we started him at Fairfax

Christian."

Evelyn and I chatted awhile longer and then I said, "I'd better get back to the hospital. Wright has to go to the Naval Air Station and fill out some papers for our flight."

I said goodbye to Beth and then turning to Evelyn, I said, "Thanks for taking such good care of Beth."

"Don't mention it." she responded. "Now, take good care of yourself and give me a call when you get a chance."

"I will, Evelyn," I replied, "and thanks again—bye."

I returned to the hospital and Wright left immediately for the air station. After he was through at the base, he planned to spend a little time at home with Beth.

Wright returned early that Monday morning and we waited for the neurologist. We were going to tell him of our decision. But, much to our surprise, the specialist walked in first.

After greeting one another, I told him of our decision to take Wrightsie to Boston for consultation. At first he seemed surprised, and then he asked if we were going to see Dr. Shaw. His question came as a shock to me. The doctor knew about this Boston physician because he had attended seminars conducted by Dr. Shaw. He felt that our decision was a good one. We were very much relieved by this confirmation of our plans.

After checking Wrightsie, the doctor left the room. Wright stayed with us throughout the morning, then he left to pick up Beth from school and help her get ready for her flight. That evening he brought Beth by the hospital on their way to Love Field. Under the circumstances, she was permitted to come up to the room to see her brother. Wrightsie and I were watching TV when they arrived, and Beth tiptoed into the room and surprised her brother.

Wright and I let them talk alone for a while. I noticed Beth held Wrightsie's hand as they chatted. And then, all too soon it was time for Beth to leave.

"Goodbye, Wrightsie," she said. "I hope you have a good

trip. I'll come up to Boston and see you. And I'll write too." Then she bent over the bed and kissed her brother.

"Here," Wrightsie said, and he picked up a brown paper bag from beside his pillow. "Bethy, this is for you. Mom and I went shopping the first night I was in the hospital. And I got this for you."

"Wrightsie," Beth said, "thank you."

"You can eat the candy and chew the gum on the airplane," Wrightsie suggested.

Beth nodded. The two children looked at each other for a moment—"Oh, Wrightsie, I'm going to miss you," Beth said. And then she kissed her brother again. "Bye, Wrightsie."

I gave Beth a big hug and a kiss. "Now remember, Beth," I instructed, "let the stewardess take you off the airplane. Uncle Tom will be there to meet you."

"I will, mom," Beth answered. "Don't worry 'bout me."

"And, Beth," I said, "I love you."

"Love you, mom," she replied. "Bye, mom. Bye, Wrightsie."

Wright returned to the hospital after he'd put Beth on the airplane. We talked for a while then we decided to turn in early. We said prayers with Wrightsie and then my husband went home. He returned about nine o'clock Tuesday morning.

After we'd packed and loaded the car, I had intended to call Joy Jeffrey to tell her about Wrightsie. I also wanted to discuss some unfinished Vietnam prisoner-of-war work we were both engaged in. That brought something else to mind, and I asked Wrightsie if he had his Major Jeffrey prisoner-of-war bracelet ready. He answered me by holding up his right arm.

Two POW bracelets slid down his forearm. One read: Commander Kenneth Coskey. Ken had been the best man at our wedding and his wife, Donna, had been my matron of honor; and the other read: Major Robert Jeffrey. Bob was Joy's husband. Both men were prisoners of war in Hanoi, North Vietnam.

At that moment the Navy corpsmen knocked at the door. They had come to pick up Wrightsie. They apologized for being early and explained that they had to have Wrightsie ready when the medivac flight landed. They were going to keep Wrightsie at the air station dispensary, just a few minutes from the airfield.

The next half-hour was chaotic. A nurse arrived carrying Wrightsie's records, x-rays and reports; a woman from the laundry arrived carrying Wrightsie's favorite fringed cowboy pajama tops that had been lost; an aid arrived pushing the hospital's wheeled stretcher with a regulation military canvas litter on top of it.

Then the neurologist came in. The corpsmen were strapping Wrightsie on the litter, the doctor watched them for a moment and then said to my husband, "Commander Brunson, we have duplicates of all your son's records and x-rays. Could we have your permission to use them in our work with medical students?"

Wright nodded and I said, "Yes, doctor. If some good can come from this—if some other child can be helped—please use anything you need. I'm thrilled you asked. Thank you."

"Thank you very much," the doctor replied. Next he strode over to Wrightsie and shook his hand. Then Wrightsie took Major Jeffrey's POW bracelet off his wrist and handed it to the doctor. "Doctor," he said, "will you give this to your wife for me? My mother told me she's sick too. Maybe this will make her feel better."

The doctor read the name and then slipped the bracelet into the pocket of his white lab coat. "Thank you, Wrightsie," he said, "I'll be sure to give it to her. Now, will you do something for me."

Wrightsie nodded.

"I've written a good friend of mine up in Boston. He'll be one of your doctors up there. Would you tell him hello for me and that I said he's to take good care of you?"

"I will," Wrightsie answered.

The doctor gently patted Wrightsie on the shoulder and turned to me and said, "Mrs. Brunson, take care of yourself."

"I will, doctor," I answered. "Thank you for everything. We'll be thinking of you and your wife."

"Thank you," he replied. "I wish you luck in Boston."

# 8

## *Mom, This Is My Funnest Day Ever*

The corpsmen wheeled Wrightsie down the hallway. He was bundled in his sleeping bag with one arm wrapped around Tigeree's neck. We all took the elevator down to the first floor and then the corpsmen pushed Wrightsie out to the gray Navy ambulance. They gently lifted him into the ambulance and invited me to ride with Wrightsie.

I readily accepted their considerate offer and Wright followed us in the car. Within thirty minutes we'd arrived at the Naval Air Station and Wrightsie was settled in a room at the dispensary.

Wright went over to the Navy exchange to buy Wrightsie a cassette player. We wanted him to be able to play the tape Evelyn gave him. I also suggested he buy some Christmas tapes.

Wrightsie was very surprised. "For me, dad!" Wrightsie exclaimed. "Hey, mom, look what dad got me! Oh, boy! Look at this!" he shouted. "The Jackson Five, and—and the Partridge Family; all Christmas songs! Oh, boy!"

Then Wright inserted the tape Evelyn had given me. Wrightsie pushed the start button and listened a few seconds. He was delighted when he heard the children's voices on the tape. Wright and I just stood back and watched. What a pleasure it was to see our son excited and happy again.

A little while later my husband's cousin from Dallas—Chuck Brunson—walked into the room. Chuck was talking with Wrightsie when the commanding officer of the base and his wife—Captain and Mrs. Muery—also walked into the room. I was surprised to see them. I'd never met Captain Muery and I'd only talked with Mrs. Muery briefly at one or two of the wives' social functions at the Naval Air Station. They had heard about Wrightsie's condition from Val Swor.

I introduced the Muerys to Cousin Chuck, then Captain Muery walked over to Wrightsie's bed. "Here's a little gift for you, young man," he said in a fatherly voice. And then he presented Wrightsie with a sailor's white hat. "Now, when you get on that Air Force airplane I want you to show the pilot these," Captain Muery said, and he pointed to a Navy officer's shield and underneath it, a pair of gold Navy wings both pinned to the hat brim. "You tell the pilot you're skipper of that airplane. Will you do that for me?"

"Yes, sir," Wrightsie answered with a grin.

"Here, let's see if it fits," Captain Muery said, placing the white hat on Wrightsie's head. "Ah, perfect."

"Thank you," Wrightsie said.

And then a very special guest arrived—Wrightsie's best friend Mary Swor. The rest of us chatted with Mary's parents for a while out in the hall, leaving Mary and Wrightsie alone in the room.

Soon I heard the wonderful sound of happy laughter coming from the room. I couldn't help but peek in. Mary and Wrightsie were playing a game of old maid.

Mary mentioned the thank-you note she had received from Wrightsie. He had expressed his appreciation to her for going with him to the children's play on his birthday.

Wrightsie, all dressed up in a blue blazer and tie, had picked up Mary and taken her to a children's play in Fort Worth back in

October. Wright and I, Beth and Mary's older sister, Lisa, had gone along as chaperones.

"I had fun," Mary said.

"How are things at Jail Hill?" Wrightsie asked, and they both laughed at the name they'd coined for J.L. Hill Elementary School.

"All right," Mary answered, "but I miss you, Wrightsie. I miss you walking me to school when I come by your house."

"It's great to see you, Mary," Wrightsie said. "It's so good to be out of that hospital. I really feel so much better here with you."

I was surprised by the adult tone and the sincere honesty of their conversation. And I felt very proud as my handsome young man talked with his lovely, petite friend. Then my eye caught sight of a child's well-worn stuffed tiger discarded and forgotten—for the moment—in a corner of the bed. What a contrast!

The Swors left and soon Chuck and the Muerys also said their farewells. About 5:00 P.M. a corpsman brought supper to our room. And then—about an hour later—a corpsman announced, "The medivac flight's inbound. They should land in thirty minutes so we're going to take your son down to the airfield now."

Two corpsmen strapped Wrightsie to the canvas litter and carried him to the ambulance. Earlier, Wright had transferred all our baggage to the ambulance, so we were cramped as we drove down to the field. Wright rode in front with the driver and a Navy doctor, and I rode in back with Wrightsie and all our suitcases.

The driver stopped the ambulance near the loading area. He left the motor running and the heater on. It was dark so he also left the headlights and the flashing red emergency light on.

When my husband spotted the incoming airplane, he pointed it out to me. I looked out of the window, but all I could see were two white pencil beams from the airplane's landing lights as it streaked over the end of the runway. The lights slowed and then stopped. Two fire trucks joined the airplane as it turned off the runway and slowly taxied towards us. The flashing and blinking white, red and green lights of the airplane and fire trucks stood out in sharp contrast to the dark winter sky.

The airplane stopped beside our ambulance and then I could see the beautiful sleek lines of the fuselage. The pilot secured the engines and the loud jet whine subsided.

Wright and I stepped out of the ambulance. A cold wind whipped around us. Suddenly, a large door swung up from the side of the plane, and a long ramp began to unfold automatically from the opening. When the ramp touched the concrete, two corpsmen hurried Wrightsie aboard the plane. As the lights from the cabin fell on Wrightsie's face, an Air Force medic—standing in the doorway—looked down and smiled; he'd recognized Wrightsie's white sailor hat.

"Welcome aboard, sailor," the medic said, and he saluted. You're the first sailor I've ever seen wrapped in a sleeping bag with cowboys and horses all over it. But then this is Texas."

Wrightsie's face broke into a grin.

My husband and I followed Wrightsie up the ramp. Two medics strapped his litter to a stanchion, and an Air Force nurse walked up. "You can sit here, if you like," she said, pointing out two empty seats across the aisle from Wrightsie.

Wright and I sat down and buckled our seat belts; the ramp refolded; the big door swung closed; the jet engines whined; and soon we were airborne.

When the plane leveled off, I got up to check Wrightsie. He was looking out the window. I watched with him as the last lights of the Dallas-Fort Worth area slid from view underneath the wing. "How's my G.I. Joe?" I asked.

"Okay, mom," he answered.

The flight nurse walked up and said, "How's he doing?"
"Just fine," I answered.

"I see from the manifest you're going to Boston," she said.
"Yes," I replied.

"Did you know we're going to land at Scott Air Force Base tonight?" she asked.

"Well, not for sure," I answered, "but my husband did say that it was a possibility."

"Yes," she said. "You see, all our medivac flights stage out of Scott, and we like to get as many planes back each night as is possible. They'll get you to Boston sometime tomorrow."

"I see," I replied.

"When we land," she continued, "there will be a bus to take you to the base hospital. They'll probably let you and your son sleep in the women's ward."

I thanked her for the information, and then I sat down with Wright and told him what she'd said.

The flight to Scott took a little over two hours. When we landed, I felt the tug of my seat belt as the pilot reversed the engines. The jet exhaust blew snow around the windows. We taxied off the runway and I glanced over at Wrightsie. He was looking out the window; I followed his gaze and saw thousands of tiny snowflakes rushing into the beam of the landing lights.

When the plane stopped, I unbuckled my seat belt and stood next to Wrightsie. "Mom," he said, "this is my funnest day ever; my tape recorder, seeing Mary, riding in an Air Force hospital plane and landing in the snow."

"Oh, Wrightsie, I love you," was all I could say. I kissed him, hugged him, then turned my head so he wouldn't see my tears.

# 9
## You've Just Got to Be the Answer to My Prayers

My husband rode the bus with Wrightsie and me to the base hospital. When we arrived, he checked in with a medic standing behind a counter. He found out that they would bring Wrightsie in from the bus in a few minutes and that Wrightsie and I would sleep in the women's ward while Wright would stay in the visiting officers' quarters.

After Wrightsie and I said good night to Wright, I followed the medics as they carried Wrightsie down to the ward. They unstrapped him from the litter and lifted him into the bed. No sooner had I tucked him in when he said, "Mom, I don't feel good. I think I'm going to throw up."

"Hang on if you can, Wrightsie," I said. I pulled open the doors to a bedside stand, grabbed a small, curved, stainless steel basin and quickly put it under his chin—just in time. He almost filled it.

"Are you okay now, Wrightsie?" I asked after a few minutes.

He nodded and I wiped his mouth and chin. Then, so the other women in the ward wouldn't hear, I whispered, "Would you like to go to the bathroom now?"

"Yes," he answered weakly.

I took his plaid robe and Indian slippers from the big blue suitcase and helped him into them. Then I lifted him off the

bed and slowly lowered him until his feet touched the floor.
"I can't walk very well, mom," he said.

"I know, Wrightsie. I'll help you." I held him under his arms
and nudged his legs along with one knee. When we reached the
bathroom, Wrightsie wrapped his arms around the sink to hold
himself up as I brushed his teeth and washed his face. My poor
Wrightsie couldn't even stand by himself, much less walk.

After tucking Wrightsie in and preparing myself for bed, I
pushed our beds closer together, held his hand as we said
prayers, and soon we were both sound asleep. The next
morning we were awakened at five o'clock to get ready for the
next leg of our trip.

Wright met us in the entrance to the hospital as the medics
were carrying Wrightsie out to the bus. We got to the airfield
around seven and by eight-thirty we were airborne.

Through a chat with the flight nurse I learned that we would
have two stops before we reached Boston: Andrews Air Force
Base outside of Washington and the municipal airport in
Providence, Rhode Island. Finally—sometime around three or
four in the afternoon—we would land at Hanscom Field in
Bedford, just outside of Boston.

I was standing beside Wrightsie's litter talking with him
when I felt the airplane start its descent for Andrews Air Base.
As our altitude lowered I started to make out the details of the
Virginia countryside.

"Wrightsie," I exclaimed, "look at the beautiful fall colors.
Daddy said we could fly over Fairfax; let me know if you see
Fairfax Christian School or our old house."

We both stared out the window. And then Wrightsie said,
"Mom, I miss Alberto and Scott and Jimmie," naming three of
his best friends in Virginia.

"I know you do, Wrightsie," I answered.

How my own heart ached for the past. I wanted to be back
with my children, showing them the sights in Washington,

D.C.; I wanted to be back in my cozy kitchen in Fairfax planning birthday and Halloween parties for Beth and Wrightsie; I wanted to be back in Japan on a family picnic in the beautiful countryside; I wanted to be back on the ocean liner between Japan and the United States playing shuffleboard with my strong, healthy son; I wanted to be back in Arlington meeting my son at the door and lifting the bunch of small wild daisies from his outstretched hands.

"Mom," I was startled from my dreams. "Mom," Wrightsie repeated, "I didn't see my school; I didn't see our house."

"I'm sorry, Wrightsie. I'm sorry." And I hugged my son. No, we couldn't go back.

A few minutes later we landed at Andrews. When the airplane stopped at the loading area I noticed a line of ambulances making their way towards the airplane. They were painted Air Force blue, Army green and Navy gray; and each had a flashing red light mounted on the roof. The ambulatory patients walked down the ramp; others were carried off in litters. And many patients were met by loved ones. As an ambulance stopped at the ramp, two medics jumped out, came aboard, and removed a litter from its stanchion. Then they carried the patient back down the ramp to the waiting ambulance. And so it went until nearly half the stanchions were empty and then the new patients were carried aboard.

The whole process took better than an hour and then we were airborne again. The same scene—on a smaller scale—was repeated at Providence except this time two Red Cross volunteers came aboard and they served beverages and cookies. Even though we'd had lunch on the airplane, they were a welcome sight. Wrightsie had a couple of sips of hot chocolate and I gobbled down some cookies. I hadn't realized how hungry I was. The two women rushed to complete their mission and soon we were airborne again.

We landed at Hanscom Field some time after three o'clock.

My eyes caught sight of a gray Navy ambulance waiting in line at the ramp. Finally it was Wrightsie's turn. I said goodbye to the flight nurse. She took my hand and said, "I hope the doctors in Dallas are wrong."

"Thank you," I answered.

Two Navy corpsmen dressed in their winter blues and white hats walked up the ramp. The nurse motioned them to Wrightsie's litter. They unstrapped the litter and carried him down to the ambulance; I sat with Wrightsie in the back. The corpsmen helped Wright load our baggage and in a few minutes we were on the road to Boston.

Towards the end of the trip we were driving down a narrow street lined with stores and my eye caught the reflection of our ambulance in the store windows. It was like watching a movie and I felt I was only a spectator to a sad story. Then we drove by a park, the reflections ended and I was jolted back to reality.

Finally the driver turned right onto Longwood Avenue and after four or five blocks we stopped at the entrance to Boston's Children's Hospital. The corpsmen carried Wrightsie through the emergency room entrance and lowered the litter to the floor. "Don't put him on the floor!" the harsh female voice of the receptionist lashed out. "Put him on a stretcher!" she commanded.

The corpsmen looked around frantically for a wheeled hospital stretcher. They spotted the stretcher near the entrance and one corpsman ran over to get it. I couldn't believe what was happening. These two Navy men had handled Wrightsie with great care and concern ever since they'd met us at the airfield. And it angered me when I heard the receptionist attack them. As the corpsmen pushed the stretcher by me I brushed some dirt off the stained sheet with all the disdain I could muster. My husband walked over to the counter and started talking to the receptionist. I don't know what he said but it silenced her.

After the corpsmen had lifted Wrightsie to the stretcher I said to them, "Thank you for all your help. I'm sorry you had to put up with this sort of thing."

"Don't worry about that, Mrs. Brunson," one of the men replied. "We just hope your son will be okay."

The corpsmen volunteered to take Wright to the hotel—the Children's Inn—while two hospital aids pushed Wrightsie's stretcher into a nearby elevator. When the doors of the elevator opened, the aids wheeled Wrightsie down a long corridor, through two wide, full, swinging doors and into the neurosurgical ward.

I'd begun to have doubts concerning our decision to come to Boston since we'd first entered the hospital. And with each passing moment my doubts were increasing. The aids had difficulty maneuvering the stretcher into the tiny, empty semi-private room. Just inside the door to the room—on the left—was a small metal crib-like bed, too small for Wrightsie. A second regular-sized bed was jammed up into the far left corner and that is where we put Wrightsie.

The aid wheeled the stretcher out of the room and I took a moment to look over what would be Wrightsie's new home—at least for a few days. The lower half of the only window in the room was occupied by an old rusty air conditioner. Cold air from around and through the air conditioner invaded the room. Beneath the window an ancient radiator hissed defiantly, waging a losing battle against the winter cold.

"Are you warm enough?" I asked as I pulled the blanket up over his shoulders.

"Yes, mom," he replied.

"Boy, did I have an experience checking in at the admission's office," Wright exclaimed as he came into the little room.

"What happened?" I asked.

"Well, I was waiting to check in when this clerk spotted the Navy wings on my uniform and she just stood there and stared at me. Finally, I asked her if something was wrong. And, peering through her granny glasses, she said, 'Are you a bomber?' "

"A what?" I asked.

"A bomber," Wright repeated. "She wanted to know if I'd dropped bombs on North Vietnam. Can you believe it? Welcome to Boston."

"Wright, I wonder if we've made a mistake by coming up here," I said.

"No," Wright answered. "No, definitely not. Just think back, everything that's happened has led us to Boston."

"Well, I guess you're right," I agreed.

"Hey, it's cold in here," Wright commented.

"It's coming in from around that air conditioner," I said.

Wright looked around the room a moment and then said, "Let's move Wrightsie's bed over here by the door and put this crib in the corner. At least it'll get him away from the window."

We'd just finished the move when a young resident walked into the room and introduced himself. He gave Wrightsie a thorough neurological exam. He didn't say anything until he was about to leave when he explained, "Dr. Shaw had late surgery today. But he should be along later this evening to see your son."

The food-serving cart could be heard coming down the hall at 5:00 P.M. Wrightsie wasn't hungry but I did convince him to eat a little to hold him through the night. After supper Wrightsie asked, "Dad, can we have a TV set?"

"I'll check and see if I can find one," his dad answered.

He was back in a few minutes. "Couldn't get one," he said. "They don't have enough for each room. But the nurse said anytime I find one in an empty room we're welcome to it."

So we gave Wrightsie his tape recorder and he played Christmas songs while we waited for the doctor.

Finally, about 8:30 P.M., Dr. Shaw arrived. Without any

introduction he said in a low, gentle voice, "Hello, Mrs. Brunson, I'm sorry I'm so late." His handshake was warm and firm. He didn't look like a doctor who'd worked a fourteen-hour day. His graying hair—parted on the side—looked freshly combed and his eyes were bright and clear.

"Hello, Commander," he said to Wright.

"Mrs. Brunson," he said turning back to me, "I want you to know your husband did a good job explaining your son's illness to me over the telephone last Saturday."

Then he walked over to Wrightsie. "Well, son, I'd like to take a look at you. I'm sure by now you've had enough of this poking and prodding."

Wrightsie nodded and managed a tired little smile.

"Let's move your friend over here," Dr. Shaw said and he moved Tigeree to the side of the bed. "This won't take long." And he gently helped Wrightsie to a sitting position.

All my previous doubts vanished as I watched that skilled and compassionate man examine my son. He projected a charisma and humility engendered by years of experience ministering to little children suffering from the worst neurological injuries, diseases and disorders.

After his examination, he carefully lowered Wrightsie to the bed and covered him with the sheet. He placed Tigeree in Wrightsie's arm and said, "Thank you. Now I know you're a long way from home, but I hope you'll enjoy your Thanksgiving dinner tomorrow," the doctor said with genuine concern. "We have roast turkey for you."

Then Dr. Shaw, Wright and I walked out into the hall. "I've only taken a quick look at his x-rays and test reports from Dallas," Dr. Shaw explained. "I'll want to study them thoroughly Friday. Then we'll decide what to do next."

"Doctor," I asked, "will it be all right if I sleep in the room with Wrightsie?"

"Yes," he replied. "Your husband and I discussed that over

the phone. The nurses have found a cot you can use if you wish. But I'd prefer you didn't."

Then, I saw another positive aspect of Dr. Shaw's personality—firmness. He knew what was best for his children and he knew how to get it across.

"You see, if we have to operate, Wrightsie will have to depend solely on the nurses," he explained. "And I think we'd better get him used to the idea as soon as possible. But you talk it over with your husband and let the nurse know what you decide."

There was no doubt in my mind but that Dr. Shaw knew what was best for his children. Therefore, I said, "I'll stay at Children's Inn, doctor."

"Good," he replied. "I'll see you Friday."

"Doctor," I said, "thank you so much for taking Wrightsie's case. You've just got to be the answer to my prayers."

Immediately, I could see I'd placed a great burden upon him. He looked down for a moment and then with compassion and humility he said, "Mrs. Brunson, I hope your prayers will be answered."

# 10
## I Love You, Mom

My husband and I returned to the room to talk with Wrightsie. I tried to explain to him that I would not be able to stay in his room as I had done in Dallas. This caused him to become concerned about having to go to the bathroom with the help of a nurse. We tried to assure him that he need not be embarrassed, but he insisted that I be there to help him. He seemed relieved when I told him I would be there to help late each evening and early each morning.

Next we said our prayers. Then I fluffed his pillow, tucked his cowboy comforter around him and kissed him good night, and told him we'd sit by the door until he fell asleep. Wrightsie was asleep in a very few minutes. "You know," I commented to Wright, "I've never seen anyone go to sleep as fast as he does. And I know he'll sleep the night through. It's a blessing for all of us."

Wright and I walked the one-half block to Children's Inn. As I dropped off to sleep, I remembered that the next day was Thanksgiving Day. I didn't feel very thankful.

The next morning I woke up around seven. I dressed quickly and hurried over to the hospital. The gray November New England sky did nothing to lift my spirits. "Mom," Wrightsie said the instant I entered the room, "I have to go to the bathroom!" I grabbed the urinal and rushed over to the bed. I was glad I'd arrived in time. Wrightsie was so very modest I knew he wouldn't let a nurse help him until the very last moment. And then, if he had an accident he would feel degraded.

Next, I washed his hands and face and combed his hair. When I'd finished I kissed the back of his perfectly shaped head—just where his neck began. Oh, how many times when he was a baby had I kissed and caressed that favorite spot? And then, as always, he hunched his little square shoulders in response.

Breakfast was served and about eight-thirty Wright walked into the room carrying two cups of steaming coffee.

"Wright," I asked my husband, "do you think there might be a TV set available this morning? We could watch Macy's Thanksgiving Day parade in New York."

"I'll check," he answered.

In a few minutes he returned, lugging a portable TV. "Hey, I found one. Somebody must have checked out early this morning." He placed the set on top of the metal clothes closet, plugged it in and turned the channel selector to the Macy's parade. The big animal floats, bands and entertainers marched across the screen and my mind drifted back to past Thanksgiving Days. I recalled the previous year when we'd spent Thanksgiving with my folks in Danbury. We all went for a walk in the crisp winter air before dinner. When we returned to the friendly warmth of my parents' house I was pleasantly overwhelmed by the delicious smell of roast turkey. For some reason, Wrightsie had mysteriously disappeared immediately after our walk. Then, as dinner was being served, he walked into the dining room and placed a little Puritan stovepipe hat beside each plate. He'd made them during his disappearance.

"Mom," Wrightsie's voice interrupted my daydreams, "do you think Bethy's watching the parade on TV—and Susan,

Tommy and David?"

"Yes, Wrightsie. I'm sure they are," I answered.

"I miss 'em, mom. I wish I was there."

"I know, Wrightsie," I said. "So do I."

Wrightsie's Thanksgiving turkey was dished up about noon. The nurses tried to brighten the meal and placed a little orange and brown paper turkey on each tray. The food was all right but it fell short of a home-cooked meal.

When he'd finished eating I said, "Wrightsie, I've got a surprise for you. We had mail waiting for us yesterday but I saved it for today."

"Who's it from, mom?" he asked.

I handed him an envelope. He opened the letter and exclaimed, "It's from Bethy! She made it!" and he held up a handmade Thanksgiving Day card. Beth had drawn and colored a turkey and other fall and harvest pictures. We all looked at the card and then I said, "Here, let's set it right beside the TV set."

Then I opened the metal closet, took out a package and said, "Wrightsie, this package is addressed to you too."

He took one look at it and said, "Mom! It's my Willie Wonka candy factory. They sent it up here?" he questioned. "I thought they'd forgotten me."

"Your dad did too," I explained. "So he called the company and asked them to send it to Boston."

"Thanks, dad," Wrightsie said. "Mom, when can we make candy?"

"When we get back home, Wrightsie," I answered. Oh, how I hoped he could make candy when and if he got back home.

We examined the candy factory with him for a few minutes and then I said, "Wrightsie, daddy and I are going downstairs to the cafeteria for our dinner now."

"Okay, mom," he said with his attention focused on his candy factory.

Wright and I walked into the hall, and then I saw a beautiful sight that more than made up for our earlier unpleasant experiences at Children's Hospital. The nurses had placed a TV set in the hall. And, seated in little chairs—and a few wheelchairs—around the TV were eight or ten children eating their dinner. Three or four nurses were spaced between the children helping them as was necessary. One nurse held a tiny baby in her arms as the child nursed from a bottle. I've never seen greater love between patients and nurses as I saw that day in Boston.

In the cafeteria, we started to eat our dinner. During the meal I noticed Wright look up and glance around the room every so often. Finally he said, "You know, Nan, even though this room is filled with people, I feel like we're all alone—isolated."

His comment gave me a start. "I feel exactly the same way," I answered.

He reached across the table, took my hand and said, "I thank God we've got each other. I couldn't go through this without you."

I nodded and squeezed his hand.

We finished our meal and returned to the neurosurgical ward. We spent the rest of the afternoon and evening with Wrightsie until he fell asleep, then we left for the inn.

Later that evening, when we were ready for bed, Wright asked, "Will the bed light bother you? I'd like to read a few minutes." He had a dark green book in his hand.

"What are you reading?" I asked.

He closed the book, showing me the cover. "It's the Bible," he answered.

I was surprised; it wasn't like Wright to read the Bible. "Was it in the room?" I asked.

"No," he answered. "Remember the night your brother took you and Beth out to supper in Arlington—the same night Sherwin McCurdy and Kris Mineau visited me? I stayed with

Wrightsie in the hospital."

"Yes," I answered.

"Well, I bought it the next day," Wright tried to explain.

"What did Mr. McCurdy and Kris have to do with it?" I asked.

"Well, Kris said I should get it."

"But, I can't see why you brought it to Boston. There's probably one here in the room."

"Yeah, I know," Wright said. "But this is a new translation. I'm beginning to understand things I've never understood before."

I was tired and dropped the subject saying, "No, the light won't bother me."

"Good night, hon," he said.

"Night," I replied.

The next morning, I awoke early. As I was dressing, I noticed the Bible on the floor next to Wright's side of the bed. And next to it were the two books Carl Wilgus had sent. I wondered what was going on in my husband's mind.

I slipped from the room and walked over to the hospital. Wrightsie had slept through the night without any problems. Wright walked into the room around nine o'clock, carrying two cups of coffee. And then just before noon, Dr. Shaw came to the room. He gave Wrightsie another thorough neurological exam. He had won Wrightsie's friendship and confidence with his warmth and gentleness, and they carried on a light conversation as Dr. Shaw went through the various procedures. When he'd completed the examination he carefully covered Wrightsie with the sheet saying, "Thank you, Wrightsie, we shouldn't have to do that again for a few days. Now, I want to talk with your mom and dad for a few minutes. We'll step out in the hall so we won't bother you with your TV program."

Wrightsie nodded.

My husband and I followed Dr. Shaw out of the room, closing the door behind us. The doctors had spotted a suspicious-looking mass on the left side of the brain stem and, as Dr. Shaw explained it to us, I felt my heart sink. I was stunned—numb. I couldn't even ask any questions.

Wright broke the silence asking, "What happens then, doctor? What if it's malignant? If it's benign, can you take it out?"

Dr. Shaw was patient with my husband's questions. "Well, there are a number of possibilities," he replied. "We would hope we could remove it—completely—without any damage to the brain tissue. But even a benign tumor can attach itself to the surrounding tissue to such an extent that severe and permanent damage would result if we removed it. I really can't say what we'll do until I find out what we have back there."

"When will you operate?" I asked.

"I've scheduled it for Monday morning," Dr. Shaw replied.

"Doctor, what should we tell Wrightsie?" I asked.

With a sympathetic voice he said, "I'll tell him, Mrs. Brunson. I'll be in to see him sometime Sunday. There's no need for him to be concerned about it over the weekend."

He waited a moment or two to see if we had any more questions and then he said good night.

Wright and I stood in the hall a few minutes to regain our composure. Later, we took turns at the pay phone as we called our families and told them that Wrightsie would be operated on Monday morning. When I told my parents the sad news they said they'd drive up to Boston and spend the weekend with us.

We stayed with Wrightsie until he fell asleep, then we left for the inn. Wright was in bed before me and I noticed him reading the Bible again. I felt sorry for my husband. I'd been able to keep my mind busy caring for Wrightsie. But Wright hadn't had a diversion and I'm sure he was worried sick, although he'd never said anything to me about his fears. I thought he might be getting some comfort from the Bible.

The next morning when I went over to the hospital, Wright stayed at the inn waiting for my folks to arrive—we'd reserved them a room next to ours. They arrived later that morning. Wrightsie was so happy to see his "Gramma" and "Feef"—the nickname Beth had coined for their grandfather.

"We've got a little something for you, Wrightsie," my mother said. And then my father handed him a gift-wrapped package. It was a game called "Battleship."

While Wright sat down with Wrightsie to play "Battleship," I took my parents back to the inn for lunch. During the meal, I brought them up-to-date concerning Wrightsie's condition and surgery. They told me they planned to stay until after the operation. I had mixed feelings about that because of mom's health, so I tried to talk them out of staying.

We finished lunch and returned to the hospital. As we walked down the hall in the neurosurgical ward towards Wrightsie's room, I glanced into a large, semi-private room. My eye caught sight of a pretty teen-age girl I'd seen before. She had a tracheotomy tube coming out of the front of her throat. I'd found out she was learning to swallow after having a number of benign tumors removed. The surgery had caused nerve damage. I shuddered and thought, "O God, I don't want Wrightsie to have something like that."

"Hey, I beat dad two out of three times," Wrightsie exclaimed when we entered the room.

"Yes," Wright explained, "I taught him how to conduct an expanding square search and he beat me at my own game."

"Feef, I challenge you to a game," Wrightsie said to his grandfather.

"Okay," Feef answered, pulling his chair up to the bed.

It warmed my heart to see my dad and Wrightsie enjoying each other's company. Theirs was a special relationship. Many times during our Navy moves I'd stayed with my folks in

Danbury while Wright settled into his new job and found us a
house. During these times Feef was more the father than
grandfather; he and Wrightsie had taken walks together; he'd
taught Wrightsie to ice fish on Lake Candlewood, and in the
summer to steer Feef's boat on the lake; and they had their
favorite TV cartoon shows.

Considering the circumstances, we had a pleasant weekend,
and all too soon it was time for my folks to leave for
Connecticut. They said their goodbyes to Wrightsie and then
Wright and I walked back to the inn with them. Wright helped
my dad load their car while I chatted with mother. "Nan," she
asked, "are you sure you don't want us to stay?"

"No, mom," I lied. "It's best this way. I'll call you tomorrow
after the surgery."

When I gave my mother a final hug, my courage collapsed.
"Oh, mom, don't go," I pleaded. "Please stay with us."

"Yes," Wright said. "Stay with us—we need you."

We all walked back to the inn—suitcases in hand and my
folks re-registered. Later that evening we'd finished supper
and were waiting in Wrightsie's room for Dr. Shaw. He walked
into the room almost unnoticed—and before I could introduce
him to my parents, he walked up to my dad, put his arm around
Feef's shoulders and said, "You must be the grandfather."

After I made the introductions, Dr. Shaw chatted with
Wrightsie for a moment. And then, turning to us, he said,
"Would you folks mind leaving the room for a few minutes?
Wrightsie and I have a little something to talk over."

We waited in the hall to find out how their little talk went.
Dr. Shaw joined us before long. He said, "I simply told him,
'Wrightsie, tomorrow morning you're going to take a little
snooze and I'm going to take a peek back here to see what's
going on.'"

And then, even knowing what his answer would be, I asked,
"Doctor, can I see him tomorrow morning?"

"No. I'm sorry," he answered, "I think it best you didn't. But, if you'd like, you can stay by the elevator and see him when he's wheeled down to the operating room."

"Thank you," I replied. I was very disappointed but I felt Dr. Shaw would not relent and that he really knew best.

He said good night to us and walked to the nurses' station to leave his orders. We walked back into the room. Wrightsie was watching TV and he never said a word about his talk with Dr. Shaw—he acted as if nothing had happened. I'm sure he felt the chat was their own secret. My folks talked with Wrightsie for a few minutes longer, kissed him good night and left for the inn.

A few minutes later, the nurse came to the room to wash Wrightsie's hair. The job took all three of us, because Wrightsie's neck was so weak he couldn't hold his head up. So while Wright held his head, the nurse and I washed and rinsed his hair.

When the washing was completed, the nurse left and I toweled his hair dry. After that we said our prayers, "Now I lay me down to sleep. . . ." This was followed by many God blesses, with an extra special one for Wrightsie.

Wright said good night to his son. "I love you, best buddy," he said and he kissed Wrightsie's cheek.

"I love you too, dad," Wrightsie answered.

"I'll see you tomorrow," his dad said. "Now, I'll wait for mom in the hall so you can say good night to her alone. Night," and he squeezed his son's hand.

I took Wrightsie's hand and said, "I wanted to come over early tomorrow morning but Dr. Shaw asked me not to. But I will be out in the hallway so I can see you when you're wheeled by on the stretcher."

He looked up at me with his courageous eyes and slowly nodded his head.

"Wrightsie, I love you so much," I said, and I put my cheek

next to his.

He put his little arm around my neck and squeezed—tightly. "I love you, mom," he said.

Fighting back tears, I cradled my cheek in the curve at the back of his neck; then I kissed my favorite spot—his hair was sweet smelling and soft as down.

We held each other a few moments longer and then I stood up. I wrapped his arm around Tigeree, squeezed his hand, and said, "Good night, Wrightsie."

"Good night, mom," he said softly.

I walked out of the room. Wright met me and we held each other closely for a moment or so. Again Wrightsie was asleep in a few minutes, and then in silence we trudged wearily to the inn.

# 11
## *No! No! No!*

We began the day at five o'clock the next morning. I dressed in a hurry, slipped out of the room, and headed for the hospital. The weather was cold and damp, and it was very, very dark. I pulled up the collar of my coat and looked down the sidewalk to the emergency room entrance. The glow of lights shining out onto the street and the sight of a security guard comforted me. I quickened my pace.

I rode the elevator to the third floor and sat down in a small waiting area just beyond the elevator doors. Every few minutes the doors to the elevator opened, and women dressed in every variety of street clothes hurried off, entering one of two doors to my right. In a few minutes they'd reappear, but this time they were dressed in identical, drab green, operating room gowns. However, each nurse's appearance was brightened just a little by a colorful skull cap, all having a different floral design.

I looked at my watch—six o'clock. "Wrightsie must be getting his pre-operative shot now," I thought. "Oh, I wish I were with him."

The double door to the neurosurgical ward opened and I immediately recognized Dr. Shaw. He was dressed in a conservative business suit. And again I noticed his precise grooming—I imagined his hair still wet from a fresh combing. I searched his face, he looked completely refreshed, alert and totally prepared for the operation. He radiated a quiet, mature confidence that lifted my spirits and somewhat calmed my fears.

Just before he entered the doctor's dressing room through the first door on my right, he looked over to me and nodded a good morning, and with an understanding tone of voice said, "He should be along any moment now." And then he walked into the dressing room.

The elevator doors opened and closed a few more times. Women rushed off and into the dressing room. I caught parts of conversations about Thanksgiving Day and the weekend as they passed by. And then the doors to the ward swung open and two operating room aids, pushing a stretcher, appeared. I knew it was Wrightsie. I jumped up and hurried over to him. The aids halted the stretcher and I looked down at my son. The pre-operative shot had worked its mercy. Wrightsie was sound asleep. But, oh, how I wished he'd seen me.

I looked at him for a few seconds trying to fix his image in my mind and then I nodded a thank you to the aids. They continued their journey up the long corridor. I stared after them and watched their progress until they turned a corner into the operating room.

Then I took the elevator down to the main lobby where Wright and my parents were waiting. A kind and pleasant-looking nurse walked up to us and introduced herself. After the introduction, we learned that she was a supervisor and Dr. Shaw had asked her to keep us informed as to the progress of the operation. Then she showed us to a waiting room just outside of her office, offered us some coffee and the use of the telephone in the waiting room.

Wright and I sat down on a comfortable couch at one end of the small, but attractive, room. My parents sat down on a second couch to our right. Two large lamps glowed from end tables and magazines overflowed from a coffee table in front of Wright and me.

We sat in silence for a minute or so and then Wright said, "Nan, the other day I found a small chapel down the hall from here. Let's go say a prayer."

"All right," I answered.

"We'll stay here," my dad said, "just in case the nurse has some information for us."

Wright and I walked down to the chapel, sat down in a pew and lowered the kneeler. We each said our prayers in silence and then we returned to the waiting room. On the way, we stopped in the lobby and drew four cups of coffee from a large coffee urn.

We all sipped our coffee and tried to carry on a light conversation. Then we tried to lose ourselves in the magazines. Of course, none of us could forget for a moment what was really happening. Each second seemed like a day.

I suppose ten to fifteen minutes passed before the nurse appeared at the door. "They've finished shaving the back of his head," she said. "He's under anesthesia and they're starting the surgery now."

"Thank you," Wright said.

Then, after what seemed like hours, she came to the waiting room again and said, "They're through the skull now. Your son's condition is stable and they're continuing."

An eternity passed. "I'm going to go to her office and see if she's heard anything," Wright said.

Just then the nurse walked into the room, "They've located the tumor," she said, "and taken a biopsy. The tissue's being studied under the microscope now."

I thought to myself, "Oh, my God, he does have a tumor! I hope it's benign. I hope they can remove it without destroying him."

In just a few minutes the nurse was back again. I screamed

inside, "No! No! No! It hasn't been long enough! They haven't had time to remove it! Oh, my God, it's malignant! Malignant!! How horrible!"

"Mrs. Brunson," the nurse said gently, "they're closing now."

I couldn't answer.

Wright looked bewildered. "What does that mean, 'They're closing now?' "

I found my voice. "It means they can't remove the tumor. It means the tumor's malignant. Oh, Wright, it means Wrightsie's going to die."

## 12
## I Think You Should Take
## Him Home to Texas

I wanted to cry but I couldn't. Mom and dad, Wright and I sat
in shocked, stunned silence. I didn't believe in hell but I
remember thinking, "If there is a hell this is surely it."
Sometime around noon, Dr. Shaw walked into the small
waiting room. He wasn't the same man I'd seen six hours
earlier: he looked older, tired, and hurt as he sat down beside
me on the arm of the couch. "I'm sorry," he said. "I'd hoped it
was a cyst. But it wasn't."

I couldn't speak.

"We'll have the biopsy studied again," he continued.
"Perhaps we'll go back in—in three or four days."

I knew he was only trying to be kind—to soften the blow.
The tumor was malignant and there would be no more
operations. I sat with my head lowered trying to pull myself
together. Then I asked, "When can we see him, doctor?"

"I should say sometime around seven o'clock tonight," he
answered. "You can stay here as long as you like."

"Thank you, doctor," Wright replied. "We would like to use
the telephone."

After the doctor left the room, Wright and I decided that
we'd better call his mother, Tom and Hilda, Evelyn, Carl
Wilgus and my sister Kathy. We also agreed that it was best not

to tell Beth about the tumor at that time.

The phone calls took most of the afternoon and when they were completed we left for Children's Inn. We all picked at our supper, then talked over our coffee trying to pass the time until we could see our Wrightsie again.

Right at seven, we walked into the recovery room. I'd seen many sad and pathetic scenes—and for that matter, even frightening scenes—in hospitals before. But I was completely unprepared for what happened next. Wrightsie was lying on his back in a hospital bed adjusted so his knees and upper body were slightly elevated. He was uncovered and nude except for a sheet covering his loins. His head, covered by a bandage above his ears and eyes, was cradled between two sand bags. I noticed his eyes were closed and his proud little chest heaved easily with each rhythmic breath. He might have looked comfortable except for a tube coming out of one nostril and a second tube in his forearm leading to an i.v. bottle.

Leaning over his bed, I said, "Wrightsie, it's me—mom. I love you."

For a moment he didn't respond, and then slowly his lips opened and I saw his tongue move. A noise arose from his throat and he tried to form words. Then I realized what was wrong. I screamed inside, "He can't talk! They've destroyed his speech center! How can I take care of him? How can he let me know his needs? How horrible! I just can't bear this!"

Frantically, I turned to my husband and then I noticed my father standing at the foot of the bed. He was staring down in shock. His face was ashen gray and I thought, "He's going to get sick, or faint or both—maybe a heart attack."

Wright saw the alarm in my face and turned to my dad, "Feef," he said taking his arm, "you'd better sit down." My dad let Wright lead him out of the recovery room to a chair in the hall.

Then I looked at my mother—the one I'd really worried

about. She was standing a little off by herself, arms lowered, holding her purse in front of her with both hands. Her eyes glistened with tears as she looked down compassionately at her grandson. I couldn't help but feel great sorrow for her.

I turned back to Wrightsie, "Oh, Wrightsie, what is it?" I said. "I didn't hear you."

His lips started to move again and I lowered my ear close to his mouth. He repeated the same series of sounds two or three times. Finally, I made out—or maybe sensed—what he was trying to say, "Please go. Please go. Please go."

"Wright, he wants us to leave," I told my husband.

Wright leaned over our son and said gently, "You're a brave, brave boy, Wrightsie. I love you. We'll go now."

Then, I leaned down and kissed Wrightsie's cheek and said, "Oh, how I love you, Wrightsie. We all love you."

I stood up. Wright's hand was on my arm gently urging me away from the bed. I knew I should leave. The whole situation was beyond me—physically, emotionally and spiritually. When we started to leave the recovery room one of the nurses walked up to us and said, "I just got out of the Navy about two months ago, and when I found out your little boy is a Navy Junior I told the rest of the girls, 'He's my special patient.'"

"Thank you," Wright replied. "Thank you very much."

As we walked out of the recovery room, I remember thinking, "Oh, I'm so thankful we can leave you in the care of these loving, skilled nurses."

We walked up the long corridor and Wright led us into the waiting room and said, "Let's sit down. I think we all need a cup of coffee."

"But Wright," I said, "I need to find Dr. Shaw. I have to find out about Wrightsie's speech."

"Okay," Wright said, "okay. But please let me get us some coffee first. Then, I'll ask the nurse in the neuro ward if she knows where we can get ahold of Dr. Shaw."

No sooner had Wright left for coffee when Dr. Shaw walked into the waiting room. "Dr. Shaw," I said, "I'm so glad you're here—we were going to call you. We've just seen Wrightsie; he can't talk."

"Yes, I know," he answered. "I saw him late this afternoon."

"Can you do something, doctor?" I asked. "Will he ever be able to talk again?"

"I don't know, Mrs. Brunson," he said very gently. "You see, we were in that part of the brain. I was extremely careful, but we were there. And, of course his larynx is swollen and sore from the intubation. This could be part of the problem. I'd say we have a fifty-fifty chance he'll be able to talk again."

At this point in time I expected the very worst, so I was somewhat relieved when he told me there was a fifty-fifty chance. "Thank you, doctor," I said.

"I wish I could be more definite, Mrs. Brunson," the doctor said, "but we'll just have to wait and see."

I nodded. Yes, we just had to wait.

As I was getting ready for bed that night, I started to relive the day. The longer I thought the more fearful I became—then extremely frustrated as I realized the hopelessness of the situation. And finally, I became very angry.

When I walked out of the bathroom I saw Wright in bed reading. "What are you reading the Bible for? That won't do anything! We've got to *do* something!" I demanded.

"Nan," Wright said, lowering the Bible, "I wish I could do something. All we can do is pray and get everyone else to pray."

"All right then," I replied, "let's start calling. Let's call Father Eby." He was our priest when we lived in Virginia. "And let's call Reverend Thoburn at Fairfax Christian School too," I said.

"All right," Wright said, "let's start calling."

Father Eby said he would put Wrightsie's name on the

prayer list at the Church of the Good Shepherd. Reverend Thoburn said he would have the children at Fairfax Christian pray for Wrightsie during their morning chapel. Everyone else we called told us they'd all keep Wrightsie in their prayers.

Just before we turned out the lights that night Wright said, "Nan, do you think the doctor will operate in three or four days? Maybe they can get the tumor out after all?"

"No," I answered. "Dr. Shaw was just trying to make it easy for us. No, they won't operate again." Then I felt guilty. I could see by the expression on my husband's face he'd still hoped there was a chance.

I took his hand and said, "I'm sorry. I thought you knew."

He shook his head.

"I love you," I said. "Thanks for reading the Bible for us."

He squeezed my hand. I didn't know why but for some reason I slept soundly and long that night.

The next morning Wright and I met with Dr. Shaw in his office. "Well, I have the biopsy report," he said. "It confirms what we saw yesterday in the operating room." And then, choosing his words carefully, he said, "Wrightsie has a highly malignant brain stem glioma. On a virulency scale of one to four, the tumor's between three and four."

Wright and I didn't say a word. We just nodded our heads as Dr. Shaw, with patience and gentleness, explained the situation.

"I'd hoped it would be extrinsic to the brain stem but it isn't," he continued. "It's intrinsic, arising out of the brain itself, and the brain stem is slightly enlarged."

"But why?" Wright asked. "What causes these things? A couple of years ago in Virginia he fell from his bicycle and hit his forehead on the pavement. He had amnesia for about half an hour. We took him to Bethesda Naval Hospital and the doctor said he had suffered a concussion. Could that have caused the tumor?"

"No," Dr. Shaw said. "We don't know the cause. We don't know why this type of tumor occurs more frequently in young children than in adults. Maybe some day we will know, but right now we don't."

"What happens now, doctor?" Wright asked.

"We'll bring him back to the neuro ward this afternoon," he said. "And then in about a week I think you should take him home to Texas."

I was surprised the doctor thought he'd be ready to travel so soon.

"Commander," Dr. Shaw said to Wright, "why don't you see if you can make arrangements for the Air Force to fly him home next Tuesday."

"Yes, sir," Wright replied.

"And if at all possible, I want him to fly straight through to Dallas—no overnight stops."

"I'll tell them," Wright said.

"I'll call your specialist in Dallas," Dr. Shaw continued, "and ask him to make the necessary arrangements down there. Wrightsie should start radiation therapy as soon as he gets to Dallas."

# 13
## Texas Is My Home

Wrightsie was moved back to the neuro ward early Tuesday afternoon. He was placed in a room with three other children, right next to the nurses' station. And he was under the watchful eye of a private duty nurse. Our visits were still restricted so we weren't permitted to see him until 3:00 P.M. Wrightsie's bed was immediately to the right of the door and up against the wall. When we walked into the room, Wrightsie was lying on his left side facing the wall. Even so, I could see he was wide awake and alert.

"Hi, Wrightsie," I said, trying to sound cheerful, but he didn't respond whatsoever.

I gave my husband a questioning look and he walked up to Wrightsie's bed and said, "Hello, best buddy." Then trying to get a response he said, "Hey, in a couple of days we can play Battleship again."

Wrightsie didn't move a muscle.

I spotted Tigeree at the top of the bed with a new bandage on the back of his head. Then, thinking Wrightsie might react to his favorite little stuffed animal, I placed Tigeree in front of him. Wrightsie's hand shot out and he angrily pushed Tigeree up against the wall.

I leaned over the bed so I could see Wrightsie's face and said,

"I'm sorry, Wrightsie."

He closed his eyes and kept them that way for the rest of the visit.

I stood there a few seconds feeling completely frustrated and helpless. Then I turned to the nurse and said, "Is everything all right?"

"Yes," she answered, "his vital signs are stable, and he's taking fluids without any problems."

"Has he spoken to you?" I asked.

"He's said a few words," the nurse answered. "I can't always understand him the first time. But when he repeats it, I can usually figure out what he wants."

All I could do was nod my head. Then Wright said gently, "Nan, we'd better go now."

Wright thanked the nurse, and as we left the room I took one last look at Wrightsie, hoping against hope he would acknowledge me. But he kept his eyes closed.

When we joined my folks in the waiting room my dad immediately asked, "How's he doing?"

"Dad," I answered, almost breaking down, "the nurse says he's all right and he's even spoken to her. But he won't talk to me—he won't even look at me. How awful! I love him more than anything in this world and he won't even look at me. I've never been so frustrated—so torn up—in my life. I ought to be delighted he's better but I can't feel that way. I don't even know how I should feel. Oh, how awful! What can I do? What can I do?"

Wright and my parents just stood there helplessly. Finally after I'd regained my composure, we walked back to the inn. That night during supper I was overcome with frustration again. I felt like standing up in the center of the room and shouting at the top of my lungs, "My son's got a brain tumor!!! My son's got a brain tumor!!!" But at the same time I knew that it wouldn't help anything. There were probably people sitting there who were experiencing emotions similar to mine. Somehow I got through the meal and the evening.

We visited Wrightsie again about nine-thirty the next morning. This time he was lying on his right side facing the center of the room. Wright and I both talked with him, but he refused to say a word. We were about to leave the room when the nurse said, "Wrightsie, it's time for you to take a few sips of water."

"No!" Wrightsie said sharply. "I don't want any water!"

I was both thrilled and shocked, thrilled that he could talk and shocked at the way he'd spoken to the nurse. I'd never heard him talk to an adult in such strong tones.

"Wrightsie," I said, "try to drink a little bit." The nurse handed me the glass and I knelt down in front of him. He closed his eyes and then I gently pushed the straw against his lips and said, "Please, take just one sip."

He pursed his lips around the straw and then, with a resigned look on his face, he sipped the water. After a few swallows he pushed the straw out of his mouth with his tongue.

"Thank you, Wrightsie," I said, and handed the glass back to the nurse.

It was time for our visit to end. I knelt before Wrightsie again and said, "We've got to leave now. Grandma and Feef are going back to Danbury. They said to tell you goodbye and they'll be back Saturday. Do you want me to say anything to them for you?"

I waited to see if Wrightsie would reply, but he didn't.

"How'd it go?" my dad asked as soon as we entered the waiting room.

I told them about the water incident and then my dad said, "I wonder why he's acting that way. It's just not like Wrightsie."

"I can't figure it out," I replied. "Maybe he's mad at me because I didn't see him before he went to surgery."

"I don't think that would cause it," Wright said. "He knew you couldn't come to the room. Well, anyway, if he doesn't change within the next few days I think we should talk it over with Dr. Shaw."

"All right," I agreed.

Later that afternoon we helped my parents pack for their trip back to Danbury. As we said our goodbyes, dad reminded me he had made reservations at the inn for themselves, Tom's family and Beth for the next Saturday.

That evening Wright and I visited Wrightsie again. As we entered the room I heard Wrightsie demand, "Nurse, I've got to go to the bathroom!"

Again I was dismayed at the way he spoke to the nurse but I was also delighted for his speech was clear and distinct. Wrightsie was facing the wall and didn't see us walk in, but the nurse did. Without speaking she handed me the little glass urinal. I nodded my head, took the urinal and said, "Let me help you, Wrightsie."

When he was through he held up his hands as usual and I wiped them very thoroughly with a wet washcloth. He still hadn't spoken directly to me, but I was thrilled to be able to help my son again.

Wrightsie did not speak to me directly until Thursday night. A little boy had just been admitted with a possible skull fracture. His face was swollen and he was both crying and vomiting at the same time. I looked at Wrightsie and saw a look of anguish and desperation on his face. I hurried over to his bed and he said in a loud whishper, "Pull the curtain. I can't stand to see that kid throw up."

Quickly I pulled the canvas curtain around his bed and saw a look of relief come over his face as he breathed a sigh. I stood silent for a few minutes. This was the first time since the recovery room that Wrightsie had spoken to me directly and I wanted to nurture our new relationship. "Wrightsie, I don't know why you won't speak to me, but if it's because you didn't see me before your operation let me tell you what happened that morning."

I paused to see if Wrightsie would respond. He did keep his eyes open and he seemed to be waiting for my explanation.

"I did see you that morning," I continued. "Remember Dr. Shaw didn't want me to come to the room? So I waited for you out by the elevator. But when they wheeled you by you were sound asleep. But I was waiting and I did see you."

Hopefully, I waited for Wrightsie to say something. He didn't answer and a feeling of despair came over me. I just couldn't understand what was wrong. I only stayed a few minutes longer and then I returned to the inn.

I told Wright about my visit and when I'd finished he said, "Well, I don't know what the problem is. But remember he hasn't just rejected you. He's rejected me and the nurses too. So it's not you. Let's talk it over with Dr. Shaw tomorrow morning. Maybe he can do something."

On Friday morning we walked into the doctor's office. After discussing our flight and hospital arrangements, I asked about Wrightsie's attitude. Dr. Shaw thought for a moment then said, "That's a little unusual for a child his age. We see this quite often in teen-agers and young adults when they've been through what your son has."

"Do you think it's because I didn't see him before surgery?" I asked—this thought was still preying on my mind.

"Oh, no," he replied. "You see, your son has been through a very difficult experience. He's been hurt and he's angry."

"Is there anything I can do?" I asked.

"No, just be patient. He'll come around," the doctor assured me. "And I'll have a little chat with him this afternoon. It may help."

I don't know what Dr. Shaw said to him, but that evening I noticed a definite change in Wrightsie's behavior. He still didn't speak to us, but at least he tolerated our presence and I sensed his anger was gone. However, the really big change occurred the next day. Beth arrived in Boston. My brother Tom and his family had brought Beth up from their home on

Long Island. They were followed immediately by my parents.

While they all registered at Children's Inn, we immediately took Beth over to the hospital to see Wrightsie. It was a tender scene.

"Hi, Wrightsie," Beth said. "I've missed you."

"Bethy, hi," Wrightsie said in a little boy voice. "I've missed you too." His personality of the past five days had changed completely. He talked easily with Beth, with Wright and with me—almost as if nothing had happened. I was thrilled.

As Wrightsie and Beth chatted I turned to the nurse and said, "How's he doing?"

"Fine," she answered. "He's much stronger."

"Mom?" Beth interrupted us. "Wrightsie's got a mean nurse at night."

"Yeah," Wrightsie chimed in, "she wakes me up every night and makes me drink a big glass of water—all at one time. Someday I'm gonna get her."

"That's not right," the nurse said, overhearing our conversation. "I'm going to check his chart."

She left the room and then returned in a few minutes saying, "Yes, she's an efficient nurse all right. She has been giving him his fluids all at one time. He needs the fluids, but he also needs love and understanding. We're going to take her off the case and put him on floor care. That should take care of the problem."

"Thank you," I said and I looked down at Wrightsie. He had a look of relief on his face.

Then I said to Beth, "We're not allowed to stay too long, Beth. Why don't you say goodbye to Wrightsie now. You can see him again this afternoon."

Beth turned to Wrightsie and said, "I have to go now, Wrightsie. I'll see you later."

"Okay, Bethy," he answered.

"Here," Beth said, spotting Tigeree off in the corner of the bed. She picked up the little, well-worn stuffed tiger and handed him to Wrightsie.

"I don't want him any more," he said in a sad, yet final, tone of voice. "He's contaminated. And please take those bandages off," he said with a hint of anger. "He doesn't need 'em."

Beth removed all the bandages from Tigeree except for the original Band-Aid on his right front paw—the one corresponding to Wrightsie's big toe injury of months before. Then she returned Tigeree to his bedside exile.

When we arrived back at the inn, we took Beth to our room. Wright and I had already decided we should tell her all about her brother.

"Beth," her dad said, "here, sit down on the bed with me. I've got something very important to tell you."

Sensing the seriousness in her dad's voice, she sat down and said apprehensively, "What is it, dad?"

"Beth, I wish we didn't have to tell you this," her dad said, "but we've always been honest with you, and I don't want you to ever regret not having been good to Wrightsie or not having loved him enough. Do you know what I mean?"

"Yes, dad," Beth answered. "But what is it? What's wrong?"

"When Dr. Shaw operated on Wrightsie last Monday," Wright continued, "he found a brain tumor." Wright hesitated a moment and then he continued, "Wrightsie's a very sick boy, Bethy. They can't remove the tumor and he may not make it."

Beth looked up at me, questioned my face and I nodded a sad yes. Then she put her head in her hands and started to cry. I sat down beside her, and we held her as she cried.

After a few minutes Wright said softly, "Beth?" She looked up at her dad. "There is one hope," and he reached under the bed and pulled out one of the books that Carl Wilgus had sent. "The Lord can heal Wrightsie," he said, giving Beth the book.

"What do you mean, dad?" Beth asked—she'd never heard her father talk like that before.

"That book says it better than I can," Wright answered. "The woman who wrote it, Kathryn Kuhlman, asks Jesus to heal people and sometimes they are healed—even from the most hopeless diseases. Beth, we all have to pray that Jesus will heal Wrightsie. There's no other hope for him."

Beth took the book her father handed her, opened it and started to read. Later we asked her to join us for lunch in my parents' room, but she wanted to stay in our room and read.

On Sunday afternoon we took Beth over to the hospital to say goodbye to Wrightsie. She held his hand and said, "I'll miss you, Wrightsie."

"I'll miss you too," Wrightsie answered. Then he picked up a small bluish-colored fluff of a dog that had decorated a potted plant he'd received.

He pressed the little dog into his sister's hand and said, "Bethy, this is for you."

Beth kissed his cheek and said, "Oh, thank you very much, Wrightsie."

My heart broke as I watched my two brave children and wondered how much longer they'd have each other.

We said our goodbyes and, as Beth climbed into Tom's station wagon, I noticed she clutched two items in her arms: the little blue dog and the book her father had given her. Wright and I watched and waved until the two cars disappeared down the street. Then I began to feel very alone and depressed.

Wright suggested we return to the hospital, but I wanted to rest in our room for a while.

Once in the room, I sat down in a chair and closed my eyes for a few moments. Then I spotted my big blue suitcase. For some reason I began to look through the clothes I'd packed for Wrightsie. My packing had reflected my hopes and fears. On the top were his get-well clothes. And hidden underneath were the clothes that reflected my worst fears. If Wrightsie had died during the operation I'd wanted him to be buried in his Cub Scout uniform.

And then I spotted his shoes—I'd packed only one pair. They

were very boyish-looking, made of brown leather with thick cord soles. I picked them up and turned them over in my hand. Memories flooded my mind. I remembered his little baby feet crossed together as he slept; I remembered how after I'd bathed and powdered him I'd kiss the bottom of his feet and he'd squirm and laugh with delight; I remembered his feet flying through tall grass as he caught a little baby rabbit he later gave to Beth; and then I remembered his last struggling effort to walk to the bathroom at Scott Air Force Base. The memories were too much. I clutched his shoes to my breast and cried my heart out.

It was about six o'clock when I walked over to the hospital to join Wright. "Have you seen Wrightsie?" I asked.

"No," he answered, "I thought I'd wait for you.

"You know," Wright continued, "I've been thinking: the other day when I told Wrightsie we'd be going back to Texas, he said, 'It'll be good to get home.' I can't remember if I told him he'd be going to a hospital or not. He may think he's going home to Arlington."

"I hope not," I answered. "I don't want him to be disappointed."

"Well, I guess I'd better make sure he knows what's going to happen," Wright said reluctantly.

We walked to Wrightsie's room and after chatting with him a few minutes, his dad said, "Wrightsie, I think I may have misled you the other day when I told you you'd be going home. You see, we have to take you to a hospital in Dallas before you can go home to Arlington."

"I know that, dad," Wrightsie said, not the least bit disappointed. "You see, when I said 'home,' I meant Texas. Texas is my home."

"Oh, Wrightsie," his dad exclaimed with a big smile, "you're—you're quite a boy."

# 14
## O God, Please Heal My Wrightsie

Monday morning Wright and I had a last conference with Dr. Shaw. Near the end of the conversation Wright asked, "Doctor, how much time do we have with Wrightsie?"

The doctor thought for a moment and then said, "Well, we're not talking about days, but we're not talking about years either—I can't be any more specific."

Wright and I were silent as we tried to assess the meaning of Dr. Shaw's words. Then, realizing that all our questions had been asked, I said, "Dr. Shaw, I want to thank you for taking Wrightsie's case, and for the wonderful care you've given him. I'll always know in my heart that he had the very best."

"Thank you, Mrs. Brunson," he said. "I hope to see you again before you leave for Dallas." Then he excused himself—he had another appointment—and Wright and I left his office for the inn.

The corpsmen arrived at the hospital around ten o'clock the next morning. I bundled Wrightsie up in his cowboy sleeping bag and after much persuasion, he consented to wear his Dallas Cowboys stocking cap over his bandaged head.

One by one, and in little groups, the nurses came to say goodbye as we walked up the hallway. There were student nurses in their blue and white bibbed uniforms and graduate nurses in crisp white. Each girl said a few words of kindness or encouragement.

And then one pretty, dark-haired nurse placed a folded piece of paper and two little, flat, painted rocks in my hand. She said, "The rocks are for Wrightsie and the poem is for you and Commander Brunson."

"Wrightsie, look," I said showing him the rocks. "Look, a little yellow smile face on this one, and—and a daisy on this one."

"Thank you so much," I said.

"You're welcome, Mrs. Brunson," she answered. "Have a good flight. Bye, Wrightsie."

As we neared the double door leading to the long corridor, I again glanced in the room where the pretty teen-age girl with the tracheotomy tube in her throat was sitting. But this time I thought, "Oh, God, I'll take my Wrightsie like that. I'll take him any way. Please, don't let him die."

When we arrived at the airfield the corpsmen parked the ambulance near the loading area. And they kept the heater on and the motor running. We sat there—in silence—a few minutes and then Wright said, "Nan, I'm going over to the canteen for coffee. Would you like a cup?"

"Please," I answered.

When he returned, we stood outside the ambulance and sipped the steaming coffee—the hot paper cup absorbed the winter chill from my hands. I stared across the gray, bleak December landscape and wondered what the future would bring. Dr. Shaw's words echoed in my ears, "Well, we're not talking about days, but we're not talking about years either."

"Oh, God," I thought, "I only have a few months, maybe only weeks, to love Wrightsie."

I looked in the ambulance. Wisps of white exhaust smoke from the motor obscured my view, then the smoke curled and whirled away and I saw Wrightsie's little freckle-faced, pug-nosed profile. I thought, "What can I do? I love him too much. What will—".

The whine of jet engines interrupted my thoughts. I looked up and saw the big blue Air Force hospital plane taxiing towards us from the runway. The plane stopped near the ambulance, the big clam shell door opened, the ramp unfolded and the corpsmen carried Wrightsie aboard.

"Put him next to the nurse's station," the flight nurse directed the corpsmen. They strapped the litter to the stanchion, checked its security and then said goodbye to Wright and me. I noticed oxygen and suction outlets next to Wrightsie's head and there were other types of emergency medical equipment in the compartment.

Wright and I took two side-by-side seats directly across the aisle from Wrightsie. We fastened our seat belts and prepared for take off. Tigeree was on my lap just in case Wrightsie wanted his little friend back.

After we were airborne, Wright and I discussed many things. He noted the date—December 7—Pearl Harbor Day, and we recalled our visit to Hiroshima's Peace Park. And then I was overcome with the sickening thought of radiation. "Oh, Wright," I said, "do you think we should go through with the radiation therapy?"

"We've got to," Wright said.

"I can't bear the thought of what it will do to his brain," I said.

"Nan," Wright said very seriously, "now this may sound strange coming from me, but you see I've changed—you've got to trust the Lord. If Jesus heals Wrightsie then the radiation damage won't mean a thing—it'd be taken care of too."

I looked at my husband in silence for a few seconds, then I said, "I hope you're right. And you have changed. I've wondered, what's happened to you?"

Wright looked straight ahead for a moment and then he said,

"Well, remember the night in Dallas when I stayed with Wrightsie at the hospital while you and Beth went out for dinner with your brother?"

I nodded.

"When you came back I told you that Sherwin McCurdy and Kris Mineau had visited," Wright said.

"Yes, I remember."

"Well, what I didn't tell you," Wright continued, "was that Kris talked with me for two hours about Christianity. After they left, I suddenly realized I'd been wrong all my life; the man-made theories and philosophies I'd believed were false—nothing but junk. Then I walked over to Wrightsie's bed—he was sleeping, and I—I, well, I accepted Jesus as my Savior.

"Now, I know that expression turns some people off," Wright said quickly, "but that's what I did. And then, as best I could remember it, I said the Apostles' Creed.

"It was wonderful; for the first time in my life I believed the creed—every word of it." There was a hint of excitement in my husband's voice.

"And then," Wright said, "I gave Wrightsie up to Jesus and asked Him to heal him. And that's what happened, Nan."

I took Wright's hand and squeezed it. We sat in silence for a few minutes and then I said, "Wright, do you really think Wrightsie will be healed?"

"I don't know," he answered. "But I'm going to keep on praying."

I looked over at our son and said a silent prayer, "O God, please heal my Wrightsie."

# 15

## *We Can't Seem to Get the Radiation to Him Fast Enough*

During the remainder of the flight to Dallas, Wright and I tried to make plans for our immediate future. We decided to have Beth return from Long Island and then ask Wright's mother—Flossy—to come and keep house while I was caring for Wrightsie in the hospital. Also, we thought it was best for Wright to report back to work.

It did not seem long before the airplane's wheels touched the runway, the pilot reversed the engines and taxied the plane to the loading area. They carried Wrightsie to the waiting Navy ambulance and soon we were on the road to the hospital in Dallas.

When we arrived I was pleasantly surprised to see Wright's cousin, Chuck, waiting for us. Heartbreak was written all over his face. The year before, his wife had died after a long, courageous fight against leukemia. And I knew he was reliving the agony as he looked down at Wrightsie.

I talked with Chuck until Wright returned from the admissions office. We invited Chuck to go with us to Wrightsie's room. He declined, saying his children were expecting him home. Before he left, Wright asked him to ask a priest to pay us a call in the hospital. Chuck assured us he would.

Wright drove on home that evening. The next morning, after Wrightsie and I had finished breakfast, an aid wheeled a stretcher into the room, and told us it was time for his "x-rays." Wrightsie nodded and I was thankful he didn't ask me any questions.

The aid rolled the stretcher parallel to his bed. As I steadied Wrightsie's head, he sidled himself onto the stretcher. We took the elevator down to the radiation area and when the aid wheeled the stretcher into the small waiting room, Wrightsie sounded out the sign over the doorway, "Ra-di-ation Ther-a-py."

"Oh, Lord," I thought, "please don't let him ask me about radiation."

And Wrightsie never said a word—although I'm certain he knew very well what was going on. It was a frightening secret we both knew, but out of our love for each other we never shared it.

The aid pushed Wrightsie's stretcher into a small examining room. Two doctors—both radiologists—were waiting in the room. One doctor—the younger of the two—turned to Wrightsie and said, "Well, son, we'd like to examine you."

After the examination, the younger doctor showed me into his office. He told me the treatment plan. There would be twenty-five Cobalt-60 treatments—five a week for five weeks After that series of treatments we would wait for two weeks for a re-evaluation. If Wrightsie responded well, he would receive five more exposures. The main objective was to halt the tumor's growth and shrink its size.

I shuddered inwardly because I was aware of the severe side effects of radiation therapy. The doctor told me Wrightsie would lose his hair—it would begin to fall out in the second or third week and he would feel very weak in general. And further, the pressure build-up around the fast-growing tumor would cause a great deal of nausea and vomiting. I wondered what the deadly radiation might do to Wrightsie's healthy brain cells, but I did not ask the question because I really didn't want to know the answer. He continued, "Now, you can take your son home on the weekends—it'll do you both good. I'm going to set up his appointments so he'll be treated early on Fridays and late on Mondays. That way you'll have a long weekend."

"Thank you, doctor," I said, too upset to really appreciate the fact we could spend our weekends at home.

"Well, Mrs. Brunson," the doctor said getting up from his chair, "I'd like to give him his first treatment now."

I left the office and returned to the small examining room. The aid and Wrightsie were busy talking with each other. When she saw me she realized it was time for Wrightsie's treatment. I helped her guide the stretcher and then just before we entered the room I said, "Wrightsie, I'll be right here waiting for you; I'm not allowed beyond this point."

Nor did I want to go any farther. I couldn't bear the thought of Wrightsie going through the radiation much less see the intricate equipment that would be used. I hurried out into the hallway. Then I noticed a sign on the wall reading "CHAPEL." I raced down the hall and turned into a large chapel. I sat down in a pew, lowered the kneeler and prayed. I felt nothing—no peace, no comfort, no assurance, nothing.

In a few minutes, I returned to the radiation area and waited. When Wrightsie was wheeled out, I searched his face to see what his reaction to the treatment was. All I noticed was a long, thin red line drawn all across his forehead. And near each temple perpendicular lines crossed the first line. Without being told, I knew the crosses were used to aim the radiation equipment so the penetrating rays could be concentrated on the brain tumor.

When we got back to the room we watched TV. The show was a comedy and it was so good to laugh together and see Wrightsie happy. We were able to forget the real world for a few minutes.

Wrightsie and I spent the rest of the day chatting and watching TV. Wright arrived about 5:30 P.M.—after work. "Well, it looks like you've settled into your new home," he said with an approving smile.

IIe was delighted to learn that we would be able to come home on weekends, and then he shared some good news with us: Beth would be returning Friday. Wrightsie was thrilled.

Wright walked over to Wrightsie's bed and said, "And guess who else is coming?"

"Who?" Wrightsie asked.

"Your Grandma Flossy, that's who," Wright said, smiling down at his son. "Think you'll be able to eat some of her apple pies?"

"Sure," Wrightsie beamed.

Finally our first weekend at home in five weeks arrived. How wonderful it was to be back in familiar surroundings. When Beth came back we had a great family weekend together. Monday morning came much too quickly.

That afternoon, after the radiation treatment, the specialist came by the room and gave Wrightsie an examination. I hadn't realized how his condition had deteriorated over the past three or four days. He could barely sit up alone and when he did his balance was poor. He weaved slightly back and forth.

"Touch your nose with your finger," the specialist said.

Wrightsie tried—almost losing his balance in the process. His little fingers missed his nose a number of times. Then he succeeded one time. I was heartsick as I watched his struggling efforts.

The next day Grandma Flossy arrived. Wright brought her directly from the airport to the hospital. She was tired from her trip and visibly upset when she saw the condition of her grandson. She stayed for a few minutes at the hospital and then Wright took her home.

By the end of the week, Wrightsie was nearly helpless. He couldn't move his right arm or leg and he had to be lifted from his bed to the stretcher and back again. Before our departure from the hospital for the weekend, the radiologist examined him.

When he'd finished, he said, "Mrs. Brunson, would you step into the hall for a minute?"

I followed him from the room, closed the door behind us and asked, "Doctor, what's wrong?"

"Mrs. Brunson," he said with grave concern, "I don't know what we're going to do: we can't seem to get the radiation to him fast enough."

For a moment I just stood there helplessly. Then I asked, "Doctor, what's causing the paralysis? Is it the radiation or the tumor?"

"It's the tumor," he answered.

"Oh, God, no!" I thought.

# 16
## Why Didn't He Heal Me, Dad?

Wright picked us up at the entrance to the emergency room around noon that Friday. He carefully bundled Wrightsie into the back seat of the car and we headed home.

As we drove along the turnpike, Wright said, "Nan, I got a call from Sherwin McCurdy this morning at work. He and his wife host a fifteen minute radio broadcast every Friday afternoon starting at four o'clock. It's sponsored by the Full Gospel Business Men. And Sherwin would like us to listen today; they're going to talk about Wrightsie."

Wrightsie's favorite teacher, Miss Carlile, visited him that afternoon. She brought many Christmas cards from his classmates, then they exchanged Christmas gifts—Wrightsie gave her a POW bracelet he'd been saving for her.

I'd been keeping my eye on the time and as four o'clock approached, I excused myself and turned the radio on. I adjusted the intercom so the radio broadcast would play in Wrightsie's room. Then I returned to his bedroom. Sure enough, Sherwin McCurdy told about Wrightsie towards the end of their broadcast. He told how he'd met our family, then in closing he requested prayer for Wrightsie and us. Wrightsie was delighted.

Wrightsie ate very little that night and we bundled him off to bed fairly early. Wright and I stayed up late talking in front of the fireplace. I told him about my conversation with the radiologist before we'd left the hospital that day. He thought for a moment and then he said, "Nan, I'm really worried. I hate to say this, but he may not make it to Christmas."

"Oh, Wright, what are we going to do?"

"I don't know. I don't know."

We stared into the flames for a few minutes, then Wright broke the silence saying, "When's your sister Kathy leaving San Francisco for Dallas?"

"Next Wednesday—the twenty-second."

"Maybe you should call her tonight and see if she can get here sooner," Wright suggested.

"Wright, I don't think so. Let's wait and see what happens. Maybe he'll be stronger tomorrow."

Wright agreed and we headed off to bed.

Wrightsie slept late the next morning. But when he did awaken I could see he felt much better and he appeared stronger. So we carried on with our plans for the weekend. The main event would be Beth's twelfth birthday.

Later in the afternoon, Wright and Beth had to go shopping. They told Wrightsie their intentions. "Wrightsie," Beth said, "Daddy and I are going to buy our Christmas tree. I wish you could go with us."

"Aw," Wrightsie said. "Mom, can I go with them?"

"I'm sorry, Wrightsie, but you'd better stay here and rest. I know you want to celebrate with us tonight," I said.

"Okay. But I want to pay for the tree with my own money," he said, referring to the money the many well-wishers had sent him.

"But, Wrightsie—" his dad started to protest and then he thought better of it. "Okay, best buddy, we'll let you buy the tree this year."

Wrightsie beamed as I fished out some of his money from its

special envelope in my purse.

Beth and Wright returned within the hour and busied themselves putting the tree up, unpacking ornaments and testing the lights. Flossy and I prepared supper.

After our meal I carried a special "birthday cake" into the den. It was an apple pie with twelve lighted candles on it—Wrightsie had requested pie instead of cake and Beth had approved the request.

I was feeding Wrightsie when a frightening incident occurred. The specialist had cautioned me that Wrightsie had lost the gag reflex on the right side of his throat. He said I should be careful that he didn't choke on his food. I was feeding Wrightsie small bites of pie when all of a sudden he started to cough and his face reddened. I jumped up, grabbed him, lifted him to a sitting position and gave him a couple of pats on the back. It was over almost as suddenly as it started. I supported his head and gently lowered him back to the pillows. Tears of fright, frustration and disappointment rolled down his cheeks.

"Wrightsie? Want to watch me open my presents?" Beth asked, thoughtfully trying to divert his attention.

Wrightsie nodded and his face brightened.

After Beth had opened her birthday gifts, we decorated the tree. Next, as was our yearly family custom, Wright and I gave Beth and Wrightsie their special Christmas ornaments to hang on the tree. That year they received identical silver crosses. We put one on the very top of the tree and the second was placed directly in the center of the tree facing the den.

Then I had one more surprise for the evening. Wrightsie had received a large package from a girl friend I'd known since my nursing days in Pensacola, Florida. "Something came in the mail for you today, Wrightsie," I announced, placing the package beside the couch.

"Bethy, would you open it for me please?" Wrightsie asked.

"Sure," Beth replied, and she started to unwrap the

package.

"Close your eyes, Wrightsie," Beth said as she started to remove the last of the wrappings.

"Okay, Bethy," he answered in an excited voice and he squeezed his eyes shut.

Beth lifted the gift from the box, then she said, "Look, Wrightsie!"

Wrightsie opened his eyes. Then he opened them wider still, his face lit up and he exclaimed, "Snoopy!"

Beth handed the large, soft, black and white, stuffed dog to her brother. Wrightsie wrapped his good left arm around the dog's neck and said, "Welcome to our home, Snoopy."

I felt a sense of pleasant delight for my son as I watched him cuddle his new companion. Then, for a moment, the feeling was replaced with sadness as I thought, "Tigeree—poor Tigeree. You're all alone in Wrightsie's closet, your fur's worn off from around your neck by Wrightsie's hugs and now you've been replaced."

"Oh, mom, I love Snoopy," Wrightsie said happily, bringing me back to the moment.

Early on Sunday afternoon Wright moved the color TV set from the den into Wrightsie's room. "Come on in and see our fifty-yard-line seats for the Dallas Cowboys' game," Wright invited.

Wrightsie was propped up in bed with two pillows, watching the TV and eagerly waiting for the game to begin. And Wright had taped two Dallas Cowboy pennants to the side of the TV.

"Oh," Wright said, "I forgot to get our drinks." And he left for the kitchen.

"Enjoy the game with your best buddy," I said as I too left the room.

Wright passed me in the hall carrying their drinks and I heard the beginning strains of the national anthem being played over the TV as I headed for the kitchen.

In a minute or so Wright walked in the kitchen with tears streaming down his cheeks.

"What's the matter, hon?" I asked with concern.

Wright didn't answer for a few seconds, then he took a deep breath and explained, "When I walked into the bedroom with our drinks, Wrightsie was trying to salute as they played, 'The Star-Spangled Banner.' He was trying to get his right arm to work and it wouldn't, so he tried to lift it to his forehead with his left hand—"

"What did you do?" I asked.

"Well, when I got ahold of myself, I said, 'That's all right, son. It's okay for a wounded Cub Scout to salute with his left hand.' Then he saluted with his left hand until the national anthem was over."

Wrightsie shouted from the bedroom, "Dad! Dad! The game's starting."

"Okay, son," Wright answered and hurried from the kitchen after he'd dried his eyes on his forearm.

Back in the hospital, on Wednesday, we planned a tea party to celebrate my sister Kathy's arrival. Wrightsie wanted to surprise her. Wright picked Kathy up at Love Field and brought her directly to the hospital, then he drove back to work.

Wrightsie was excited to see his aunt and they enjoyed their visit over cookies and tea.

Early that evening, the radiologist dropped in. After I'd introduced him to Kathy he walked over to the bed. "Wrightsie," he said, "I'm going to let you go home early this weekend. You can leave tomorrow morning after your treatment. No treatment on Friday—it's Christmas Eve."

"Thank you," Wrightsie said in a little voice. I could see he was getting tired.

Then the doctor asked, "What do you want for Christmas, Wrightsie?"

"Potato salad, steak, apple pie on Christmas Eve; and strawberries, muffins and ham for Christmas brunch."

"Well, I see you've got that all figured out," the doctor laughed. And then very genuinely and gently he said, "I wish you a merry Christmas, and I'll see you next Monday, Wrightsie."

"Merry Christmas," Wrightsie responded.

The next morning after Wrightsie's treatment I took him down to the chapel with me. I wheeled his stretcher through the doors leading into the chapel and I said, "This is where I come every morning during your treatment."

Wrightsie's eyes scanned the large sanctuary and he spotted a red wooden box fastened on the wall just inside the entrance. "What's that for?" he asked.

"That's a box where a person can leave a donation for poor people," I explained.

"Oh," he answered.

"Well, let's go back to the room," I said pushing the stretcher back through the doors. Wrightsie's eyes stayed fixed on the poor box as I rolled him into the hallway.

When we were back in his room I started to gather all the things we'd take home with us for the long weekend. Wright joined us and we were finally ready to leave. As we wheeled Wrightsie down the hall towards the elevator he said, "Mom, can we go to the chapel again—before we go home?"

"Well, yes, but what for?" I asked.

"I want to give some of my money to the poor people."

"We sure can," I answered bursting with admiration.

As we neared the chapel I heard singing. We pushed Wrightsie's stretcher through the double doors and stopped beside the poor box. A choral group, practicing Christmas carols, provided a fitting backdrop for our mission. We listened to the singing for a few minutes and then I said, "Wrightsie, how much money do you want to give?"

His reply flabbergasted me. It was a great deal for a little boy to give and a sizeable portion of what he'd received from his well-wishers.

"Wrightsie, why don't you let me write a check for the amount and you can pay me later," his dad suggested.

"Oh, no," Wrightsie answered. "I don't want anyone to know how much I gave. And you and mom have to promise you won't ever tell."

"We promise," his dad assured him.

I reached into my purse, withdrew the stated amount, folded it and handed the money to Wrightsie. He struggled with his good left arm and hand trying to put the money into the slot. Wright reached down and supported his left shoulder, then Wrightsie was able to deposit the money. His effort exhausted him and he laid back down on the stretcher with a sigh. We all bowed our heads and Wrightsie led us in prayer.

"Dear Jesus, please use this money to help the poor people have a good Christmas." We all said, "Amen."

The spirit of Christmas was upon the three of us as we left the hospital that December day.

A wave of nausea hit Wrightsie when we arrived home. Surprisingly, he became very hungry after this feeling of sickness left and he devoured waffles, bacon and potato salad. After his late brunch, he drifted off to sleep.

Wrightsie slept late into the afternoon. When he woke up I turned the TV set on for him and returned to the kitchen. Later Wright joined me for a cup of coffee. We chatted at the table for a few minutes when Wrightsie asked, "Dad, will you put me on the floor?"

Wright gave me a look that asked, "Is it okay?"

I nodded a silent yes.

Wright put a blanket on the den floor, lifted Wrightsie from the couch and lowered him to the floor—on his stomach. Then Wright returned to the kitchen.

We continued to talk for a few minutes, then Wright glanced in the den towards Wrightsie. A startled look crossed his face, and, as he motioned for me to look in the den, he asked, "Wrightsie, what are you doing?"

When I looked in the den, I saw Wrightsie struggling to move around on his stomach—using his good left arm and leg.

With a proud grin he looked up at his dad and said, "I'm practicing so I can crawl to the Christmas tree on Christmas morning."

Wright jumped up from his chair at the table and hurried into the den. "Oh, Wrightsie," he said, choked up with emotion, "you don't have to crawl. We'll ask Jesus to heal you so you can walk to that tree on Christmas morning."

Wright gently picked up his crippled son and put him back on the couch and tucked him in saying, "There. You rest a while: you've been working hard."

"Thanks, dad," Wrightsie answered.

I noticed tears in Wright's eyes when he returned to the kitchen.

The next day was Christmas Eve. We woke up to a bright and sunny morning. Wrightsie asked, "Mom, can we go see the Foxes?"

"Oh, Wrightsie, are you sure you're up to it?" I asked.

"Sure, mom. I feel fine."

"Okay. Evelyn wanted us to come over."

I bundled him up in his sleeping bag and we all—Flossy, Kathy, Beth, Wright with Wrightsie cradled in his arms, and I—walked next door to the Foxes'.

Bopo met us. His huge frame filled the doorway. "Well, now," he boomed in his strong Oklahoma voice, "here's Wrightsie coming for a visit."

Wrightsie gave a shy little grin as he looked up from his father's arms at the towering Bopo.

"Put him right over there on the couch," Bopo commanded,

"so he can watch TV with the men."

Wright laid Wrightsie down on the L-shaped divan and piled pillows under his head. Then the men and boys watched a football game.

Beth ran off with the Fox girls while we women chatted in the kitchen. Every few minutes I checked Wrightsie to see if he was tired. All too soon, an uncomfortable look came across his face. "Are you all right, Wrightsie?" I asked.

"Oh, mom," he said in a sad voice, "I'm sorry; I don't feel good. Can we go home?"

We all said hurried goodbyes and left for home. Wright put Wrightsie in his bedroom for a rest and I started to prepare our supper.

At the close of the evening we all said prayers in Wrightsie's room. Wright laid his hands on Wrightsie's head and prayed, "Holy Father, use my hands as instruments for your mercy. Let the healing power of your Holy Spirit flow from me to my son, and in the name of Jesus Christ heal him from his sickness. Strengthen his right arm and leg, restore them to use and in the morning let him walk to our Christmas tree. In Jesus' name I pray. Amen."

"Amen," Kathy, Beth, Flossy and I chorused.

Wrightsie looked up at his dad with thankful eyes, then we all gave him a kiss and said goodnight.

That Christmas morning Wright and I woke up very early. Wright made coffee, turned on the tree lights and started a fire in the fireplace while I got dressed. By eight o'clock Beth, Kathy and Flossy were up and dressed and it was time to get Wrightsie.

Wright and I slipped quietly into his room and knelt beside his bed. "Wrightsie? Wrightsie?" I said softly. "It's morning. Santa's been here."

I noticed Wright staring intently into Wrightsie's face. Slowly Wrightsie opened his eyes.

"It's morning, Wrightsie," I repeated. "And Santa's been here."

A little smile came to the right side of Wrightsie's face. But as usual the left side didn't respond. And I saw a bitter look of disappointment come across my husband's face. Then I recalled his healing prayer of the night before.

Wright fought back his disappointment, gently lifted our son from his bed and carried him out to the den. As he lowered him to the den couch, Wrightsie looked up into his father's eyes and asked in a searching, bewildered tone, "Why didn't He heal me, dad? I begged Him and begged Him."

It took a moment for Wright to compose himself before he could answer Wrightsie's question. Then he said, "I—I don't know, Wrightsie—except—except it just wasn't God's time yet."

"I didn't think about that," Wrightsie replied in a completely satisfied tone of voice, fully accepting his father's explanation.

"There's no doubt about it," Wright said to me later when we discussed this incident, "if faith alone were the answer to miraculous healings, Wrightsie would have been healed at that instant."

"I couldn't agree more," I answered.

# 17
## *Why Do These Things Have to Happen?*

We spent the rest of Christmas morning opening our gifts. Then, around noon, we had our special, traditional Christmas brunch: strawberries piled high on steaming, buttered corn meal muffins served with thin slices of hot Danish ham.

After brunch I put Wrightsie down for a nap in his bedroom. He seemed particularly tired and weak. I had to brush a great deal of his hair off the pillows—by this time it was falling out in clumps. When I walked back to the den I noticed Wright had set up our movie projector and screen.

"What are you going to show?" I asked.

"Well, we've never seen the movies we took on our vacation last summer," Wright said. "Thought I'd show them."

Soon we were all seated and Wright turned on the projector. For a few moments I was transported back to one of our most enjoyable vacations. Wright and I had wanted Beth and Wrightsie to see the old haunts in Florida where we'd met and courted. Beth and Wrightsie had loved it. For seven days we'd rented a motel room opening on the beautiful white sands of Pensacola Beach. I watched the movie screen and saw a brilliant picture of the waves from the gulf rolling and tumbling easily onto the sunlit beach. Way off in the distance, huge stark white clouds towered high into the deep blue sky. Then I saw my strong, happy son run from the beach into the sparkling, blue-green water. The camera zoomed in on Wrightsie. He was a picture of health with his square, tanned shoulders and sun-streaked hair. His eyes crinkled against the sun; a wide, perfect smile of delight lit up his face. The movie ended abruptly as home movies do. I hurried into the kitchen. I don't think anyone saw my tears.

The remainder of the Christmas weekend passed all too swiftly. On Sunday we all rode to Love Field in Dallas to see my sister off for San Francisco. I was going to miss her sweet, gentle manner and her tremendous understanding. Wrightsie and Beth would miss her too—particularly Beth. Kathy had taken Beth on jaunts here and there: out for a hamburger, or for a ride, sometimes just a stroll so they could talk. Beth had needed her tender, loving care.

On Monday afternoon, Wright took Wrightsie and me back to the hospital. We went to radiation immediately and then back to his room. Wright planned to spend the rest of the afternoon and early evening with us. So after I put Wrightsie down for a nap we sat and chatted. Before long, I noticed Wright was very restless.

"What's the matter?" I asked in a low voice so I wouldn't disturb Wrightsie.

"I don't know. I'm worried and I—I—oh, I don't know."

He was silent a moment and then he announced, "Nan, I'm going to my office."

"But why? Everything's closed down for the holidays; there's no one there."

"I know, that's why I'm going. I've got to be alone to think things through. Nan, we need help. I need help. Oh, I know we've had Sherwin McCurdy and his Full Gospel friends helping us, but I need something more and I don't even know what it is. Nan, I'm sorry, I've got to be alone to think."

Wright got up and walked towards the door. "I'll call you

from the office."

"Hey," I said, "I love you."

"I'm sorry, Nan," he said walking back to me. "I love you." We kissed each other and he held me in his arms. I looked into his eyes and felt very sorry for him. He looked tired and frustrated and a little lost. He was by nature an optimistic man, but at that moment he looked drained.

"When you're through at the office, why don't you go home," I suggested. "Please, don't come back to the hospital tonight. I'm tired and I'm going to turn in early. Why don't you too?"

"Maybe I will. Anyway I'll call you before I leave the office."

I dropped off to sleep in the chair for a while until I was awakened by Wrightsie. I freshened him up and we watched TV as we waited for supper to be served. After our meal we were again watching TV when the phone rang—it was Wright.

"Nan," he almost shouted, "I've found somebody to help us!"

"Who?"

"Well, let me tell you the whole story. When I came to the office I started to reread that Full Gospel Business Men's pamphlet Carl Wilgus sent me. Remember, the one titled *Episcopalians and the Baptism in the Holy Spirit*"?

"No," I answered, "but go ahead."

"I noticed a priest from Seattle—a Dennis Bennett—had written several of the articles in the pamphlet. Then suddenly I thought, 'That's it! That's it! I'll call Father Bennett!' "

"Well, how'd you get his number?" I asked.

"Nan, it was a miracle! I picked up the phone and called Seattle information. I just told the operator I wanted the number of an Episcopal church in Seattle and she asked, 'Which one?' and I said, 'I don't care, any one.'

" 'All right,' she said, 'I'll give you the cathedral!'

"Well, I called the cathedral and a man answered the

phone—I'm sure it was a priest. You know, he had an authoratative voice and all that. Anyway, he said, 'No, I'm sorry, you've got the wrong church. Father Bennett has Saint Luke's. I'll give you the number. But I'm afraid you won't be able to talk to him; he's a very busy man and it's almost impossible to get ahold of him.'

"So I called Saint Luke's and the secretary answered the phone. I asked to speak to Father Bennett and she said, 'I'm sorry, he's not in; may I help you?' Well, I started to tell her about Wrightsie and she said, 'Wait, wait. I think you'd better try to get Father Bennett.' She gave me a number to call—'He may have left the number by now, but try it anyway. If you don't get him call me back.'

"Nan," Wright continued, "I called the number and Father Bennett answered the phone. Can you believe it?"

"What did you tell him?"

"I'd almost memorized it. I said, 'Father, my name is Wright Brunson. My young son is dying from a brain tumor. Will you pray for him?' "

"What'd he say?" I asked.

"He said he'd put Wrightsie on his prayer list. And then he asked, 'Where are you calling from?' I told him and he said, 'I want you to call Father Ted Nelson at the Church of the Resurrection in Dallas. An associate of mine has just returned from there and he told me Father Nelson has a powerful Spirit-filled ministry out there.' "

"Wright, what does Spirit-filled mean?" I asked.

"I don't know for sure, Nan. But I think it has something to do with the Holy Spirit.

"Anyway," Wright continued, "I thanked him and then I called Father Nelson at the Church of the Resurrection—and he answered the phone too. I told him about the same thing I told Father Bennett, 'Father, my name is Wright Brunson and my young son is dying from a brain tumor. Father Dennis

Bennett told me to call you.' "

"What did—" Wright didn't wait for my question.

"I think Father Nelson was a little stunned by the whole thing. For a second or so he didn't say a word and then he asked, 'Where is your son now?' I told him, Nan, and I told him you were staying with Wrightsie. He'll be up to see you tomorrow. Isn't that wonderful?"

"Well, yes—yes," I answered. I was happy for Wright but I didn't understand his enthusiasm or why it was so important to him that Father Nelson was going to visit us. Little did I know my whole life would change soon after Father Nelson's visit.

Wright noticed my lack of enthusiasm and asked, "Is that all right? I mean, you don't mind if Father Nelson comes to see you, do you?"

"Oh, no," I answered, trying to sound a little more enthusiastic for Wright's sake.

"Great," he replied. "I'm going home now. I'll call you from the house. Love you."

"Love you," I answered, and I hung up the phone.

I got Wrightsie ready for sleep; we said our prayers and soon he was sleeping. I was watching TV with the volume turned down when I heard a quiet knock at the door. I turned the TV off and answered the knock. I opened the door to a younger, pretty, blonde woman.

"Mrs. Brunson," she said in a soft voice, "I'm Beverly Henderson and my daughter's doctor suggested I get in touch with you."

"Yes," I said. "Just a sec, let me check to see if Wrightsie's still asleep. Then we can talk over there across the hall in that empty room."

Wrightsie was sound asleep so I slipped out of the room quietly and joined Beverly. "Excuse me," I said, "I don't leave him alone very often."

"I understand, Mrs. Brunson."

"Please, call me Nancy," I said. "You said your daughter's doctor wanted you to talk with me?"

"Yes," Beverly answered. My nine-year-old daughter Kimberli has a brain tumor too."

"Oh, no!" I exclaimed. "How long has she been sick?"

Beverly's pretty blue eyes were tired and worried as she told me of the onset and history of her daughter's illness. In many ways the story was very similar to Wrightsie's. And her fears, dashed hopes, frustrations and apprehensions were similar to mine. Next, we talked about our children's lives before their illnesses. I suppose we'd talked for ten or fifteen minutes when I said, "Let me check Wrightsie again."

Beverly waited at the door for me. "Yes," I said, "he's all right."

"Well, I should get back to Kim," Beverly said. "Would you like to see her?"

"Oh, yes," I answered.

We walked down the hall and into their room. I noticed an older looking woman sitting beside the bed. "Mother, I'd like you to meet Nancy Brunson. Nan, this is my mother, Mrs. Lane."

"Hello," I said.

"How do you do," Mrs. Lane responded. "How's your boy doing?"

"He's asleep now," I answered.

Beverly leaned over her daughter's bed and said, "Kim? Kim, you have a visitor—Mrs. Brunson; her little boy has the same problem you do."

"Hello, Kimmy," I said.

"Hello, Mrs. Brunson," she answered, looking up at me with sleepy blue eyes. Her long blonde hair fanned out over the pillow framing her beautiful face.

"It's not right," I thought, "it's not right that children should have to go through such things."

105

"What is your son's name?" Kimmy asked in a gentle, little-girl voice.

"Wright," I answered, "but we call him Wrightsie."

"How old is he?"

"He's one year younger than you," I answered.

"I'd like to meet him sometime," Kimmy said.

"All right," I assured her. "When you both get a little better I'll bring him down to see you."

She gave me a warm smile.

I could see she was drowsy so I said, "Kimmy, I have to go now to check on Wrightsie. I'm glad I met you."

"Bye, Mrs. Brunson," she said in a sleepy voice.

Beverly and her mother walked into the hall with me and we all chatted a few minutes longer. Then Mrs. Lane asked, "Could I see your son?"

"Yes," I answered. "Certainly."

Wrightsie was still asleep when we slipped into the room. Mrs. Lane peeked down at him and whispered, "Oh, what a handsome boy. Why do these things have to happen?"

I couldn't answer her question.

She seemed very upset as I walked her to the door. When I said goodnight I took her hand saying, "You're going through the worst time right now—when you first find out it's a brain tumor."

"Yes," she answered sadly. "I guess all we can do at a time like this is trust in the Lord."

I nodded my head.

"Well, good night, Nancy. Thank you."

She walked slowly down the hall back to Kimmy's room. Little did I realize then what soul-stirring events the future held for Kimmy and Wrightsie—together.

# 18
## *Would You Believe, That Was the Lord!*

As I was getting ready for bed, I started to think about the Christian faith Beverly and her mother had exhibited during our conversations. I thought about Sherwin McCurdy, Carl Wilgus and Wright's acceptance of Jesus Christ. And I thought about Wright's conversation with Father Bennett and the next day's visit by Father Nelson. I can't say I was troubled but I realized they all seemed to have a stronger faith than I had.

Then I thought back to my childhood. I'd been raised a Lutheran. Although my dad was a Roman Catholic, my mother had directed my religious training. I'd spent my first eight years of schooling in the Lutheran parochial school in Danbury, Connecticut. Oh, I'd memorized the catechism and required Scriptures and learned the Bible stories, but my life was not centered on Christ.

Wright and I had been married by a Lutheran minister in the chapel of the United States Naval Postgraduate School in Monterey, California. The minister, during our premarital counseling, encouraged us to become members of the same denomination. So, after we were married, we started to attend Saint James Episcopal Mission in Monterey. I found the dignity, the ceremony of the high Episcopal services appealed to my spirit and decided to become an Episcopalian.

I smiled as I recalled the events. The rector at Saint James instructed me and soon it was time for my confirmation. The bishop of California, then Bishop Pike, was scheduled to ordain a priest at All Saint's Episcopal Church in nearby Carmel. Arrangements were made for the bishop to confirm me alone before the ordination ceremony and I was assured I would have a private confirmation.

Our priest, Wright, and I arrived at the appointed time. But the bishop had been delayed. I watched in panic as more and more people arrived and finally filled the church. Then our priest indicated it was time for us to walk to the altar rail in front of the large church. Bishop Pike appeared and as he administered the sacramental rite of confirmation by the laying on of hands, the pipe organ boomed and trumpets blared an old majestic hymn. Then, to the same accompaniment, the Bishop blessed our marriage. It was all a stirring experience to say the least.

During our married life Wright and I often talked about religion. He'd soon partially converted me to his beliefs: there was a loving God, He loved everybody, therefore, there was no hell—a loving God would not condemn anyone to hell. But where Wright believed Jesus to be just a man, I considered that He was part of the Trinity—although I didn't know what it meant to receive Jesus as my Savior.

Next, I recalled an incident that took place during our second tour of duty in Monterey, California. Beth was four years old and Wrightsie was just a few months old. One night, Wright checked Beth to see if she'd gone to sleep and he came out of her bedroom shaking his head. "We've got to do something about that!" he said.

"What's the trouble?"

"You know how I like to ask Beth what she's thinking about before she goes to sleep?"

"Yes," I answered.

"Well, tonight she said, 'I'm thinking how I'd like to die and go live with God in heaven.' Next thing you know she'll start believing in hell and all that stuff. Must be that little Catholic girl she plays with that's giving her these ideas."

I didn't say anything.

"You know what I'm gonna do?" Wright continued. "I'm gonna start taking Beth to church."

"Take her to church!" I exclaimed. "I should think that's the last place you'd take her."

Wright looked confused and embarrassed. "Well, that's what I'm going to do—take her to church. You understand, don't you?"

No, I really didn't understand and I didn't answer his question. I just let the subject drop. But Wright and Beth started attending church.

I dropped off to sleep that night in the hospital recalling that Wright had called a priest in Seattle, Washington, who gave him the name of a priest in Dallas, Texas, who was coming to visit me sometime the next day. I was, to say the least, confused.

The next morning Wrightsie and I were waiting in the hall for his turn in radiation therapy when another stretcher rolled up. It was Kimmy.

"Hi, Beverly. Hello, Kimmy," I said. "Oh, Wrightsie, I want you to meet Mrs. Henderson and her daughter Kimmy. I met them last night after you'd gone to sleep."

Wrightsie looked at Kimmy and said, "Hello."

"Hi, Wrightsie," Kimmy answered with a smile.

"Wrightsie," I said, "Kimmy has a problem like yours."

Beverly and I chatted until it was Wrightsie's turn for treatment. I don't recall that we met again at radiation, but Wrightsie and Kimmy would meet each other again.

After the treatment Wrightsie and I returned to his room and, about mid-morning, Father Ted Nelson visited us.

Wrightsie and I were watching TV and when the priest entered the room I got up and turned the set off. "Mrs. Brunson, my name is Ted Nelson," he said in a strong, confident voice. "Your husband asked me to come up and see you."

"Yes, he mentioned you'd be here. Please call me Nancy," I said, shaking his hand.

He walked over to the bed and I said, "Father, this is my son Wright the Third but we call him Wrightsie. Wrightsie, this is Father Nelson. Daddy asked him to come and see us."

"How are you, Wright the Third?" Father Nelson asked enthusiastically.

Wrightsie said cautiously, "Fine." I don't think he could quite figure out Father Nelson.

They chatted a few minutes and I tried to figure him out myself. He reminded me of the convivial Roman Catholic priests who used to visit the hospital in Danbury, Connecticut, where I took my nurse's training. He was wearing the traditional black suit with the white collar, and there was just the hint of a paunch beneath his suit coat. There was a touch of gray in his otherwise dark hair and his sparkling brown eyes provided a window for his exuberant personality. I also sensed he was trying to size up our situation.

Turning to me he said, "Let's have a cup of coffee down in the cafeteria."

I glanced hesitantly over to Wrightsie and Father Nelson said, "You don't mind if I borrow your mom for a few minutes, do you?"

Wrightsie didn't answer for a second or two and then he said very reluctantly, "Oh, all right."

"Fine. I promise I won't keep her long," Father Nelson replied.

I turned the TV on again and gave Wrightsie the call button saying, "If you need anything ring for the nurse." Then I stopped at the nurses' station on the way to the elevator and told them where I was going.

We walked into the same type of cold, automated cafeteria Wright and I had sat in nearly six weeks before when Wrightsie had undergone his last test before going to Boston.

Father Nelson drew two cups of coffee from a vending machine and we sat down at one end of a long metal table. "Well, Nan," he said, "tell me about it."

I summarized the whole situation, telling him of my early hopes and then of the fears and dreads. The longer I talked the more nervous and anxious I became. I must have appeared very distraught to him—I guess I was—for later he said he was more concerned about me during his first visit than about Wrightsie.

I took the last swallow of my coffee and said, "I've prayed and it hasn't helped. Every morning when he's getting his radiation I run down to the chapel and pray. I feel like I'm praying to a stone."

Father Ted didn't answer but he nodded his head as if he understood. I'm sure he did.

"Let's go back up to the room and say a prayer with your son," he suggested.

When we got back to the room Wrightsie was still watching TV. I turned the set off again and then Father Ted said to Wrightsie, "Now, Wright, I'm going to say a prayer and we're going to ask Jesus to clear up this problem for you."

Wrightsie gave a cooperative nod and closed his eyes.

Father Ted pulled a small, circular, metal container from his pocket and unscrewed the cover. Then he prayed for Wrightsie, laid his hands on Wrightsie's head and anointed his forehead with oil from the metal container, making the sign of the cross.

I walked Father Ted to the door. Before saying goodbye he reached in his coat pocket, took my hand and gently pressed a small silver cross into my palm saying, "Nancy, I want you to have this. There's nothing magic about it—it's only a symbol. But I've carried it through many difficulties and I'd like you to have it."

"Thank you, father," I answered. "Thank you very much."

We said goodbye to each other and his parting words were, "Nan, hang on to the cross." I didn't realize it then, but there was a double meaning to his words.

Later that day Wright called from work and said, "Father Ted called and said he'd seen you."

"Yes."

"Well, what'd you think of him?" Wright asked with hopeful enthusiasm.

"He was nice," I answered. "We talked for a while and he prayed for Wrightsie."

"Was that all? I mean, don't you have anything more to say about him?"

"Well, yes. He said he'd be back to see us and he gave me a small pocket cross."

"Is that all?" Wright asked in a disappointed tone of voice.

"Oh, honey," I said, "don't get me wrong. I really liked him and I'm glad he'll be back to see us."

"Good, good," Wright replied. "Say, when he called me he said we should come out to the Friday night prayer meeting at the Church of the Resurrection if possible."

"This Friday?" I asked. "It's New Year's Eve."

"Well, yes," Wright replied. "We might as well. It sure will be a different way to spend New Year's Eve."

"What about Wrightsie?"

"Let's take him if he's up to it," Wright answered. "How's he doing?"

"He's done better today. Seems a little stronger. But let's see how he does for a few days before we plan on going to the prayer meeting."

"Okay," Wright agreed.

"Oh," I said, "the radiologist told me there won't be any treatment this Friday, so we can come home Thursday morning—another long weekend."

"Great," Wright replied. "Well, gotta go now. Tell my best buddy I love him. Bye."

"I will. Love you. Bye."

Wrightsie improved a little during the rest of the week. We were home for the weekend by mid-morning Thursday and that night Flossy, Beth and I made plans to go shopping in Dallas so we could show Flossy the city, particularly the Neiman-Marcus downtown store. Wright would stay with Wrightsie and have a father-son day.

"Okay," Wright said, agreeing with our plans. "But don't forget we're going to the prayer meeting. It begins at 7:30 P.M. and we have to drive way over to northeast Dallas—probably take an hour."

"I don't know, Wright," I said. "Do you really want to go to the prayer meeting?"

"I sure do," Wright replied.

"Well, let's see how Wrightsie feels tomorrow," I suggested.

We enjoyed our shopping trip Friday, and when we got home Wright was chomping at the bit to go to the Church of the Resurrection. Wrightsie had had a good day so I agreed to the journey.

That was Wrightsie's first outing since he'd been admitted to the hospital way back in November. I dressed him in his blue blazer, denim shirt and tie, white trousers and the rough, leather shoes with the cord soles—the same ones I'd taken to Boston. Wrightsie had lost a great deal of weight and the clothes looked big for him. After I finished dressing him Wright carried him to our car. He wrapped the sleeping bag around him and put a pillow under his head.

We did very little talking on the way to Dallas. But Wrightsie did make one comment, "Some happy new year," he said.

"Why? What's the matter?" I asked.

"I want to be well," he replied.

"You will be, Wrightsie," I answered, but I suppose there wasn't much conviction in my voice.

We parked the car. Wright gently lifted Wrightsie from the back seat, cradled him in his arms and we walked into the church. The building was made of brown stained wood. There was no steeple. We entered the back of the church and I noticed there were no pews—just gray metal folding chairs. Later, Wright called them Episcopal chairs because each one had a kneeler that could be unfolded. The chairs were placed in a circle and I suppose there were twenty-five to thirty people seated around an opening in the center. And in the center were a couple of chairs occupied by two guitar players. Many eyes turned our way and I sensed that Father Nelson had briefed them on our circumstances.

We must have been quite a sight, now that I think of it. Wrightsie, bald except for a shock of hair in front, being carried by his father. A worried mother, sister and grandmother all looking apprehensive and a little embarrassed as we searched for a place to sit. We found four chairs side-by-side in the outermost circle near the door. Wrightsie was weak from the trip and he didn't have the strength to sit up anyway so Wright held him in his arms.

After we were seated, Father Nelson opened the meeting with a prayer and then the guitar players started a song and the people began to sing. I suppose we'd been there about ten minutes when Wright whispered, "I've got to take Wrightsie out to the car; he's too tired. Please stay here, we'll be all right." Wright got up and carried Wrightsie out the entranceway and I noticed two men immediately got up and followed them out the door.

The songs continued and I lowered my head and started to silently pray for Wrightsie. And then something happened. I began to feel a gentle quickening, deep in my soul. It was a quiet yet enlivening sensation of spirit I'd never experienced before in my life. Then I thought, "I can't let this happen. I might do something foolish like jump up out of my chair." With that I purposely shrugged away the feeling—just turned it off. Then, I sat and observed the service a few minutes longer.

Next, I decided to walk out to the car to see how Wrightsie was doing. Wright was talking with the two men who'd followed him out of the church. After the introductions I said to the shorter of the two men, "I started to feel something I'd never felt before back there in the church."

I went on to describe the experience and he nodded knowingly and said, "Would you believe, that was the Lord!"

"Oh, no," I thought to myself. "Now I've lost it. I shrugged Him away. I'm going back in the church."

I took my seat and started to pray again and nothing happened. I guess it was about an hour later, the singing was over and people were asking for special prayers for sick or troubled loved ones and friends. The person requesting the prayer sat in a chair in the center of the circle. Then he or she would give only the first name of the person involved, relate the situation, then the other members of the group would gather around the requester and pray. Some would gently lay one hand on the shoulder of the person in the chair during the prayer. Flossy, Beth and I remained seated in the back row of chairs as these prayers were being said.

Then Father Nelson looked over at me and said, "Nancy, would you like to sit in proxy for Wrightsie?"

I nodded my head, got up and made my way into the center of the group. I sat down in the chair, folded my hands in my lap, lowered my head and closed my eyes. Father Nelson started to pray. I felt loving hands gently lowered on my shoulders and other people started to pray also but in a lower voice than Father Nelson's. I heard the word "shalom" a few times and a few people seemed to be praying very softly and gently in different foreign languages. I thought, "Oh, maybe I'll get that feeling again and Wrightsie will be healed."

Nothing happened and I said to myself, "I've lost it, I've lost it."

And then, would you believe, a TV horror scene I'd seen many months before came to my mind. A woman had sold her soul to Satan and when it came time to pay her debt she tried to renege. The scene that came to my mind was her futile struggle to escape a circle of witches that kept pushing her into the ground. I thought, "How can I think such things when these loving people are laying hands on me and praying for Wrightsie's healing?"

In a few minutes the prayers ended. I thanked the people and returned to my chair, a very disappointed woman. Shortly after that the communion service began, and since it was late—we slipped out of the church and headed home. During the drive I told Wright of my experience—both when I entered the church and the one in the prayer chair. I finished by saying, "And I don't understand why I should think of witches and hell and Satan; I don't even believe in Satan."

"Well, I don't know about that," Wright said. "I think—" and then he let the subject drop.

"What did those men who came out to the car have to say? Who were they?" I asked.

"The shorter man—Gordon Bell—was healed from cancer of the lymphatic system and the other man had a son healed from spinal meningitis. After they told me about the healings they asked if they could pray for Wrightsie. I agreed and they laid hands on Wrightsie and asked the Lord to heal him. They prayed for the whole family. They sure are fine people."

"Yes," I agreed. "I've never met such a large group of loving, concerned people. I know their hearts really went out to us."

"I was surprised to see so many people at a New Year's Eve

prayer meeting," Wright commented.

"I know," I replied. "By the way, I think I saw two couples there from our church in Arlington."

"You're right, Nan," Wright said. "I noticed them when we first arrived but I couldn't figure out where I'd seen them before. It was at Saint Alban's."

It was after midnight when we got home. "Let's have a midnight snack," I suggested.

"Yeah," Wrightsie was the first to answer. "Can I have a dish of Flossy's potato salad with a glass of milk?" he asked.

After our meal the phone rang. It was my sister Kathy and my folks who were visiting her in San Francisco over the holiday. Of course, as each one came to the phone I had to tell them about my night at the prayer meeting. Each time I ended my story by saying in a discouraged voice, "I think I blew it."

As I got Wrightsie ready for bed, he asked if he could sleep with me that night. I could not resist his request. We said our prayers, I tucked Wrightsie into bed, making sure his Snoopy was comfortable too, and soon he was sound asleep.

After everyone was in bed for the night, I began to think over the evening's events. I'd certainly met a wonderful group of strong and faithful Christians. But they also had another quality I couldn't quite identify. "I'll have to ask Wright about that tomorrow," I thought.

Next, I thought about the feeling I'd had when we'd first entered the Church of the Resurrection and I'd started to pray for Wrightsie. As I turned that over in my mind, I felt a strong desire to pray for him again. So I got up from the table and walked into the laundry room just off the kitchen and closed the door. Then I knelt on my knees and began to pray.

I suppose five—maybe ten—minutes passed. Then I realized I was totally surrounded, enclosed within a capsule of perfect and indescribable spiritual love. Time disappeared. For the first time in my life I knew God was real, I knew He was a personal God, and I knew He loved me!

I got up from my knees and walked back to our bedroom. As I looked at my son in our bed in the darkened room, I thought I should do what they did at the Resurrection, I should lay my hands on his head and pray for his healing—and then I realized my hands were warm, tingling. I laid my hands on Wrightsie's head and prayed, "Oh, Lord, please heal my dear son Wrightsie—please heal him." Then I climbed into bed, lay down next to him, put my hand in his, and fell soundly asleep.

# 19
## Mom, Why Did God Choose Me as a Victim?

The next morning I couldn't wait to tell Wright about my introduction to God. I ended my story by saying, "I don't understand it; all those times I've prayed in the chapel at the hospital and then He comes to me in our laundry room?"

"I can't answer your question, Nan," Wright said with a broad grin.

"Maybe it has something to do with those wonderful people at the Church of the Resurrection," I suggested.

"Could be," he answered. "I really don't know."

"Well, what is it that makes them seem different?" I questioned. "What do they have that other Christians don't have?"

"I don't think they have anything more than other Christians have," Wright explained. "From reading the pamphlet Carl Wilgus sent me, I'd say it's just that the people at the Resurrection believe something additional about what's available to all Christians."

"Additional? What do you mean?"

"Here's how I see it," Wright answered. "Before His Ascension, Jesus told His disciples to wait in Jerusalem 'til the Holy Spirit came and filled them with power from heaven. And remember, Jesus had talked about the Holy Spirit before. One time He told them that John baptized with water but He, Jesus, would baptize them with the Holy Spirit. And another time Jesus said He must go so the Father would send them the Holy Spirit.

"Anyway, the disciples did what Jesus told them to do. They stayed in Jerusalem, and on the Day of Pentecost they were baptized in the Holy Spirit. And after that, they worked all sorts of miracles. In fact, that was the birth of the Church."

"Where'd you learn all that?" I asked.

Wright laughed and said, "Well, hon, while you've been taking care of Wrightsie all these months I've been reading everything I could get my hands on."

"Okay. But what does the Holy Spirit and the Day of Pentecost have to do with Father Nelson and the people at the Resurrection?" I asked.

"When the disciples were baptized in the Holy Spirit they received a number of gifts, and the people at the Resurrection believe those gifts are just as available to Christians today as they were back on the Day of Pentecost."

"Gifts?"

"Yes."

"What are they?"

"Well, later on in 1 Corinthians—chapter 12, I think—Paul lists the gifts. There's the gift of wisdom; the gift of knowledge; the gift of healing; working of miracles; prophesy; discerning of spirits; tongues and the interpretation of tongues." Wright raised a finger to number each gift.

"Let's see, that's only eight. There's one more," he said. "Oh, yeah, faith—the gift of faith. That's what I need," he laughed.

"But, Wright, you said healing, didn't you?"

"Yes, that's one of 'em."

"That's what I want—healing. I want Wrightsie healed! And that's what the people prayed for at the Resurrection. Oh, Wright, do you think it's possible he can be healed?"

"Yes, I do."

"You really believe all this, don't you? I mean about the Holy Spirit and the gifts?"

"Yes, I do," Wright answered. "You know there are some highly educated men that believe it also. There's Father Dennis Bennett, Father Nelson, and I read about a neurosurgeon out in California. And another thing, I'm amazed at the number of passages in the Bible—both Old and New Testaments—that refer to the Holy Spirit.

"I can't figure out why I haven't heard about Him before," Wright continued. "I mean I knew about God the Father and God the Son, but not God the Holy Spirit."

"Well, I've always believed in the Trinity, but I guess I never knew that much about God the Holy Spirit either," I answered.

"Anyway," Wright said, "I know where we can learn about the Holy Spirit now."

"Yes," I said. "And I want to go back to the Church of the Resurrection next week."

"Great," Wright answered. "We will."

The next day—Sunday—we had visitors late in the afternoon. Wright answered the door and escorted a husband, wife and their young daughter into the den, and introduced them to Flossy and me. Their thoughtful visit was explained when the husband and wife, Fred and Mary Bingaman, said they were members of our Saint Alban's Episcopal Church.

Then their daughter, Camy, said, "And Wrightsie and I are in the same grade at J.L. Hill."

We talked about many things that afternoon and Camy visited Wrightsie in his room and presented him with a little gift.

Towards the end of their visit Mary Bingaman mentioned a book she'd read recently: "It's entitled *Nine O'clock in the Morning,* and it's written by Father Dennis Bennett, an Episcopal priest."

"Dennis Bennett!" Wright exclaimed.

Then he went on to tell the Bingamans about his phone call to Father Bennett the previous week, and our resulting visit to the Church of the Resurrection.

When the family left later that afternoon, Mary Bingaman offered, "If you'd like, I'll leave Father Bennett's book in your mailbox tomorrow morning."

"Yes, please," Wright replied. "I'd like to read it. Thank you."

The next morning Wright checked the mailbox two or three times and finally the book arrived. He sat down to read it immediately.

Meanwhile, I was gathering up the things Wrightsie and I would need at the hospital.

And poor Wrightsie had a rough day. He'd enjoyed his two long weekends at home and he wasn't looking forward to the hospital. "Oh, mom," he said in a tormented voice, "today the vampires come after me." (This was the name he'd given to the lab technicians who took a blood sample from his finger each Monday—it was the only routine he really dreaded.)

"Wrightsie, I know it's hard for you; I don't like blood tests either. But they are trying to help you get better. Look, you've been so brave about everything else, if you keep it up through the blood tests I'll—I'll buy you the official trousers for your Cub Scout uniform."

"Really, mom?"

"Yes," I nodded.

"Okay. I'll try hard. Real hard," he said trying to convince me and himself.

When we were packed and ready to go back to the hospital, Wright said, "Do you want to take this book with you," as he handed me Father Bennett's book.

"No, thanks," I answered. "You read it and tell me what it says."

"Okay."

We arrived at the hospital mid-afternoon and settled in for the week. And Wrightsie was very courageous when his blood sample was taken. Our stay that week was routine until early Wednesday when Father Nelson visited us again. We chatted for a while and then he prayed for Wrightsie.

That night I was getting Wrightsie ready for sleep and he said, "Mom, I felt a tingling in my brain when Father Nelson prayed for me."

"Are you sure, Wrightsie?" I asked, feeling excitement.

"Yes, mom," he assured me.

"Well, we'll ask the doctor about it tomorrow morning."

We said our prayers and then Wrightsie asked, "Mom, will you help me? I want to roll over on my stomach."

"Okay, here," I said, as I helped him roll over. "Now what?"

As I watched, he struggled with a great effort and managed to pull his knees up, underneath his stomach. Then, using his elbows, he raised his chest up from the bed. He managed to hold that position a few moments before he toppled over on his right side. He beamed a smile of accomplishment.

The next morning when I mentioned to his specialist the tingling Wrightsie had felt in his brain, the doctor dismissed it saying, "I suppose it's possible. It may have something to do with the radiation."

Nevertheless, Wrightsie improved dramatically in the next few days. Wright took us home Friday afternoon and that evening we—Wright and I—went to the Church of the Resurrection while Flossy baby-sat with Beth and Wrightsie. We returned home after midnight and the first thing I heard over the intercom when I entered the house was, "Mom, mom!"

I walked to Wrightsie's bedroom, opened the door and in mock sternness said, "Are you still awake?"

"Yeah," Wrightsie grinned, "I've been waiting for you and

dad. I had fun with Bethy and Flossy tonight."

Flossy looked into his room and said, "You should have seen him; he sat on his knees and played cards with Beth for over forty-five minutes."

"Wrightsie," I exclaimed, "that's wonderful."

Wrightsie smiled a proud grin.

"Now you'd better get to sleep," I said. "Here, gimme a kiss and hug. Love you."

Wrightsie squeezed me around the neck with his good arm, then he tried to put his right arm around my neck too. He didn't quite make it but I was thrilled; he was definitely getting stronger.

The following Sunday afternoon when Wrightsie woke up from his nap he called, "Mom, will you get me my tape recorder?"

I was surprised by his request. Along with Tigeree, he'd lost interest in his tape recorder after his operation in Boston. "Here it is," I said, retrieving the recorder from his closet.

"Mom, is that Tigeree I see in there?" he said, looking into his closet.

"Yes."

"Can I have him, please?" Wrightsie's voice was almost apologetic.

I handed him the long exiled stuffed tiger and he said, "Snoopy, meet Tigeree."

"Wrightsie, what's going on here—wanting the tape recorder and Tigeree after all these weeks?"

"Oh, mom," he explained as if I should have known the answer, "I didn't want to play with 'em 'til I was all better.

"Mom, can I have the tape Bethy and the Foxes made for me?"

I took the tape from his desk drawer and inserted it in the recorder. Wrightsie pushed the play button, adjusted the volume and gave me a big grin when Nicky Fox's voice filled the room. He listened for a few moments then turned the volume down and said, "Will you ask Grandma Flossy to come and hear my tape?"

Just as Flossy walked into his bedroom the telephone rang. "I'll get it," I said.

"Hello."

"Hello, Nan," a woman's voice said—I could tell it was long distance—"this is Marie-Louise. Kenneth and I have been wondering about you folks. How's everything?"

"Oh, Dr. Johnson," I exclaimed. "What a surprise. How wonderful of you to call. We're doing fine. Wrightsie's had the best weekend since he first went to the hospital. And this will be our last week. Wrightsie has his twenty-fifth treatment Thursday."

"Good, good," Dr. Johnson replied.

I talked for some time, bringing her up-to-date and then I asked, "How was your trip to Hiroshima?"

"We had a fine time," she answered. "We renewed many old friendships. Oh, by the way—I don't know if you remember—but we have some Roman Catholic nuns in Hiroshima who are very good friends."

"Yes, I remember."

"Well, we told them about you and your problems; they're praying for your family."

"Thank you," I answered.

"You folks seem to have had your share of troubles—and I know prayers are answered."

"Yes," I agreed with her. "And I must admit I wonder why these things happen."

"Well, Nancy—this may not help—but it seems to me the Lord only tests the ones He loves the very most."

"Yes, it helps some," I answered. "And the Lord has been good to us. I don't know what we'd do if it weren't for the wonderful friends He's sent to help us."

We chatted for a while longer and then she asked, "May I speak with Beth?"

I called Beth to the phone and after they'd talked for a few minutes I said a few last words.

"I'll keep in touch with you," Dr. Johnson said, "And you're in our prayers."

"Thank you, Dr. Johnson. Thanks for calling."

As I hung up the phone I thought, "How wonderful of her to call. But I wonder what prompted her to call today?" My question was answered in a few days.

The next day as we prepared for our return to the hospital, not one word was said about the "vampires." I knew Wrightsie was still thinking about his official Cub Scout trousers.

Wrightsie continued to improve during that week in the hospital. And so much so, that on Wednesday afternoon he asked, "Mom, do they have a gift shop here?"

"Yes," I answered. "It's down on the first floor."

"Can we go shopping? I want to get Bethy and Mary Swor a present."

"Are you sure you feel strong enough?" I questioned him.

"Yep," he said confidently.

"All right," I answered. "But let me see what the nurses say. And I'll have to find a wheelchair. I'll be back in a minute."

The nurses had no objections, so I found a wheelchair and returned to the room.

I lifted Wrightsie into the chair and explained, "Now, Wrightsie, I'm afraid you might get tired so I'm going to tie this cotton blanket underneath your arms and around the back of the chair. Okay?"

"Okay," he answered.

Soon we were in the gift shop. I wheeled him beside the shelves. "Mom, can you go slower?" he asked. "I want to see everything."

"All right," I laughed, proud of my careful shopper.

"There!" he said pointing. "I'll get that ice cream soda set for Bethy."

"That would be good for Mary too," I suggested.

"Nooo," he answered thoughtfully. "That's not like Mary."

I pushed him a little farther, then he pointed again and exclaimed, "That's it! That tea set over there."

He was right: it was the perfect gift for little Mary Swor.

We paid for our purchases and returned to the room. And no sooner did I get him back into bed when he vomited. Oh, I felt so sorry for him.

But his spirits weren't dampened, for late that evening about ten o'clock, he said, "Gee, mom, I feel like a midnight spin."

Again I bundled him in the wheelchair and off we went down the hall. We stopped by the windows opposite from the elevators. The city lights of Dallas sparkled in the clear night air.

"Mom," Wrightsie said, "look at the airplanes."

We watched the airliners make their approaches to Love Field. Their flashing red and green lights and bright landing lights stirred memories of past journeys—most were pleasant except for our last two flights.

We headed back to the room and as we passed the darkened playroom, Wrightsie said, "Wait, mom. Can we go in there?"

I flipped on the lights and wheeled him in the room. "Mom, look at all the games and toys." His eyes sparkled as he examined each item. We stopped by the bookcase and he selected a book about President Lincoln. Then we returned to his room and settled in for our last night at the hospital.

Thursday morning, he was given his twenty-fifth treatment and before we left the radiation area the radiologist came out to speak with us. "Wrightsie, you've made very good progress. I want you to keep it up."

Wrightsie nodded seriously.

"And when you get home I want you to mind your mother.

She's taken wonderful care of you but now you're getting better and you can help her."

Again Wrightsie nodded.

Then the doctor took me aside, "Mrs. Brunson," he said gently, "I've got some advice for you too. When you get home you'll have to discipline Wrightsie as you would a normal healthy child. I've seen families where, through misguided love, they've overindulged their child and he's become a tyrant. At times it will be very difficult, but if you really love him, you'll lay the law down."

"I will, doctor," I assured him. "Thank you for the advice. Thank you for everything."

"You're welcome," he answered. "I'll set you up with an appointment for two weeks from today: we'll re-evaluate him. If he's responded well, we'll give him the additional series of five treatments. And we can do it on an outpatient basis."

Then turning to Wrightsie he smiled and said, "Goodbye, Wrightsie. You've been a good patient. Now remember: mind your mom and keep up the good work."

"I will," Wrightsie said earnestly. "Bye, doctor."

Next, Wrightsie and I returned to our room and I started to pack for our trip home.

Later, after the specialist examined Wrightsie, he said, "I'll want to see him in my office toward the last of February. In the meantime, I'll be in touch with the radiologist. And, after his re-evaluation, give my office a call to set up a definite appointment."

"Fine," I agreed.

Wright arrived at the room and soon he'd loaded the car with all our belongings. Then in high spirits we headed for Arlington and home.

The next morning I gave Wrightsie his first tub bath in over eight weeks. I guess you might say Wrightsie was an unusual little boy when it came to baths and showers; if I'd let him, he'd sit in a tub or stand in a shower for hours.

He sat in the tub and I steadied him with one hand on his square shoulders and with the other hand I gently scrubbed away. I can only imagine how luxurious he felt as the warm sudsy water slowly moistened his dry skin.

We chatted away as I washed him and then he caught me off guard with the question, "Mom, why did God choose me as a victim?" There wasn't a hint of self-pity or anger in his voice—just a straightforward question.

I swallowed hard as I searched my mind for an answer. Suddenly I remembered Dr. Marie-Louise's comment during our phone conversation the previous Sunday: "Wrightsie, the Lord only tests the ones He loves the very most," I repeated.

He considered my reply for a moment and then with the faith and trust only a child can muster he expressed a satisfied, "Oh, I see."

Silently, I thanked God for Dr. Marie-Louise.

## 20
### Oh, Baloney!

The next day, Friday, when Wright came home from work, he pushed a child's wheelchair into the house. Wrightsie smiled when he saw his new transportation. "Here, let's go for a ride," his dad suggested. Wright lifted Wrightsie from the couch and placed him in the wheelchair. They zipped from room to room for a few minutes, ending up in the kitchen where I was preparing supper.

"Hey, mom," Wrightsie said in an excited voice, "what do ya think of my race car?"

"Are you Robin or Speed Racer?" I asked, referring to two of his favorite TV characters.

"Speed Racer," he answered with a grin.

"Okay, Speed Racer," I joked, "please start your engine and clear out of my kitchen so I can get supper. Otherwise your dad and I'll never get to the prayer meeting on time."

"Zoom, zoom, zoom," Wrightsie responded. "Let's go, dad."

Grandma Flossy baby-sat with Beth and Wrightsie that night while Wright and I attended the prayer meeting at the Resurrection. We returned late and they were all asleep.

We got into our pajamas, put on our robes and walked out to the kitchen. I made some coffee, then we sat at the table and started to discuss the prayer meeting. "You know, except for New Year's Eve when I felt the presence of the Lord, I haven't gotten much out of the prayer meetings," I commented.

"Oh," Wright answered with genuine surprise. "What's the problem?"

"I've felt—well, sort of left out," I answered. "Everyone looks so happy—it's kinda like going to a party where everyone's having a good time but me. I felt that way tonight. And then on top of that, when Father Ted talked about hell it frightened me—depressed me. I just don't want to believe a loving God would allow hell to exist."

"Oh, honey," Wright replied, "Father Ted wasn't trying to frighten anybody. He was trying to explain that Christians don't have to worry about hell; Christ has taken care of that."

"You sound like you believe in hell," I commented. "You didn't used to."

"Look, Nan," Wright said gently, "when I used to read the Bible—before I became a Christian—I believed the things in the Bible I liked and discarded the things I didn't like. That was pretty foolish of me. Just because I choose to believe something exists doesn't make it exist and vice versa. You know, if I say to myself, 'Hah, I don't believe in gravity,' and then I jump off a building, I'm not going to float away. I'm going to get hurt because regardless of what I think, or want to think, gravity does exist. That's the way with hell; the Bible speaks about it—Jesus talked about it. Yes, I believe in hell."

"Well, I don't," I said. "If God is love then I don't see how there can be a hell."

Wright shook his head slowly and took a drink of coffee. "I think it's important for you to get this squared away in your thinking. Why don't you make an appointment with Father Ted and talk it over with him?"

"Maybe I will," I replied. "And I want to ask him about healings too—Wrightsie's healing."

But as the days flew by I forgot about our discussion and making an appointment with Father Nelson. My days were filled with homemaking chores and taking care of Wrightsie. We had many wonderful and memorable moments together. One warm, sunny afternoon towards the last of January I decided to take Wrightsie down to the Woodland West Shopping Center about five blocks from our house.

"Great, mom," he said, thrilled with the idea. "Bethy told me they have some turtles at the five-and-dime store. Can we see them?"

"Sure," I replied.

I dressed him in jeans and his big green sweat shirt—the one with the bright yellow smile face on it, and helped him into his wheelchair. As I pushed him out of his room, I said, "Wrightsie, I know it's warm but I think you should wear your tennis hat."

"Aw, mom," he protested.

"Now, Wrightsie," I answered. "The doctor said he wanted you to keep your head warm. Let's go into Beth's room; I think your hat is with hers in the bottom drawer of her dresser."

I stopped his wheelchair in front of the dresser, searched through the bottom drawer and found his tennis hat. Just as I stood up, Wrightsie caught sight of his reflection in the big mirror over the dresser—it was the first time the realization had dawned on him that his hair had fallen out. His first reaction was one of wide-eyed surprise. Then his face registered a look of shock and disbelief. Next, a cloud of heartache started to move across his face. But, at that moment, our eyes met in the mirror. Immediately, he put on a look of complete nonchalance and said, "Oh! You found my tennis hat. But maybe I should wear my ski hat instead?"

"No," I answered, "you'd be too warm. Your tennis hat's perfect."

"Okay, let's go," he said, trying to sound impatient. "And

remember, we have to look at the turtles."

I knew he'd covered up his heartache about his appearance to protect me. With a heart full of pride for my brave son, I pushed him in his wheelchair down the street towards the shopping center.

Towards the end of our shopping adventure we looked at the turtles at the five-and-dime store. Because we couldn't make up our minds about which turtle to buy, I suggested that we wait until Beth came home from school so she could help us with the decision. That night, with Beth's help, we bought Wrightsie a turtle.

A few days later, on the twenty-seventh of January, I took Wrightsie back to the hospital for his two-week re-evaluation. The radiologist was satisfied with his progress and prescribed the additional series of five radiation treatments—on an outpatient basis. Then the next Wednesday, after Wrightsie had received his fifth treatment, the radiologist had some final words of advice.

"Wrightsie," he said, "you're doing fine. Are you minding your mother?"

"Yes," Wrightsie answered in a serious tone of voice.

"Good."

Then turning to me the doctor said, "Well, he's come a long way. You know, I think you should get him started on school work."

"School work?" I asked, surprised by his suggestion.

"Yes," he assured me. "If you'll check with your school district, I think you'll find they have a home-bound program. A teacher will come to your house and tutor Wrightsie."

"Oh, that's wonderful!" I replied. "I'll call this afternoon."

"And another consideration," the doctor continued, "he'll be able to start physiotherapy in the next month or so. I'll have my office make the arrangements. They'll call you when they have an opening."

As soon as we returned home, I called the Arlington School District and made arrangements for Wrightsie's home-bound teacher. I discovered that she would be coming each Tuesday and Thursday morning.

That night after supper I surprised Wright with the news. He was delighted, and Wrightsie seemed eager to begin. Beth promised to help Wrightsie with his homework.

Later that evening the telephone rang. "It's Father Ted for you," Wright said handing me the phone.

"Nan, there's a woman up here from Florida for a few days—her name's Anne White. I want you folks to see her," Father Ted explained in a hurried voice, not wasting any words. "She's an Episcopal laywoman and she has a powerful healing ministry. She's booked up solid during her visit, but when I told her about you folks she squeezed you in for an appointment tomorrow at noon—during the lunch break. Can you make it?"

"Yes," I answered, "where should we meet her?"

"She's giving a healing seminar at a retired minister's house in Fort Worth. Got a pencil? I'll give you the address."

I copied the address and said, "Okay, Wrightsie and I'll be there at noon."

"Oh, no," Father Ted replied emphatically. "I want the whole family prayed for."

"Well, I don't know if Wright can get off from work."

I looked at Wright and he nodded his head.

"Wright says he can get off," I continued. "We'll be there."

"Fine," Father Ted replied. "Oh, say, tell Wright I got the message he left with the secretary; I've set him up with an appointment here in my office for 1:00 P.M. this Saturday."

"All right, father," I answered. "I'll tell him."

"And, Nan," Father Ted continued.

"Yes?"

"I love you all and you're in my prayers. Goodbye."

"Thanks, father. I appreciate your prayers. Bye."

After I'd hung up the phone, Wright asked, "What's that all about?"

I explained the situation, then I said, "I didn't know you'd called Father Ted for an appointment."

"Yes," Wright said. "I need to talk to him about a few things."

"Oh?"

"Look, Nan," he said. "We've been through some pretty rough times together. When you think back to all the Navy deployments I had when we were first married; then there was almost three years of rotating shift duty in the Pentagon plus I was working on my master's degree; then when we came to Texas I thought we'd get it all together and the worst thing of all happened. It's been rough—really rough."

I agreed.

"Well, Nan," Wright continued, "I think there's more to life than what we've been through and I need to talk to Father Ted about it. Maybe he can show me a different way, a different approach to life—or something like that."

We sat in silence for a few minutes. I could feel a weariness come over me. The months of worry and fear, dashed hopes and frustrations had finally overtaken me.

"Well, I hope Father Ted can help you—help us," I said.

"We'll see," Wright said in a tired voice. "We'll see."

The next day we were winding our way through the streets of a suburban area of Fort Worth. "Here it is," Wright said, stopping in front of a small, neat house. Wright carried Wrightsie in his arms and we walked to the door. Father Ted's wife, Lee Ann, ushered us into the house and made the introductions. Then we were hurried into the den that was serving as the conference room. Beth, Wright—with Wrightsie in his arms—and I sat down in three chairs in the center of the room. The members of the seminar—mostly clergymen and their wives—gathered around and then Mrs. White led the prayers. She first prayed for Wrightsie to be healed, and next she prayed for the rest of us. Even though it was a hurried meeting I couldn't help but be impressed by the genuine love, great compassion and deep faith those wonderful Christians displayed for me and my family.

Two days later, Wright kept his appointment with Father Ted. When he returned later in the afternoon I asked him about his visit.

"He's really great," Wright answered. "I mean he doesn't waste any words and he seems to know what you're thinking before you say it. Of course I'm sure he's heard everything I said many times before from many people. And I think the thing that impressed me most was the way he started the talk with a prayer and ended it with a prayer."

"Well, did he help you?" I asked.

"Yeah," Wright said thoughtfully. "Yes, I think he did. But, Nan, you know there are no pat answers to these things. Mainly we had a man-to-man talk that was centered around Christ."

"When do you have another appointment with him?"

"I don't," Wright answered, "but *you* do."

"Me?"

"Yes. You see, I told him you have some questions I can't answer," Wright explained, "so he set you up for an appointment next Saturday at one o'clock.

"Now, you don't have to go," Wright hastened to add. "But I wish you would. I'm sure he can answer your questions."

"I'll go. But the main thing I want to talk about is healing—Wrightsie's healing."

"Great," Wright said.

Sunday morning at breakfast Wright asked if I would like to go to church with Beth. He assured me that he and Flossy would take care of Wrightsie. Beth seemed eager to attend church and although I hesitated at first, I decided to go. It was to be the rector's last Sunday at Saint Alban's.

The church was practically filled with people when we arrived, but Beth and I managed to find a seat in the very first pew.

During the sermon I was pleasantly surprised to hear the rector preach about the power of the Holy Spirit. And he recommended that his parishoners attend a Friday night prayer meeting at the Church of the Resurrection. I remember thinking, "I wonder if Sherwin McCurdy and Kris Mineau had anything to do with his comments about the power of the Holy Spirit, and his suggestion to attend the Resurrection."

The following Tuesday was an important day on Wrightsie's road to recovery. His home-bound teacher arrived at the house for his first lessons. After the session, I was thrilled to hear her say, "Your son shouldn't have any difficulties with his school work. He's up to par with his classmates in reading ability and arithmetic."

Then that afternoon Wrightsie attended his second Cub Scout meeting since he'd been released from the hospital. As I was about to help him dress in his uniform, I called Grandma Flossy and Beth to his room for a little ceremony.

"Wrightsie," I said, "you were a good, brave boy when those 'vampires' came after you in the hospital, so—," and then I reached in his closet, pulled out a hanger and continued, "here!"

"Mom!" he exclaimed. "Cub Scout pants! Oh, boy! Thanks, mom!"

"Beth helped me pick them out at the store and Grandma Flossy hemmed 'em for you," I explained.

"Thanks, Bethy. Thank you, grandma. Oh, boy!" he said again.

After he'd dressed I drove him to the meeting that was being held on the athletic field at nearby Bailey Junior High School. I held Wrightsie underneath his arms and he tried to walk from the car to the field. The rest of the boys were running relay races so Wrightsie and I sat on the dry, straw-colored winter grass and watched them. I began to think Wrightsie was feeling sad because he couldn't run. I was about to say something to divert his attention from the races when he said, "Gee, mom, I'm the luckiest boy; I'm the first one to have my official Cub Scout pants." With that he reached over and tugged at one pant leg.

All I could say was, "Oh, Wrightsie," as I fought to keep the tears from my eyes. And I thought, "If only I could have your courage."

The next two days were very busy—preparing for a Valentine party at J.L. Hill Elementary School. Wrightsie's third grade teacher had called and invited him to the Friday afternoon party to be held in her classroom. We had shopped for the cards together and I addressed them for him. It rained Friday afternoon so I drove the three blocks to the school. I carried Wrightsie from the car to the building as he clutched his bag of valentines in his good hand. The teacher greeted us with a warm, sunny smile and pulled up a chair for him to sit in. His classmates gathered around, all talking at once: "Hi, Wrightsie!"—"I've missed you, Wrightsie"—"Here, I've made a box for your valentines"—"When you coming back to school?" Wrightsie had a wonderful time and so did I.

That night we all went to the Resurrection for the prayer meeting. When we drove into the parking lot, I recognized one of the men who'd prayed for Wrightsie New Year's Eve, standing by the entrance to the church. He recognized our car and started walking towards us.

"It's Gordon Bell," Wright said.

We got out of the car, Wright carried Wrightsie and we walked towards the church. Gordon met us and said, "Hi, folks. How's he doing?"

"Much better," I answered. "He's stronger now; he can sit

up and he's even stood up a couple of times."

"That's great," Gordon replied. "Praise the Lord!

"Here, let me get that for you," Gordon said, opening the door.

We found some chairs; Wright sat on one side of Wrightsie, I was on the other side and Gordon sat immediately behind him—Beth joined the kids sitting up in the center with the guitar players. From that night on we began to refer to Gordon Bell as Wrightsie's earthly guardian angel, for whenever we attended the meetings Gordon was waiting for us when we drove up.

During the service, Father Ted came up and said a few words to Wrightsie, then turning to me he said, "Don't forget our appointment tomorrow."

"I won't. If I can find my way I'll be here."

On the drive home that night Wright pointed out important landmarks and highway signs so I could find my way the next day.

As I drove back to the Resurrection the next morning, I mulled over in my mind what I wanted to ask Father Ted. Of course the topic that first came to mind was healing. When I entered the church I spotted Father Ted walking towards his office carrying a steaming cup of hot coffee. "Hi, Nan," he exclaimed with enthusiasm. "Grab yourself a cup of coffee from the kitchen and come on in my office."

"Thanks," I replied.

He waited until I drew a cup of coffee and then I followed him into his office. It was a small room. An old roll top desk was placed against the wall at one end of the room near the door. A swivel chair was pulled up to the desk and in back of it was a table that served as a second desk. One wall was lined with books and the other end of the room was filled with a large draped window. Across from the book shelves was a davenport on which I sat. Father Ted sat in the swivel chair and pivoted towards me placing his coffee cup on the second desk.

"Nan, what do you think of our prayer meetings?" he asked.

"Oh, they're all right, I guess."

He thought for a moment then said, "Before we get started let's say a prayer."

I lowered my head.

"Praise you, Jesus," he began in a strong voice. "Thank you, Jesus. Thank you for Nan; thank you for bringing Nan and her family to the Church of the Resurrection so we can minister to them in your name.

"We lift up little Wrightsie to you, Jesus. We ask that the healing power of the Holy Spirit restore him to perfect health.

"Lord, Nan and I are gathered together in your name. We ask you to be present with us, to guide our hearts and our minds, to teach us so we may have a closer walk with you. We give you all the honor and the glory. Thank you, Jesus. Amen."

"Amen," I repeated.

Father Ted took a drink of coffee, then he repeated his previous question, "What about the prayer meetings?"

"Well, I don't feel I'm a part of them," I answered. "And the night when you started talking about hell it frightened me. But, father, I don't want to talk about that. I want to talk about Wrightsie's healing."

"Look, Nan," he answered, leaning forward over the table. "I'm not worried about Wrightsie's healing. He's been prayed for, he's been anointed and he's got a strong faith in Jesus. He's all right. It's you I'm concerned about."

"Me?" I exclaimed.

"You bet! Nan, when I first met you at the hospital I saw an exhausted, worried and defeated woman. Ever since that day my prayers have been as much for you as they have been for Wrightsie. Now, if I'm going to help you—if you want me to help you—I've got to find out a few things about your faith. Let's get on with it."

I nodded my head.

"All right," he continued. "Now tell me. Who is Jesus?"

"Well—well, He's part of the Trinity. I studied about Him in parochial school. And I—"

"No, no. That's not what I mean," Father Ted interrupted. "Do you know Him personally—as your Savior? Is He the center of your life? Does your whole being center around Him?"

"Well, I've never thought about Him that way before," I answered, feeling uncomfortable under Father Ted's questioning.

"Do you realize He went to the cross because He loves Nancy Brunson? Do you realize He went to the cross because He loves everybody in the world?"

I tried to divert his questions away from me and said, "If He loves everybody in the world why does He permit the slums to exist? Why doesn't He do something about the poor little black kids in the slums?"

"Oh, baloney!" Father Ted exploded. "You're in no shape to worry about what Jesus Christ is doing in the slums! Believe me, He's got plenty of His people doing His work in the slums! So right now, you'd better be concerned about Jesus Christ and Nancy Brunson!"

I can assure you, Father Ted had my undivided attention for the rest of our conversation. And when I left his office that afternoon I had an entirely different concept of Jesus and His relationship to my life.

# 21
## *The Lord Can Do Anything*

February 14—Valentine's Day—was supposed to be a red-letter day. Wrightsie had an appointment with the specialist in Dallas. All in all, he had made steady and noticeable progress since he'd last been seen by the specialist—back in January when he'd been discharged from the hospital. So we were positive the doctor would be impressed with Wrightsie's progress.

After his bath that morning, I was dressing Wrightsie in his bedroom when I heard Grandma Flossy call from the den, "Nan, Nick Fox is here; he'd like to talk to you. Can he come back there?"

"Sure. Come on back, Nick. I'm in Wrightsie's room."

I'd just helped Wrightsie into his wheelchair when Nick walked into the room. Immediately I noticed a hurt and worried look on his face. "Nan, I've got bad news," he said. "Evelyn wanted me to tell you that Bopo died this morning."

"Oh, no!" I exclaimed. "Oh, poor Evelyn. When? What happened?"

"Her mother called a few minutes ago. He died early this morning—massive heart attack." Then Nick went on to explain the circumstances.

When he'd finished I asked, "Is there anything I can do?"

"I don't think so," he answered. "At least not right now. Thanks. We haven't decided when we'll go up to Oklahoma. I'll call you when we make up our minds. Well, I'd better get back to Evelyn."

Nick hurried down the hall and I called after him, "I'll be over in a few minutes."

Then I went back into the room and looked at Wrightsie. He was sitting quietly in his wheelchair, head lowered. "Oh, Wrightsie," I said, kneeling in front of him. He had a lost, bewildered look on his face and tears glistened in his eyes.

I took his hand in mine and said, "Are you going to be all right?"

He nodded his head sadly.

Then I wheeled him into the den and said to Flossy, "Will you watch Wrightsie? I'm going over to see if I can help the Foxes."

"Mom, let me go. I want to help too," Wrightsie pleaded.

"I'm sorry, Wrightsie," I answered, "but you stay with Flossy. I won't be gone long."

"Aw, mom," he protested as I hurried over to the Foxes'—sliding closed the glass door to the den as I left the house.

I could see Evelyn had been crying. "Thanks for coming over," she said as she hugged me.

"I'm so sorry, Evelyn," I said. "Can I do anything?"

"Well, Nick's going to pick up the kids at school. We're going to Oklahoma as soon as we can get packed," she answered.

I did what I could to get them on their way and then I returned home. Wrightsie was sitting in his wheelchair watching TV and he looked like he was sulking. Flossy walked into the den from the kitchen, drying her hands on her apron. "Nan, please don't ever leave me alone with Wrightsie like that again," she said, shaking her head.

"Why? What happened?" I asked.

"He scared us both half to death," Flossy answered—and Wrightsie avoided my eyes. "Not long after you left I was cleaning up the kitchen and I heard him grunt a couple of times. I rushed into the den. The wheelchair was tipped forward resting on the foot rests and Wrightsie's head was against the glass door. Why the glass didn't break I'll never know."

"Wrightsie," I said trying to sound stern, "what were you doing?"

"I was trying to open the door and my wheelchair tipped up. I hit my head on the glass," he said, and tears came to his eyes. "I wanted to help. I loved Bopo."

"Oh, Wrightsie," I said, kneeling beside him. "I know you did."

Then, trying to take his mind off the subject, I put my arm around him and said, "You can help me check their house later. We have to be sure everything's turned off and they've left water for their dog."

Wrightsie nodded through his tears.

I called Wright at work to tell him about Bopo's death and Wrightsie's accident. Wright suggested that we cancel the appointment with the specialist.

"I think you're right," I agreed. "I'll set up another appointment for a week from today."

Later that afternoon—after we checked the Foxes' house—Wrightsie and I decided to go to a store where he could buy some Valentine cards. After he'd selected cards for his dad and sister he said, "Mom, do you think you could leave me alone for a few minutes?"

I'd been steadying Wrightsie as he'd picked out the other cards and I didn't know how he could stand alone without me supporting him.

"That's all right," a salesgirl said, overhearing our conversation, "I'll help him if you like."

"Thank you," I replied. Then I made myself scarce in another part of the card shop. I peeked back once and noticed the salesgirl holding Wrightsie by the back of his belt as he searched intently through the cards underneath the sign, "MOTHER."

Our Valentine's Day celebration that night was rather subdued as our thoughts and talk kept going back to Bopo and the Fox family. But there was one bright spot; Beth had a special gift for Wrightsie. At the appropriate time she walked up to her brother, hiding something behind her back. Wrightsie was completely puzzled as she started to sing the wedding march.

"What is it, Bethy?" he asked.

Beth showed him a pint container and his eyes brightened when he recognized the white carton the five-and-dime store used for turtles. "I bought a bride for your turtle," Beth explained.

"Oh, Bethy!" Wrightsie exclaimed. "Thank you!"

Then we all sang, "Here comes the bride—"

Later that night we all gathered in Wrightsie's bedroom for our prayers. The new turtle was placed in the little aquarium on the night stand beside the bed. We ended our prayers with a special request for peace and comfort for the Fox family. Wrightsie started to cry. "Mom, why did God have to take Bopo?" he asked.

"I don't understand either, Wrightsie," I said. "We probably won't know the answer 'til we get to heaven. We just have to remember he's so much happier there than here."

"I know," Wrightsie sniffed, "but I'm sure going to miss him."

"I know you will, Wrightsie," I answered. "I know how you feel."

I pulled the cowboy sleeping bag up over his shoulders and—as usual—tucked him in securely so he wouldn't roll out of bed. Then I kissed him goodnight and asked, "You gonna be okay?"

"Yes," he answered in his little boy voice.

I turned out the light on his bedside table, closed the door to his room and joined Wright and Flossy in the kitchen. Wright was adjusting the intercom system so we could monitor Wrightsie's room when he said, "Listen."

Very slowly and solemnly, Wrightsie was singing his favorite patriotic song, "When Johnny comes marching home again, hurrah, hurrah—"

"I think he's singing that for Bopo," Wright said with a sad smile.

From then on Wrightsie accepted Bopo's death in a very positive manner. Whenever we'd reminisce about Bopo, Wrightsie would remind us all that he was happy in heaven.

Wrightsie's remarkable progress continued but on the next Saturday he—we all—had a bad scare. His dad worked outside, taking care of the lawn, and Wrightsie followed him around using his wheelchair for support. Wright finished in the front yard and walked down the driveway with Wrightsie right behind pushing his wheelchair. Suddenly he got his feet tangled together, lost control of the wheelchair and fell, hitting his head on the pavement.

Wright rushed over, picked him up and carried him to the couch in the den. Wrightsie cried in a frightened voice, "Oh, I hope I don't have a setback. I hope I don't have a setback."

Beth came into the den carrying the sunglasses Wrightsie had been wearing—they were broken.

"I'm sorry, mom," Wrightsie sobbed when he saw the glasses. Then he said again, "Oh, I hope I don't have a setback."

I guess it was at that point I fully realized the intense desire Wrightsie had to recover from the crippling effects of his brain tumor.

"Wrightsie," I said, "don't worry about the sunglasses. We'll get you another pair. And I know you're going to be all right. Don't worry about a setback."

He recovered quickly from his scare and returned to the yard to watch his father.

The next day we all attended Sunday services at Saint Alban's Episcopal Church for the first time—as a family—since the onset of Wrightsie's illness. Wright helped Wrightsie to the altar and we all took communion. After the service the young priest, who'd temporarily replaced the previous rector, greeted us warmly at the door and said, "If it's convenient, I'd like to bring communion to your son some time during the week."

"That would be wonderful," I answered.

"Fine," the priest continued. "I'll call you before I come over to your house."

"Thank you, father."

As we walked to our car, Wright commented, "I like that young priest."

Later we would find out many people watched us go to the altar that Sunday morning and their hearts and prayers went out to us.

After church we drove to Dallas for lunch—we wanted to take Grandma Flossy to one of our favorite restaurants. When we returned home that afternoon Wright said to Wrightsie, "Hey, best buddy, what do you say we fly your kite in the back yard?"

"Yeah, dad," Wrightsie said enthusiastically.

"Want to help us, Nan?" Wright asked.

"No, thanks," I answered. "I've got a little laundry to fold, then I think I'll read the paper."

I finished my work in the laundry room, gathered up the Sunday paper and walked into the den. I sat down on the couch and glanced through the sliding glass doors into the back yard.

Evidently, Wright and Wrightsie had tired of kite flying for they were sitting side-by-side on the patio with fishing poles in their hands.

I watched them for a few minutes and my thoughts slipped back to the previous year when we'd bought the house—it had been quite an experience. When Wright reported to his new duty station in Dallas, Beth, Wrightsie and I stayed with my folks in Connecticut until Wright could find a house. After looking all over the Dallas-Fort Worth area he'd decided Arlington was the best place to live because of its superior schools. And, just before he came to Danbury for Christmas leave, he'd finally found an acceptable house in southwest Arlington.

During his leave he explained the housing situation in the area and the schooling consideration. Then, after describing and drawing diagrams of the house he'd found, he finally convinced me we should buy it.

On his third night back in Texas, Wright called and without any preliminaries he said, "Nan, I lost the house."

"Oh, no!" I exclaimed. "What happened?"

"Well, this afternoon—after work—I asked my boss if he would look at the house; you know, he owns a couple of houses and since we've never bought one before I wanted to get his opinion."

"Did he think it was a good buy?" I asked with a sinking feeling.

"He said it was a fair price," Wright answered. "And so, since the real estate agent was with us, I signed the contract right then and there."

"Well, why did we lose it?"

"Nan, that house has been empty for more than five months and, would you believe, somebody else put in his contract right after I did. And he offered the owner a down payment. But since I want to refinance with a no-down-payment veteran's loan, the owner accepted the other guy's offer. And that was that," Wright said in a disgusted, hopeless voice.

Beth picked up the extension phone and said excitedly, "Hi, dad. When are we moving into our new house?"

"Beth," Wright said wearily, "I'm sorry. I lost the house. Somebody else got it."

"Mom," Beth cried, "did you hear that! Oh, daddy, I want to be with you in Texas. I miss you. Please find another house, daddy."

"I'll try, Beth, I'll try. That's what mom and I are talking about. I miss you too," Wright said trying to comfort Beth. "I'll call you just as soon as I find another house."

"Okay, daddy," Beth said, still crying. "I love you. Bye."

"Bye, Beth. Love you."

Beth hung up the extension and I said, "Oh, Wright, I feel like Beth does and I'm angry; it just doesn't seem fair. After all the separations we've had and now this."

"I know, Nan. I know."

"I mean, we've had great fun up here with my folks, but I want to be together again as a family. What are you going to do?" I asked.

"Well, I'll start looking again," Wright answered. "I'll ask the boss if I can have tomorrow off. If I find a house, I'll call you."

"Good luck," I said half-heartedly. "I hope it doesn't take you as long with the second house as it did with the first one."

"So do I," Wright agreed.

Two days later, Beth and I were still trying to recover from our disappointment when Wright called again. He told me about another house he'd found. He was very enthusiastic about its good location and financing. I asked him if he was sure he was doing the right thing.

"Absolutely!" he countered. "Nan, you won't believe this. After I talked to you night before last—I went up to my room here in the Bachelor Officer's Quarters and for the first time in my adult life, except for our family prayers, I knelt down and prayed to God."

"You *what*?" I asked in a surprised voice.

"I prayed to God," Wright stated. "First, I told Him I thought He wanted us to be together as a family. And if this were the case, then He had to find us a house. Next, I asked Him for a house we could afford; then, I asked Him to find us a house close to an elementary school and a junior high school so the kids won't have to ride a bus. And finally—" Wright laughed, "this is funny—I prayed, 'God, three bedrooms would be fine but four would be better.' Nan, this house has *four* bedrooms!"

"How'd you find out about it?" I asked.

"Well, yesterday the boss gave me the day off. I looked all over Arlington and late in the afternoon I found a fairly good house in the northwest part of town. But it wasn't really what I thought you'd like. So I told the owner I'd have to call you before I made my decision. When I got back to the BOQ, I was about to call you when I noticed a note in my mailbox. It was from my boss. He wanted me to call him. I did, and he told me about the house."

"How did he know?"

"Nan, I tell you this whole thing is a miracle. Remember, I told you my boss looked at the first house with me?"

"Yes."

"Well, a woman who lives across the street saw us in our Navy uniforms. Her husband's in the Navy Reserve and he'd told her earlier about my arrival in Texas. When she saw us she figured I was still looking for a house. Then, the very next day—the day after my prayer—her best friend in the neighborhood popped in for a visit. Her friend announced that her husband had just received and accepted an offer for a new job in Tennessee that very morning—they own the house,

Nan," Wright said.

"The Navy Reserve wife asked her friend what they were going to do with their house. 'Sell it, I guess,' her friend answered. And then the wife said, 'I know somebody that might buy it.' And then she called my boss.

"This morning I called the owner," Wright continued. "I went to look at the house and we both signed the contract."

"Oh, Wright, are you sure we're doing the right thing?"

"Nan, I'm telling you God answered my prayer. Oh, I wish you could see this house. It's perfect. It's a three-block walk in one direction to the best elementary school in Arlington and a three-block walk in the other direction to the best junior high school in Arlington. It has dark-stained wood paneling in the den that matches our furniture. Oh, and the den has a cathedral ceiling too."

For some reason I sensed Wright was holding something back, so I asked, "Wright, why is it better than the other house—I feel like there's something you're not telling me?"

"Well, Nan, it—it has another—" he hesitated a moment. "It has another feature—but I want to save it. I want to surprise you when you all get down here."

"Oh, Wright," I said in a worried voice, "I just don't know what to say—we've never bought a house before and I—"

"Yes, I know," Wright interrupted. "My boss says we have rentitis. Look, Nan, I'll tell you this much; it's got a place to swim."

"You mean a pool!"

"No, no, not a pool," Wright answered. "It's even better than a pool. Now, I'm not going to say any more. Just take my word for it; God answered my prayer and then some. And I want to surprise you."

Six weeks later Beth, Wrightsie and I flew into Dallas. Wright drove us to a motel where we waited until sunset before he took us to see our new home. As we drove down the driveway and turned into the back of the house, Beth exclaimed, "Look, mom! We've got a canal in our back yard!"

It was a beautiful home in a perfect location. When we stepped from the car I noticed the houses across the canal were sharply silhouetted against the clear, warm twilight of the western sky. Gas lanterns lighted the lawns facing the canal and their reflections rippled and sparkled from the surface of the water like thousands of tiny fireflies. It had been a beautiful introduction to our new home.

And now, a year later, as I watched Wright and Wrightsie fishing in the canal I realized again that God had indeed answered my husband's prayer.

Later that evening, over our traditional Sunday taco supper, our conversation turned to Wrightsie's Monday appointment with the specialist. "Nan," Wright said, "I'm going to call my boss and see if I can have tomorrow off. I'd like to go to the doctor's with you."

"That's a good idea," I agreed. "Let's make it an outing. We can take Flossy shopping at the Quadrangle in Dallas and then take her to lunch before the appointment."

The next afternoon, our outing completed, we arrived at the specialist's office. We had a short wait and then we were ushered into the examining room. Wright carried Wrightsie and sat him on the examining table, then I undressed him to his waist. Wrightsie asked, "Should I show him how I can walk?"

"We'll see," his dad answered.

The specialist entered the room, nodded a quick greeting to Wright and me and said to Wrightsie, "Well, let's have a look at you."

We waited with anticipation for a favorable comment from the doctor during his examination but none was forthcoming. When he'd finished the examination he turned to me and said, "You can dress him now. I'll be back in a few minutes."

I dressed Wrightsie and when the doctor returned he asked, "Has he been having any problems?"

"He's still constipated," I said.

"Well, that's probably due to lack of exercise. Just keep using those suppositories and stool softeners I prescribed."

Then Wrightsie whispered into his father's ear, "Dad, please put me down. I want to show him I can walk."

Wright lifted Wrightsie from the table and gently lowered his feet to the floor. Then unaided, he took two difficult, struggling steps to a nearby chair. As Wright helped him into the chair I noticed a look of accomplishment on Wrightsie's face. But the specialist paid no notice to his efforts.

Next my husband asked, "Doctor, will it be all right for him to go swimming when the weather's warmer—I mean, will it help him regain the use of his arm and leg?"

"It can't hurt," the specialist said matter-of-factly. "Just make sure he wears a hat. He could get a severe sunburn 'til his hair grows back."

Hair was an important issue with Wrightsie. He'd already secured his father's permission to let his hair grow long enough to cover the surgical scar on the back of his head and neck.

The specialist's remark prompted a question from Wrightsie. "Doctor," he asked hopefully, "how long before my hair will grow back?"

" 'Bout a year or so," the doctor commented.

The expectant expression on Wrightsie's face turned to disappointment—"a year or so" was a long time in the life of an eight-year-old.

Even so, Wrightsie was undaunted and he then asked his most important question, "How long before I'll walk normal again?"

The specialist answered, "I'm going to tell it like it is; you'll never walk right again."

Wrightsie's face reflected a look of utter dejection mixed

with angry disbelief. Then he doubled up his fists, placed them to his eyes and slowly shook his lowered head from side to side.

Suddenly I was sick to my stomach; I couldn't believe what I'd heard or the way it was said.

I didn't want to break down and cry in front of Wrightsie, but for the first time since his illness I couldn't control my tears. I quickly put on my sunglasses and left the examining room saying, "I'll be in the waiting room."

A few minutes later Wright, stern-faced and angry, carried Wrightsie into the waiting room and we hurried out of the doctor's office. On the drive home to Arlington I sat in the back seat with Wrightsie. He stared out the window during the entire trip and never said a word. Once I tried to comfort him by putting my arm around his shoulders. But he never acknowledged my gesture.

Later that evening—at sunset—Wright carried him out to the back yard. He sat Wrightsie on the hood of the car and started to talk with him when two neighborhood boys came over to say hello. They were both wearing identical military-looking hats and I guess that gave Wrightsie an idea. He spotted me standing in the doorway to the den and said, "Mom, will you get me the sailor hat Captain Muery gave me—the one I wore to Boston?"

I got the hat from his room and took it out to him "Thanks, mom," he said. Then making sure the little Navy gold wings and officer's shield were in front, he placed it on his head.

I went back into the house and in five or ten minutes I noticed Wright and Wrightsie were sitting together on the patio by the canal. They seemed to be deep in conversation. It was almost dark when they returned to the house. Wright turned the TV set on for Wrightsie and then he joined me in the kitchen. "How's he doing?" I asked.

"A little better," Wright answered. "I think he'll snap out of it. How are you?"

"I'll be all right," I answered. "But I still can't believe what happened. What did you say to Wrightsie?"

"Well, those military hats gave me a great opening," Wright explained. "When we were sitting on the patio, I asked him, 'Wrightsie, do you know what courage is?' and he said, 'Well, not exactly, dad.'

"So, I explained, 'Wrightsie, when a person stands up and fights against all odds then he is courageous. And that's what you are, best buddy. In fact, you're the most courageous boy I've ever known.' And then he said, 'Aw, come on, dad.'

"Then I said, 'I'm not kidding, Wrightsie. Why, there're many men who've fought in Vietnam and they'd rather go back there again than go through what you've been through. You're more courageous than they are.' "

"What did he say to that?" I asked.

" 'You mean it, dad?' Then I said, 'You bet I do, Wrightsie.' And that got a big smile out of him. I think he'll come out of it okay, Nan."

But the next morning Wrightsie was still talking about his devastating experience. I was dressing him in his Cub Scout uniform—he had a meeting that afternoon—when he asked, "Mom, do you think that doctor was right about me never walking right?"

"No, I don't!" I said angrily. "He can make a mistake just like anybody else."

Wrightsie seemed satisfied with my answer. But I hadn't convinced myself, for after his home-bound teacher arrived I walked into my bedroom and had a good cry. Later, I'd barely finished repairing my make-up when the teacher called, "Mrs. Brunson?"

"Yes," I answered, walking into the dining room that doubled as a classroom.

"I think we'd better end his lessons early today—he seems to be having a little difficulty."

I looked at Wrightsie sitting at the table. His face was reddened with frustration and I saw tears in his eyes. I walked his teacher to the front door, said goodbye and then I returned to the dining room. Wrightsie was staring off into space. "Are you all right?" I asked.

He looked at me and answered, "I'm okay, mom." But the sadness in his eyes spoke louder than his words. I knew he was thinking about what the specialist had told him.

"Let's go into the den," I suggested. "You can watch TV 'til lunch is ready. I've invited Mrs. Fox for lunch—we'll eat in the kitchen and you can eat in the den. Then you can rest 'til it's time for your Cub Scout meeting. You still want to go to your meeting, don't you?"

"Sure," he answered; his spirits picked up a little at the mention of Cub Scouts.

After a late lunch, Evelyn Fox, Grandma Flossy and I were still chatting around the kitchen table when the phone rang. "Dr. Johnson!" I exclaimed when I recognized her voice. "Where are you?"

"In Dallas," Dr. Marie-Louise answered. "I'm on my way to a meeting in San Antonio and I had to change planes in Dallas."

"Do you have time to see us?" I asked hopefully. "Wright can pick you up within fifteen or twenty minutes and it's only a thirty minute drive to Arlington from Love Field."

"I'd like to see you;" she answered. "Let me see if I can catch a later flight. I'll call you right back."

In a few minutes the phone rang again and Marie-Louise said, "I've got a seven-thirty flight to San Antonio."

"Wonderful," I answered. "I'll call Wright at work. He'll meet you at the baggage claim area."

"Fine, fine," she answered. "I'll see you shortly. Bye."

After straightening the house a bit, I took Wrightsie to his Cub Scout meeting. He was greeted by a chorus of young, healthy yells when we arrived. I helped him sit on the floor with his back against an overstuffed chair. Then his den mother said, "Nan, I'm going to take the boys for an ice cream after the meeting. So, if you like, I'll bring Wrightsie home."

"Oh, Shirley, that'll be perfect," I said. "I'm having unexpected company this afternoon and that will really help me out. Thanks."

I returned home and in a few minutes I heard Wright's car. I walked out to the driveway to meet them and I was surprised to see Beth grinning from ear to ear, sitting in the back seat. "Mom!" she exclaimed as she leaped from the car, "daddy and Dr. Johnson picked me up when I was walking home from school!"

Dr. Johnson stepped from the car and gave me a warm hug. "Nancy, it's good to see you," she said. "You look wonderful."

"Oh, thank you," I replied.

Marie-Louise put her arm around Beth's shoulders as we walked into the house.

After I'd introduced Marie-Louise to Flossy I said, "Beth, why don't you take Dr. Johnson on a tour of the house while I make some tea?"

"Okay, mom," Beth answered and she led Marie-Louise towards her bedroom.

A few minutes later we gathered in the den for our tea party. Marie-Louise and Flossy sat on the den couch while Beth, Wright and I sat on cushions placed around the coffee table in front of the couch.

The tea had been poured and we were munching on cookies when I asked, "Marie-Louise, please tell me more about your trip to Japan."

"Well, like I told you when I called on the phone last month, we had a wonderful time," she answered. "But it is so good to be back and to see our friends again."

"By the way," she continued, "I don't know if I mentioned it during our phone conversation, but the Catholic nuns in Hiroshima are keeping you in their prayers."

"Thank you, Marie-Louise," I replied gratefully. "I don't know what we'd do if it weren't for the prayers of everyone—especially during the rough times. Oh, did Wright tell you about our visit to the specialist yesterday?"

"No," Marie-Louise answered.

"I thought I'd let you tell her," Wright explained.

So I told her the story in detail. I'd just finished when the doorbell rang—it was Wrightsie home from his meeting. He joined us on the floor around the coffee table.

Then Marie-Louise reached into a brightly colored shopping bag she'd placed beside the couch. "Here," she said, pulling two gift-wrapped packages from the bag. "I brought a little something for you, Beth." She handed Beth one package. "And for you, Wrightsie," she handed him the second.

Beth helped Wrightsie unwrap his package. When the gift came into view, Marie-Louise explained, "It's a book of Chinese proverbs."

Wrightsie smiled and said, "Thank you." Then he started to leaf through the pages.

Beth unwrapped her package and exclaimed with delight, "Look, mom! It's a Japanese cookbook. Thank you, Dr. Johnson."

Then Wright got up from the coffee table saying, "My legs are cramped. Think I'll sit in my chair. Wrightsie, want to sit with me?"

Wrightsie nodded his approval and Wright helped him walk over to the overstuffed green leather chair. When he was situated on his dad's lap Marie-Louise said, "Wrightsie, your mother told me you saw the doctor yesterday."

"Yeah," Wrightsie answered quickly, his voice tinged with involuntary anger. "He told me I'd never walk right again!"

"Well, I wouldn't be too concerned about what he said," Marie-Louise replied in a gentle, matter-of-fact, yet confident, tone of voice. "Remember this, Wrightsie: even though doctors are highly trained and skilled professionals they can still be wrong."

Wrightsie's face lit up with a smile that said, "I knew he was wrong." Then he nodded with determination. From that moment on Wrightsie regained his confidence and, if anything, he was more determined than ever to fully recover from the crippling effects of his brain tumor.

"And besides," Marie-Louise continued, "it doesn't make any difference what the doctor said; the Lord can do anything."

Wrightsie, hanging on every word Marie-Louise spoke, again nodded his head—this time in serious agreement.

Then Marie-Louise turned to Beth and said, "Beth, let's go over to the light. I'd like to look at your face."

They walked over to the sunlight which was shining through the den's glass door. After a careful examination of Beth's face, she nodded her approval and said, "You're taking good care of your complexion. Keep it up and don't get too much of this Texas sunshine."

We continued our chat for a while and then it was time to take Marie-Louise back to the airport—we all made the trip to Dallas.

After our final farewells—she had a special hug for Beth—we watched her disappear down the boarding ramp to the airplane. I turned to Wright and said, "You know, the Lord always seems to send Marie-Louise to us just when we need her most."

"What do you mean?" Wright asked.

"Well, I realize now He was looking out for us in Japan when He provided her for Beth's dermatology problem—even though we weren't what you could really call a Christian family. And then she called on the phone the day before Wrightsie asked the question, 'Why did God choose me as a victim?' I was given an answer before the question. And today she arrived to repair the damage done by the specialist. Marie-Louise was right when she said, 'The Lord can do anything.' "

# 22

## Let's Call It Old Ironsides

On the drive back to Arlington, we talked about Dr. Marie-Louise's visit until Wrightsie changed the subject by announcing, "Hey, dad, I almost forgot. We're having a Cub Scout parade this Saturday. Can I be in it?"

"You mean, can you march in the parade?" his father asked. Wrightsie nodded, "Yes."

"Well, I don't know, Wrightsie," his dad said. "How can you—I mean—you can't—" Wright searched for the words to explain to Wrightsie he couldn't possibly march in a parade with his partially paralyzed right leg.

Sensing his father's dilemma, Wrightsie spoke up and said, "Don't worry 'bout that, dad. Some of the guys said they'll push me in my wheelchair."

"What do you think, Nan?" Wright asked.

"Fine with me. I think it'll be fun."

"Oh, boy!" Wrightsie exclaimed. "Gee, thanks, mom. I've always wanted to be in a parade."

"But you've got to help me get ready," Wrightsie continued. "Our den's theme is fishing, so I have to dress up like I'm going fishing."

"Don't worry, we'll help you," I assured him. And for the rest of the drive to Arlington we discussed his fishing costume.

When we arrived home, Wright lifted his son from the car. Then Wrightsie said, "Dad, let me walk by myself. Can I?"

Wright lowered him to the driveway and walked close to his side as Wrightsie struggled towards the house. After a couple of steps he stumbled. Wright's hand shot out and he caught Wrightsie before he fell to the pavement. "Here, best buddy," Wright suggested, "you'd better let me help you."

"Okay," Wrightsie reluctantly agreed.

Wright helped Wrightsie into his bedroom, turned on the TV for him and came into the kitchen. "There's no doubt about it," he said, "Dr. Marie-Louise was just what he needed. He's bound and determined he's going to walk again."

Wright and I continued our chat in the kitchen while I prepared supper. Half an hour had gone by when we heard a noise coming from the hallway leading into the bedrooms. I looked up and watched Wrightsie as he struggled to walk into the den.

"Wrightsie, please be careful," I pleaded. My heart filled with a mixture of pride and sorrow as I watched my son's courageous battle.

"I'm—all—right, mom." His strained voice reflected his herculean efforts. "I'm—going to—show that—doctor!"

Then too exhausted to go any farther, he stopped and leaned against the wall at a precarious angle trying to regain his strength.

"Here, Wrightsie," his dad said, getting up from the kitchen table. "You've done a good job; let me help you the rest of the way."

Wrightsie gave his dad a grateful smile as he took his hand for the last few steps into the den. "Thanks, dad."

That night after supper, Wrightsie was unusually tired and I put him to bed early. After we said our family prayers I stayed in his bedroom and talked with him awhile. Finally, I tucked him in again and said, "I'm proud of you, Wrightsie. You're a brave boy. I love you."

"Thanks, mom. I love you too. And I love my cozy bed," he said in a sleepy voice. Then he wrapped his arm around Snoopy's neck and snuggled deeper into the covers. "And thanks for changing my sheets today."

I gave him a quick kiss goodnight and tears came to my eyes. I hurried out of his bedroom and shut the door.

Two nights later—Thursday—when Wright came home from work, he walked into the kitchen carrying several large sheets of white cardboard.

"What's that for?" I asked.

"I got an idea for Wrightsie's Cub Scout parade," he answered.

"Hey, Wrightsie," he called into the den. "I know how we're going to fix you up for your parade Saturday."

Wrightsie looked up from the TV set and asked, "How, dad?"

"We'll tape these cardboard sheets together to form the shape of a boat—without a bottom. Then we'll fit it over your wheelchair. It'll look like you're sitting in a fishing boat."

"Great, dad!" Wrightsie exclaimed. "But what about my feet? They'll show."

"No," his dad answered. "We'll lift the leg rests up 'til they're parallel with the ground. That way your feet will be covered by the sides of the boat.

"Great!" Wrightsie said again. "Let's make the boat now."

"In a few minutes," Wright answered. "Let me talk to mom first. Okay?"

Wright walked over to the stove and poured himself a cup of coffee. Then he said, "Carl Wilgus called me at the office today. He said Father Dennis Bennett had been in Washington, D.C., for a few days and he talked to him about Wrightsie."

"Did Father Bennett remember your phone call—the one you made right after Christmas?" I asked.

"He sure did," Wright answered. "In fact Carl said Father Bennett told a Full Gospel Business Men's meeting about Wrightsie and they all prayed for him."

"Isn't that wonderful?" I replied. "I don't think we could make it if it weren't for all these prayers. The Lord has sure sent some wonderful people our way."

"Yes," Wright agreed thoughtfully. "And He seems to send them just at the right time."

"By the way," he continued, "have you finished Father Bennett's book—*Nine O'clock in the Morning*—yet?"

"No," I said, a bit embarrassed. "Oh, Wright, you know how I read books. I've flipped through some of the pages, but I haven't really read it."

"Nan," Wright said with mock exasperation, "you've got to read it from cover to cover."

"I know. I will, I will."

"I almost forgot to tell you," Wright said. "Where's Flossy?"

"She's over talking with Evelyn. Why?"

"I made her airline reservations today," Wright answered.

My heart sank a little at Wright's words. I'd tried to forget that Flossy would be going home to New York. I said, "I hate to see her go."

"I do too," Wright said. "But she does have responsibilities to attend to at home."

"Well, I know she'll be happy to get back to her home. Especially since she's stayed longer than she'd planned."

"Yes," Wright agreed. "I'm glad she stayed the extra two weeks after Wrightsie came home from the hospital."

"Well, he's improved a lot in that time and I'm sure we can get along now. But I'm going to miss her."

"Me too," Wright said, and then he smiled. "What's Wrightsie going to do for apple pies?"

Beth overheard her father's comment and hollered in from

the den, "I'll bake 'em for you, dad."

"Okay, Beth," Wright answered with a laugh. "I'll hold you to that promise."

"Well, I'm thankful your mom stayed as long as she has," I said. "I know it's been hard for her to see Wrightsie in this condition."

"I know," Wright answered. "But I've seen a change come over her since she's been here."

"What do you mean?"

"It's difficult to explain, Nan," Wright answered. "You see, mom's never gotten over my father's death—even after all these years—until now. And for some reason I think Wrightsie had something to do with it. I don't know why; maybe it's his courage, or his faith or both. But he's definitely had an effect on his grandmother."

"Hey, dad," Wrightsie yelled in from the den, "can we make my boat now?"

Wright smiled at me and answered, "Sure, buddy. Let's get started."

Wright put Wrightsie into his wheelchair, pushed him out to the garage and they started their construction. When supper was ready, I opened the door to the garage and said, "Come on in, supper's—"

"Mom!" Wrightsie yelled urgently. "Don't look. We want to surprise you!"

"Okay. But come on in. You can finish the boat later. Supper's ready."

The conversation during supper was entirely devoted to the parade and the boat. "Wrightsie?" Beth asked. "What are you going to name your boat?"

"Gee, I don't know, Bethy. Can you think of a name?"

Beth thought a few minutes then shook her head. The rest of us suggested a few names but none seemed to click.

Then Wright exclaimed, "Hey, I've got it—the perfect

name! Let's call it Old Ironsides."

"Yeah!" Wrightsie agreed. "Yeah, just like the name of the detective on TV who needs a wheelchair."

"Exactly," Wright said. "But it's got another meaning too. You're a Navy Junior, Wrightsie, and the Navy's most famous ship was nicknamed Old Ironsides."

"Hey, that's right," Beth said.

"Come on, dad," Wrightsie said with excitement, "let's finish Old Ironsides and put the name on it."

"Okay," Wright laughed getting up from the table. "Let's go!"

Father and son left the table and about an hour later Wrightsie called from the garage, "Mom, Bethy, Grandma Flossy! Come and see my boat!"

We walked into the garage. Wrightsie, a fishing pole resting over his right shoulder, was sitting in Old Ironsides as his dad pushed him across the garage towards us. "Dad's going to be my outboard motor in the parade," Wrightsie said.

Then Wright turned the wheelchair around and started to push it away from us. Strapped to his back was a large, white, four-bladed propeller. "What—how'd you do that?" I asked with a laugh.

"I cut and folded one of the cardboard sheets into a pinwheel," Wright explained. "Then I fastened it to this old web belt with a small bolt and nut. Look!" Wright flipped the propeller with his hand and it spun freely as he circled the garage with Old Ironsides. "It'll spin in the wind during the parade."

And there was plenty of wind that Saturday morning—a cold, blustery north wind backed up by a winter gray sky.

For some reason Wrightsie's mood matched the weather. "Wrightsie, I want you to wear your winter jacket," I said as I dressed him for the parade.

"Aw, mom," he protested with obvious displeasure. "None

of the other guys will have jackets. It'll cover up my fishing outfit."

"That doesn't make any difference. I don't want you to catch cold."

"Aw, mom," he said again.

His disposition didn't improve as we drove into downtown Arlington. When we arrived at the marshalling point for the parade I noticed all his little Cub Scout friends were also dressed in their warmest winter jackets. Wrightsie's face brightened a little as his friends clustered around him and exclaimed over Old Ironsides. But it didn't last, for as they stepped off into the parade, Wright accidentally hit the edge of the curb with the wheelchair. Wrightsie was jostled and he turned around and gave his father an annoyed look. Wright missed the expression—he was waving to Beth and me. "See you at the end of the parade," he yelled as they marched off down the street.

"Okay," I called back. "Beth and I will be taking movies, so smile."

Wright answered with a final wave and off they went. The pinwheel propeller spinning rapidly in the cold wind seemed to hurry them along.

Beth and I rushed up the sidewalk along the line of march to the vanguard of the parade. Then we stopped and I shot movies when Old Ironsides came into range. We then advanced to another vantage point for more pictures. After one series of shots, I lowered the camera and called, "Wrightsie! Wrightsie! Over here! Hi! Hi!"

Wright searched the crowd, caught sight of Beth and me and waved. Then he bent over and said something close to his son's ear. But Wrightsie refused to look our way. All I could see was the profile of his nose and fat, little red cheeks from beneath the hood of his jacket.

A pleading thought came to my mind, "Oh, Wrightsie,

what's the matter? Please look at me, please smile. You'll be able to march in a parade some day. Please smile!"

Beth must have seen the sadness in my face. "What's wrong, mom?" she asked.

"Nothing, hon. Just a thought. Nothing."

Beth tugged on my hand and pointed down the sidewalk. "Come on, mom," she encouraged. "Let's go to the next corner. We can take some more movies from the steps down there."

I turned my head away and quickly brushed a few tears from my eyes with the back of my hand. Then I followed Beth down the sidewalk.

After the parade we hurried back to our warm home. Grandma Flossy met us at the door—the delicious aroma of hot apple pie swirled from the open door. "I heard all about the parade on the radio while I baked. The announcer described Old Ironsides."

"You're kidding," I said. "Wrightsie, did you hear that? You were on the radio."

For the first time that day Wrightsie grinned. "The announcer was very much impressed with the whole idea," Flossy continued.

Many months later we were to find out that a scouting official viewing the parade had also been very much impressed. And as a result, he started a new and wonderful ministry for a unique group of boys.

Wrightsie's spirits brightened a little and we took a few more movie pictures of Old Ironsides in the back yard. Then he asked, "Mom, can I have a piece of pie—just a sliver?"

After he finished his pie, he said, "Mom, I'm tired. Can I have a nap?"

A hint of fear tugged at my heart. "Do you feel all right?" I asked.

He nodded slowly, "I'm okay, mom. I'm just a little

tired—and cold."

"Okay, let's go," I said, helping him to his bedroom.

When I removed his shoes, he asked, "Mom, can I sleep on the floor in my sleeping bag?"

"Sure," I answered. "Here, let me spread it out on the floor for you." Then I helped him lie down.

"Mom, don't forget Snoopy," he reminded me.

"Here you go," I said, handing him his stuffed dog. Then I zippered the sleeping bag around him, closed the drapes, gave him a quick kiss and left the room.

He seemed to sleep forever that afternoon. And I worried more and more with each passing minute. Finally, I said to Wright, "I'm worried sick. He's slept so long. And he did the same thing yesterday."

"Nan, he's all right," Wright tried to reassure me. "He's been excited about the parade and all. Don't worry, the sleep's good for him."

But I wasn't reassured.

Finally, after about three hours, Wrightsie awoke and he did seem a little more cheerful. But even that didn't revive my spirits and that night when I went to bed I was exhausted from worry and very much depressed.

# 23
## *I've Got It! I've Got It!*

The weather changed overnight and the new day dawned warm and sunny. It was Flossy's last Sunday with us and we tried to make it a special day. When Wright returned from church he borrowed a neighbor's boat—with a small electric outboard motor—and we cruised up and down the canal sightseeing. And that evening Wright prepared our usual Sunday night taco supper.

The next day friends and neighbors dropped in to say their goodbyes to Flossy. Some had gifts, including Evelyn Fox who gave her a prisoner-of-war bracelet with Commander Ken Coskey's name on it. The farewell ceremonies were capped Monday night when we all attended a Cub Scout blue and gold dinner at J.L. Hill Elementary School. Wrightsie was all decked out in full uniform. We were a proud family as Wrightsie was presented with his wolf badge.

Then Tuesday afternoon we drove Flossy to Love Field in Dallas. After many hugs and kisses she walked down the boarding ramp to her plane. Of course we didn't know it then, but that was the last time Wrightsie and Grandma Flossy would ever see each other. We watched the plane taxi to the runway and then headed home.

During the drive my thoughts retreated to all the events that had occurred during Flossy's stay with us. I felt kind of blue by the time I got to Arlington. Then I realized it was two weeks to the day since Evelyn's dad had died. So I decided to put Wrightsie in his wheelchair and we dropped over to see her. When Evelyn came to the door I noticed she had company. "Oh, I'm sorry, Evelyn," I said. "We'll come back later."

"No, no," she insisted. "Come on in; I want you and Wrightsie to meet Marty. We were just talking about you."

Evelyn made the introductions and we talked for some time. When I got up to leave, Marty said, "Nan, I'm so happy I got to meet you. I've heard so much about you and Wrightsie. We've got to get together again."

"Oh, yes," I agreed. "Please come by anytime." I liked Marty immediately. Her warmth and outgoing personality—and enthusiasm—had really lifted my spirits. I looked forward to seeing her again.

I didn't have to wait long. Two days later—Thursday afternoon—she dropped by with a friend for a visit. Marty introduced me to her friend, Hazel, then I showed them to the kitchen. We chatted over coffee and in no time our conversation turned to Christianity. It didn't take me long to realize that Marty and Hazel were loving, devout Christians—and charismatics.

Soon our talk centered around the Christian healing ministry. The conversation was even more meaningful when I found Marty was also a registered nurse. Towards the end of our visit Marty said, "Nan, I brought you a number of booklets that discuss healing. Please read them when you have time."

"Thank you, Marty," I said taking the booklets.

"And remember, Nan," Marty continued, "when you pray for Wrightsie's healing don't concentrate on his condition now. Just believe in the healing power of the Holy Spirit and pray for his complete and perfect recovery."

"Thanks. I will," I assured her.

Then Hazel said, "Nan, I had some books on healing I wanted to bring you too. But when I prayed about it I was led to only this one pamphlet."

I took the pamphlet and read the title out loud—*Authority of the Believer*.

"Yes," Hazel replied. "It's written by Kenneth Hagin. He talks about the authority a Christian has to counteract the power of Satan."

I was surprised she'd been led to bring me a book on that subject. I had no hang-ups whatsoever concerning Satan. I'd heard about Satan in my Lutheran elementary parochial school days. But I didn't really believe he existed. Nevertheless, as soon as they left, I picked up Hazel's booklet and read it from cover to cover.

When Wright came home from work that night I told him about their visit. Then I said, "You know, after I finished reading the pamphlet I suddenly realized that Satan does exist."

"No kidding," Wright answered good-naturedly.

"Well, I can remember when you didn't believe he existed," I chided him.

Then Wright became serious and said, "Yes, I know. I had a lot of foolish theories before I became a Christian. And I'm afraid some of my hairbrained ideas rubbed off on you. But you're right; Satan's all too real."

"There's no doubt in my mind about that now," I said emphatically. "Many times I've been angry at God because I believed it was His fault Wrightsie had a brain tumor. It's Satan's fault; he's the destroyer, not God."

"Exactly," Wright said. "And that's why it's so dangerous when people don't believe in Satan. They end up blaming God for all the horrors in this world, and that drives them even further away from Jesus and His salvation. And you can bet Satan delights in that."

That night when we said our bedtime prayers, I felt a new sense of Christian confidence and security as we prayed to our loving Father.

The next afternoon I was surprised by a telephone call from Beverly Henderson. She said her little Kim was doing poorly. It was sad; poor Kim wanted to walk again, but she hadn't improved at all. I tried to comfort Beverly and at the end of our conversation I said, "We're going to the Church of the Resurrection this evening. I'll ask Father Ted to say special prayers for Kimmy tonight."

I really looked forward to the prayer meeting. I too intended to say special prayers for Kimmy and I wanted to exercise my newfound Christian confidence I'd gained since reading *Authority of the Believer*. During the general confession before communion I confessed my sins to God. First, I confessed my previous disbelief in the existence of Satan. And second, I confessed my previous disbelief that Wrightsie could be healed. Then I felt as if a tremendous burden had been lifted from my shoulders.

After Holy Communion the church emptied rapidly except for those who wanted special prayers. Father Ted stepped down from the altar and walked up to me with sort of a questioning look on his face. "Nan," he said with a slight shake of his head, "I've never been led to do this before but I feel that you're ready to ask for the baptism in the Holy Spirit."

"Oh, Father Ted, yes," I exclaimed. It's funny; I hadn't really considered asking for the baptism that night and yet when Father Ted spoke I knew in my heart it was right. "Yes," I said again, "I'd like to ask for the baptism."

Wright and Wrightsie were at the back of the church visiting, but Beth had stayed with me and taken in the conversation. "Mom," she asked, "can I go with you? I want to ask for the baptism too."

Father Ted smiled his approval and together we walked to

the altar rail. Beth and I knelt at the rail and a lovely woman started to pray with Beth. Father Ted knelt in front of me and said, "Nan, I want to give you a few words of instruction before we ask Jesus to baptize you in the Spirit. Now, if you've ever dealt with anything that has to do with the occult—you know, fortune telling, Ouija board, horoscopes, anything like that—I want you to confess it and renounce it right now. Many people think such things are innocent but they're not. They're of Satan and they're dangerous.

"Now, Nan, say this prayer after me," Father Ted continued. "Holy Father, I confess I have—name those things you wish to confess," Father Ted interjected. I named the Ouija board and a fortuneteller I'd visited many years before as a teen-ager. And then I ended my prayer under Father Ted's guidance by saying, "I renounce these acts and bind them under the blood of Jesus Christ never to return, in Jesus' name. Thank you, Father."

Then Father Ted said, "Now, Nan, I'm going to ask Jesus to baptize you in His Holy Spirit. If you feel your throat start to fill up or feel like you should pray, just open your mouth and let the words come out."

I nodded and lowered my head. Father Ted placed his hands gently on my head and started to pray, "Dear Jesus, precious Savior, I thank you that your servant Nancy is under your protection. I ask you to baptize her with your Holy Spirit. Fill her heart with joy and peace and comfort. Let her sing praises to your glory. . . ."

As Father Ted prayed I became conscious of the prayers for Beth who was kneeling beside me. Then I heard Beth quietly speak a few beautiful words I didn't understand. My heart thrilled as I realized she'd received her prayer language. Father Ted continued to pray with me. I thought I started to feel a fullness in my throat but then I wasn't sure. Then Father Ted ended his prayer. "Oh, Father Ted," I said in a disappointed voice, "I didn't feel a thing."

"I did," Father Ted answered. "But it makes no difference. We're not dealing with feelings or emotions. We've asked Jesus to baptize you in His Holy Spirit and it is done. It's as simple, as complicated, as wonderful as that. You *have* received."

Then Father Ted gave me a big hug and said, "I love you, Nan."

Father Ted moved along the altar rail and began to pray with another woman. Beth and I left the church to find Wright and Wrightsie. We couldn't wait to tell them. When we finally located them, Beth was bursting with exuberance as she described her experience.

Wrightsie rode with his father in the front seat of the car on the way home to Arlington. Beth sat beside me in the back seat. We were about halfway home—driving south on Loop 12—the conversation had ceased and I was silently praying. All of a sudden my throat filled and words started to flow from my mouth—unknown words. And my heart leaped with joy. Then I exclaimed, "I've got it! I've got it!"

The car swerved as Wright snapped to attention and yelled, "What! What's the matter!"

"I've got it!" I repeated. "I've got my prayer language!"

# 24
## *O Ye of Little Faith!*

That night after the family was in bed, I walked out to the kitchen and sat down at the table—oh, how many family experiences, decisions, joy and sorrows had been discussed around our kitchen table. Immediately, I began to pray—very quietly—in my new prayer language. The unknown words of praise and thanksgiving rolled freely from my tongue. My heart filled with joy as I was overwhelmed by the reality of my Savior, Jesus, the power of His Holy Spirit and the love of God.

As I continued praying, a vivid thought was placed in my mind. "His mercy endureth forever. His mercy endureth forever." Over and over again the thought repeated itself—it was almost as if I'd been given the interpretation of my prayer language.

Then a second thought—my own thought—filled my mind, "Wrightsie's healed! He's going to be all right! Praise the Lord!" I went to bed floating on a cloud of peace and love.

I told Wright about my experience at the kitchen table the next morning. He was excited for me, but I detected a note of caution in his voice. Nevertheless Wrightsie's continued improvement supported my interpretation of the thought, "His mercy endureth forever." For instance, that Tuesday after his lessons, the home-bound teacher said, "Wrightsie's really doing well with his schoolwork. Maybe you should think about putting him in school this fall. He'll be able to go right into fourth grade."

"Wonderful!" I exclaimed. "And you mean he won't have to repeat third grade?"

"No," she smiled. "He's right up with his classmates. He'll do fine in fourth grade."

I glanced over at Wrightsie and he was beaming over his success. His teacher continued, "We have a special school in the district for children who are—well, shall we say—need special consideration. They have a special school bus with a lift, ramps at the school for wheelchairs and special programs. Maybe you and Wrightsie could visit the school.

Wrightsie nodded his enthusiastic approval.

"We will," I assured the teacher. "Thank you for the information."

The first part of March flew by in a flurry of happy activities: school lessons, Cub Scouts and Friday night prayer meetings at the Resurrection. The only bad news concerned little Kim Henderson. I'd kept in touch with either Kimmy's mother, Beverly, or her grandmother, Mrs. Lane. And they reported Kim's condition had slowly worsened.

All the activities must have gotten to me towards the end of the month. One Thursday night, after a particularly long day, we had gathered in Wrightsie's bedroom for our evening prayers. When I knelt down beside his bed I complained wearily, "I'm so tired. And my right arm and shoulder have ached for days."

We all said our prayers and Wright and Beth left the room as I tucked Wrightsie in for the night. He looked so comfortable I was prompted to ask, "Are you happy, Wrightsie?"

"Yes, mom," he answered with a little boy smile, and he gave Snoopy an extra loving squeeze with his good left arm. "I've been happier than ever since I left Boston; the Holy Spirit leaped in my brain during surgery and I have the gift of healing."

I was amazed by his statement and I just stood and looked down at him. Then he asked, "Mom, can I pray for your arm?"

"Yes, please." I knelt beside his bed again. I helped him as he pushed himself into a sitting position with his left arm. Then he placed his left hand on my shoulder and, struggling, he managed to put his right hand on my forearm. Next, he lowered his head and started to pray silently. I lowered my head for a few seconds then I looked up into his face. His eyes were closed and I could see he was deep in prayer. I lowered my head again until I felt the pressure of his hands lessen.

"Did you feel anything, mom?" he asked in an expectant tone of voice.

"Well, no. I don't think so," I answered, hoping he wouldn't be disappointed.

"I did. I felt my hands tingle. You're gonna be okay."

"Oh, Wrightsie, I love you," I said giving him a big hug.

He looked into my eyes, and in a serious, almost mature voice, he said, "And I love you, mom. I love you more than you'll ever know." Then he said, "Mom, can we say another prayer?"

"Sure. What for?"

"I want to pray for Dr. Shaw and his continued success in brain surgery."

"All right. Here, let me take your hands." We lowered our heads and prayed for Dr. Shaw and his work.

When I left his room that night I felt specially blessed by the Lord. And the next morning all my aches and pains had disappeared.

Good Friday arrived on the last day of March that year. The three Episcopal churches in Arlington coordinated their Lenten observances so we attended Good Friday services at Saint Bartholemew's. I was overwhelmed by the solemnity and meaning of the occasion and wiped away tears during most of the service. When we left Saint Bart's, Wright asked sympathetically, "What were the tears for?"

"For Jesus," I answered. "For the first time in my life I've realized what Jesus did for me, for you and Beth and Wrightsie—for all mankind. And I thought of the jeers from the crowd around the cross, His suffering and His Father forsaking Him and I couldn't help but weep for Him."

"You're wonderful," Wright replied. "I love you!"

Sunday we attended Easter morning services at our own Saint Alban's. What a glorious day it was! Wrightsie's recovery could be measured each Sunday when we went forward for Communion. When he'd recovered sufficiently so we could take him to church, Wright had carried him to the altar rail. Then, as he improved, he'd walk part of the way. Next, he'd walk the full distance—up and back—while Wright held his hand. But that Easter morning when Wright reached for his son's hand to help him, Wrightsie whispered as he pushed his father's hand aside, "No, dad. Please let me do it alone." Then he held his head up, squared his shoulders, took a deep breath and marched unaided to the Lord's Supper. Oh, he had a bad limp—but he made it all the way. A few days later we were to find out that a couple at Saint Alban's had been watching Wrightsie's progress. They'd thrilled with us that Easter morning as he soloed to the altar rail and it started a change in their lives.

The next Friday was another important first day for Wrightsie. He started physiotherapy. The guard at the hospital emergency room entrance remembered us from Wrightsie's radiation therapy and he saw to it we could park as close as possible to the entrance.

Then that night we attended the prayer meeting at the Resurrection. When we walked into the church a couple interrupted us. The wife said, "Excuse me, but aren't you the

Brunsons? I'm Lorena Hamilton and this is my husband Wingo. We've wanted to meet you."

Wright made the introductions and we were pleasantly surprised to find out they were members of Saint Alban's in Arlington. We also found out Wingo was a professor of mathematics at the University of Texas at Arlington.

"Is this your first time at the Resurrection?" I asked.

"Yes, it is," Lorena answered. Then she smiled and explained, "You see, we first saw you and your family on Palm Sunday and I asked some friends who you were. But no one seemed to know your name. Then, last Sunday, we watched your son push his father's hand aside and walk to the altar rail alone. Well, we were more determined than ever to meet you. We finally found somebody who knew you and we also found out you come over to the Resurrection every Friday night. So here we are."

A few months before Lorena's story would have amazed me but I had begun to learn how the Lord works in people's lives. And I recognized this as one of His "coincidences."

As we looked for a place to sit, Beth whispered, "Mom, Dr. Hamilton looks so much like grandpa!"

"Yes, I know," I answered. "It's amazing."

Lorena and Wingo soon became our very close friends and were to play an important part in our lives.

We all took seats close to the center of the circle of chairs. As usual, Gordon Bell, Wrightsie's earthly guardian angel, appeared and slapped Wrightsie gently on the shoulder. "How are you, Wrightsie?" he asked.

"Fine," Wrightsie answered with a shy, big grin.

Father Ted strode into the back of the church. He tossed off greetings to various people who were gathering for the prayer meeting, "Hello there, Stan—Hutch, how's it going?— Allene, get those books on sale—Hi, Brunsons." Before we could answer he'd disappeared into his office.

I turned to Gordon, introduced him to the Hamiltons, and we discussed Wrightsie's progress including his physiotherapy and his Easter walk to Communion.

"Praise the Lord," Gordon replied after each report.

Then the prayer meeting began. Oh, how good it was to be with God's people. Their warmth, their compassion, their Christian love was wonderful and I let it surround me. I needed it all. And without question my new life in the Spirit sustained me. Otherwise I couldn't have kept the pace I was maintaining.

We left the prayer meeting late that night, yet we were up early Saturday with a full weekend ahead of us. Sunday night ended with a late, delicious taco supper. Wright and I were in the midst of cleaning up and the kids were getting ready for bed when the phone rang. Wright answered. "Hello—Tom!" he exclaimed. "Wait a minute."

"Hey, Nan, it's your brother Tom. Get the phone in our bedroom."

I ran to our room, picked up the extension and Wright asked, "How are things on Long Island?"

"Great. Great," Tom answered, "But we want to come down to Texas and see the Brunsons."

"Wonderful!" I exclaimed. "When?"

"Hi, Nan," Tom said when he heard my voice. "Well, how's Friday the twenty-first—for the weekend?" he continued. "I'll have flown my April schedule by the twentieth. I'm pretty sure we can get down there Friday and come back here Monday. You folks have anything on over that weekend?"

"No. No," I assured him. "Oh, it'll be great to see you and Hilda and the kids."

We must have talked on the phone an hour that night. Beth and Wrightsie talked to Susan, Tommy and David. Before they got on the phone I cautioned, "Let's not tell them Wrightsie can walk; we'll surprise them when they come down here."

Beth and Wrightsie nodded their heads in gleeful delight

over our secret.

I started preparations for their visit the very next day. Meanwhile, Wrightsie's schoolwork, physiotherapy and Cub Scout efforts continued. And Wrightsie made steady improvement. However, one night for a few minutes the old fears returned. I'd put Wrightsie to bed and we'd said our prayers when he complained, "Mom, my stomach hurts. It feels like it's being eaten."

"Oh, Wrightsie," I said trying to hide my fears as I had visions of cancer destroying his stomach. "How long has it hurt?"

"Since supper," he answered.

"I'm sure you'll be all right in the morning," I said trying to convince myself more than Wrightsie. Then I had an idea. "Wrightsie, would you like to sleep with me tonight?"

He nodded his head in his little boy way. Wright carried him into our bedroom and Beth followed behind, carrying his stuffed menagerie including Tigeree and Snoopy.

I tucked him in our bed, gave him an extra hug and kiss, turned out the light and hurried out to the kitchen. I sat down at the table and tears came to my eyes. Beth walked into the kitchen, saw my despair and asked, "Oh, mom, what's wrong?"

"Beth, I'm exhausted—and I'm frightened about Wrightsie's stomach ache."

"Don't be worried," she said gently. "Remember when Peter and the disciples were in the boat with Jesus? A storm came up and they were so scared they woke Him up. And He said, 'O ye of little faith'? Then He stopped the storm."

"You're right, Beth," I said with an apologetic smile. "I've got to have more faith. Thank you. You've taught me something. Would you pray with me?"

Bethy nodded.

We held hands and I prayed, "Holy Father, thank you for Wrightsie's healing. Now we pray for his complete and speedy recovery. And we lift up his tummy to you tonight. Take away the pain and give him a restful night. Thank you, Father, for giving me Beth. In Jesus' name. Amen."

A few minutes later, I quietly peeked into our room. Wrightsie, his arm around Snoopy, was sound asleep.

# 25
## The Lord's Used Wrightsie to Heal Me!

Wrightsie's stomach ache was gone the next morning. That afternoon, when Beth returned from school, she and Wrightsie went around the neighborhood selling tickets to an upcoming Boy Scout jamboree. The Scoutarama was to be held in Fort Worth the Saturday before Mother's Day in May.

It was a cold, windy day and I reminded them, "Now I want you to bundle up." I saw them to the door and then peeked out the window as they walked to a house across the street. Oh, Beth was so loving and careful with her brother. She held his hand all the way and carefully helped him up on the neighbor's porch. Then she pushed the doorbell and hurried to the side so she wouldn't be seen when the door opened. The neighbor bought a ticket, and when she closed the door Beth hurried to Wrightsie's side. He held up a dollar bill—I just imagined him saying, "Look, Bethy! I sold my first ticket." Then Beth helped him down the porch and off they went to the next house, fighting against the wind.

Friday night we attended the Resurrection. Father Ted and most of the men were on a retreat, but not Gordon Bell. He was waiting for us when we arrived.

It was a glorious evening with a very special ending. The last song we sang was "Amazing Grace." And we usually ended the

183

hymn with a chorus of "Praise God, Praise God. . . ." During the chorus, I held my arms high and closed my eyes as I sang the words of praise. Wright nudged me and looked down at Wrightsie. I followed his gaze and my heart thrilled; for the first time in his recovery Wrightsie had managed to raise his right arm over his head. And there he stood, praising God in song at the top of his voice with both arms raised high. It was a beautiful sight.

By the time Thursday rolled around I was prepared for my brother Tom and his family. We had also known for some time that Carl and Jean Wilgus would be in Dallas. Carl had been invited down by the Full Gospel Business Men for various speaking engagements. Wright and Carl had agreed that they would call us after their arrival in Dallas and Carl had managed to firm up his speaking schedule. I wanted very much to meet Carl and Jean, and I hoped they would be able to meet Tom and Hilda.

We'd reviewed our plans for the weekend. Wright remarked, "The captain's going to let me off from work tomorrow so I can go to the airport with you to pick up Tom and Hilda and the kids."

But the next morning, Wright called around nine-thirty and said, "Nan, I can't go to the airport with you. An A-7 just crashed at the Waco airport and I've got to go down there."

"Oh, no!" I exclaimed. "Who was the pilot? Is he okay?"

"Yes," Wright answered. "But I don't think you know him. It was a company test pilot. And he got out of it okay. He's not hurt, but the plane was built under government contract so our office has to investigate the accident. I've got to head up the investigation. And be prepared; I'll have to work Saturday and maybe Sunday."

"Oh, Wright," I said, disappointed in the fact he'd miss much of the weekend activities we'd planned.

"I know. I'm sorry," Wright answered. "I've got to rush now; there's a plane waiting to fly us down to Waco."

"Bye now. Be careful." I said.

The Harkins family arrived on schedule later that day. Wrightsie and I were at Love Field to greet them as they walked off the plane. When we spotted them, Wrightsie proudly hurried forward. "Wrightsie!" Hilda exclaimed. "Wrightsie! You're walking! How wonderful!" Big tears rolled down her cheeks as she bent over and hugged her nephew.

On the drive back to Arlington, I outlined our plans for their visit. Wrightsie joined in and said, "And I'm going to be your guide Sunday. We're going to take you on a tour of my favorite place: Six Flags Over Texas." Then he told Susan, Tommy and David all about the rides and shows at his favorite amusement park.

Just before supper Wright came home from work. After greeting Tom, Hilda and the kids, he said, "Well, I've got to fly back down to Waco tomorrow and I'll be down there most of the day on the accident investigation. But I will be free Sunday—can't miss Six Flags Over Texas you know."

"Great, dad!" Wrightsie responded.

We had a relaxed, leisurely dinner that night; then after the children were in bed, we chatted a long time—catching up on our lives since we'd last met in Boston way back in December. The next morning after Wright had left again for Waco, I served brunch on the patio. At Wrightsie's request, I'd prepared my special menu reserved for notable occasions—like Christmas, Easter and visits by special people. The fresh strawberries, steaming cornmeal muffins and thinly sliced hot ham disappeared quickly.

Hilda and I had just finished cleaning up after the meal when the phone rang.

"Hello. This is Carl Wilgus."

"Hello, Carl. This is Nancy. Oh, I've been hoping you'd call." We talked for a few minutes, then I explained Wright's absence and mentioned that my brother and his family were visiting. Next we tried to figure out when it would be best for him and his wife Jean to come out to Arlington—they'd already checked into a downtown Dallas hotel. As it worked out, they were free that afternoon. We agreed that I'd pick them up in front of the Neiman-Marcus Gourmet Shoppe on Commerce Street.

Leaving the children under Susan's watchful eye, Tom, Hilda and I were about to climb into the car when Wrightsie asked, "Mom, I'd like to pick up Commander Wilgus with you. Can I go?"

"Sure," I answered. "I know he wants to talk with you. Let's go."

We had a wonderful visit that afternoon. Carl and Jean enriched our lives with their quiet, gentle—yet strong—Christian spirits. Jean gave me a gift of solid chocolate candies she'd bought at Neiman's. I passed these out as Tom and Carl started to discuss their first years in the Navy. Their early careers had paralleled; both entered the Navy about the same time, both were assigned to patrol squadrons after flight training and although they didn't know each other they had many mutual friends.

Then Carl began to relate a miraculous event that had occurred some years before when he had an engine fire on a flight. We adults gathered in the den around the coffee table and the children were playing a game on the floor. But, as Carl neared the thrilling climax of his story, I noticed the children had forgotten their game and hung on his every word. From then on until we took Carl and Jean back to Dallas our conversation centered on Christianity. I'm sure Tom and Hilda had never participated in such a discussion before. I must say they received a crash course in the Holy Spirit, Christian healing and the charismatic renewal.

The next day—Sunday—Wrightsie proved to be an enthusiastic guide as we toured Six Flags Over Texas. He headed up our procession through the amusement park in his wheelchair, climbing out for each ride and show.

We were a tired, happy group when we arrived home that night. Even so, just before bedtime Wrightsie had his own show to perform. For weeks he'd been practicing for an important part he was to play in a Cub Scout skit Monday night. And he wanted to practice one more time for Susan, Tommy and David—sort of a dress rehearsal. It came off perfectly, then we all fell into our beds.

Monday morning, Wrightsie and I took the Harkins family to the airport. We said long, lingering goodbyes and Wrightsie and I watched sadly as they boarded. As their plane climbed steeply skyward over Dallas, Wrightsie turned to me and said, "I'm going to miss 'em, mom."

"I know. Me too." And we walked slowly back to the car.

The rest of Monday was a nervous day for Wrightsie. On the drive back from the airport he practiced his lines again in preparation for his stage debut. The skit was about clowns and I painted the appropriate face on Wrightsie hours before the play was to begin. He dressed in his red and white striped nightshirt with a matching nightcap Beth had sewn for him. At the appointed time and place—about 7:30 P.M. in the auditorium at J.L. Hill Elementary School—Wrightsie and his Cub Scout friends—also clowns—were gathered around a cardboard box. Another Cub Scout was hiding in the box—I don't know why; I can't remember the plot. Then Wrightsie proclaimed his memorable lines, "Hey, Jojo! Are you in there?" Everything was perfect. The play was a success, the boys loved it, the audience loved it—their applause was loud and Wrightsie was a very happy Cub Scout.

We certainly had had a long, wonderful, busy four days. Then Wednesday night we came back to earth when I called Beverly Henderson to see how Kimmy was doing. Beverly sounded depressed and she said Kim was doing very poorly. "Beverly," I said, "would you mind if I called some people at the Church of the Resurrection—and asked them to come over and pray for Kimmy?"

"Oh, Nancy," she answered. "Please have them come."

Thursday night I called Beverly again and while we were talking her doorbell rang. It was Gordon Bell and a group from the Resurrection. Then, the next night, at the Resurrection prayer meeting, we all prayed for Kimmy's healing.

Before I knew it we were in the month of May. On the second, Wrightsie had his last day of physiotherapy at the hospital, for a vacancy had occurred for him at a rehabilitation center. And the next day he started this program. We were thrilled with his progress and every night we thanked the Lord for his healing and prayed for his rapid recovery. Then we'd pray for Kimmy.

Our lives were centered around the Lord and His people. About that time we were also awakened to the fact that Jesus was using Wrightsie in a powerful way to help change people's lives. The first incident was revealed to us during the Resurrection prayer meeting the first Friday in May. When we walked into the church Father Ted spotted us and said, "Here, Wrightsie. How about passing out these song books?"

Wrightsie beamed, grabbed an armload of books and placed one book on every other chair.

Then, during the prayer meeting, a number of people stood up and told what the Lord had done in their lives. During one testimony, Wrightsie leaned across my lap and whispered, "Dad, when are you going to tell them about me?"

I could see Wright was caught off guard by Wrightsie's question. Then he answered positively, "Tonight, Wrightsie. Tonight."

Wrightsie smiled and sat back in his chair. A few seconds passed and then he whispered to me, "Mom, can I leave and go play with the kids?"

How perfect! We had never discussed the fact that he'd had a tumor. It was still a secret we kept from him and—I'm sure—a secret he kept from us. With Wrightsie out of church, his dad could tell everything. I nodded my approval and Wrightsie left the meeting.

The previous speaker finished, and immediately Wright stood up and told the whole story. It was a beautiful witness. Later, after Communion, a young woman walked up and introduced herself. "My name is Anne," she said, bubbling over with excitement and enthusiasm. "Your son was used to bring you and your husband to Christ. And I've got to tell you how Jesus used him in my life."

Before she could take a breath, Anne continued, "You see, I'd ruined my life. I'd walked out on my husband. I drank too much. I partied too much. I let my kids fend for themselves. Believe me, I didn't care what happened to me or anybody else. Oh, I knew I needed help. In fact, I'd seen psychiatrists off and on for most of my life—I've even had shock therapy. But nothing helped. Another thing—I never remember ever crying in all my life. I'd go to any extremes so I wouldn't cry."

Anne rushed on saying, "In fact, one psychiatrist said, 'That's one of the reasons for your difficulties; you need to cry.' When I talked with him, I'd get to a point in my story where you'd expect a human being to cry and I'd laugh and laugh—even cackle. I'd really hardened my heart to the world. Why, if I saw a little kid sick like Wrightsie, I'd say to myself, 'Tough luck, kid, it's a rotten world.' "

Anne took a quick breath and said, "Then, a couple of months ago a priest got ahold of me and said I should come to these prayer meetings. I was at the end of my rope and ready to agree to anything. So I came. Well, of course I couldn't miss Wrightsie with his little bald head and scar and all. I've watched him improve from where he could hardly move to where he's walking. Then, three weeks ago tonight, we were singing 'Amazing Grace' at the end of the prayer meeting and for some reason I was watching Wrightsie."

Wright and I nodded; we remembered the night.

"Well, Wrightsie had his good left arm in the air, praising the Lord. Then he tried to raise his right arm. Oh, what a struggle. It was like he was trying to lift a heavy barbell. Then with a tremendous effort he made it—both arms in the air, praising God. That did it. Suddenly I thought, 'Look at that; after all Wrightsie's been through he stands there and praises God.' I started to cry. Just a whimper at first, then the tears really came. And I couldn't stop for days—I didn't want to. I tell you, the Lord's used Wrightsie to heal me!"

# 26
## Keep Up What You're Doing

As we drove home from the meeting that night, Beth and Wrightsie slept in the back seat of the car. Wright and I discussed Anne's witness. "You know," Wright commented, "I get the feeling that Wrightsie is more than just our son."

"What do you mean?" I asked.

"Well, we seem to be sharing him with more and more people. And, as a result, their lives are being changed."

"You're right," I agreed. "It's almost as if he has a special ministry. First, there was Lorena and Wingo and tonight Anne. I wonder how many more lives the Lord will touch through Wrightsie."

"Many, unless I miss my guess," Wright answered, and then he laughed. "Last Saturday, when Wrightsie and I drove to pick up the cleaning he said, 'Hey, dad, you think we can go around the country and tell everybody how the Lord healed me?' "

"Well, that's one thing," I said laughing, "he's not shy when it comes to talking about Jesus."

The following Monday, I was cleaning house when the phone rang. "Hello, Nancy. This is Mrs. Lane—Kim's grandmother."

I sensed a sadness in her voice. "Mrs. Lane, is there

something wrong with Kimmy?" I asked.

"Yes," she answered. "Beverly asked me to call you; Kim's in the hospital with pneumonia."

"Oh, no! How bad is it?"

"Well, our doctor said not too bad. But he wanted her in the hospital so they could keep an eye on her."

"When did she come down with it?" I asked.

"A few days ago. She was eating a hamburger and choked on it—she has swallowing problems like Wrightsie had. Scared us half to death. I guess she got some of it in her lungs. At least that's what the doctor said. She was admitted to the hospital last Friday."

"Well, if you think it's all right, we'll go up to see her tomorrow. Wrightsie has physiotherapy. We'll drop by after that."

"Oh, yes," Mrs. Lane answered. "I know Kim and Beverly will be happy to see you."

We walked into Kimmy's room about three o'clock the next day. Her pretty blonde hair was spread out over the pillow—miraculously, she had lost very little of her hair—and a big smile appeared on her face when she recognized us. I pulled a chair up beside her bed for Wrightsie, then I sat down next to Beverly. We chatted and the children watched a cartoon on TV. A few minutes passed and I glanced over at Kimmy and Wrightsie. They weren't watching TV. Kimmy's eyes were closed, and Wrightsie's hands were clasped together in his lap and he was praying so intently he was almost shaking. What a touching scene it was.

We stayed about half an hour that day and before we left we again prayed for Kimmy. After the prayer, Wrightsie noticed a little stuffed Snoopy dog lost in the bed clothes. "I've got a Snoopy too," Wrightsie said.

"That's not mine," Kimmy explained. "It belongs to one of my sisters. She let me borrow it."

"Ooh," Wrightsie answered thoughtfully. I knew something was going on in his mind.

As soon as we left the room, he said, "We've got to do something about that!"

"About what?"

"Snoopy!" he said emphatically. "He's not hers."

"But, Wrightsie, Kimmy's sister was very loving to let her borrow Snoopy."

"I know, mom. But I want her to have one of her own—just like mine."

"He's an expensive one," I reminded him.

"I don't care how much he costs. She's gonna have him! I'll pay for it with my money."

He was very determined. "All right," I said. "Say, I remember seeing a Snoopy just like yours at Park Row Pharmacy in Arlington."

"Let's go!" Wrightsie exclaimed and he rushed me out to the car.

We bought the Snoopy and had it gift-wrapped with paper that was covered with at least a hundred little yellow smile faces. "Mom, can we take it up to Kimmy now?" Wrightsie asked impatiently.

"No. I'm sorry, Wrightsie. There's not time. We'll see Kimmy on Thursday, after your therapy."

The next evening we attended a prayer meeting in the parish hall at Saint Alban's Episcopal Church in Arlington. As far as I know it was the first time a charismatic meeting had been held at Saint Alban's. When we walked into the hall I said, "Oh, Wright. There are the Hamiltons. Let's sit with them." We joined Lorena and Wingo and chatted until the meeting began.

Saint Alban's had lost the rector it had had for many years. (He was the same one who—way back the previous November—had walked in the hospital room when the Air Force officer, Kris Mineau, and Sherwin McCurdy had prayed for Wrightsie.) While the church was looking for a new rector, a young priest was filling in. He was a brilliant young man who, for some reason, had watched Wrightsie's progress very closely. He'd been to the house numerous times to give Wrightsie Communion and one day he'd fished with him in the canal.

Although he seemed unsympathetic to the charismatic renewal, he agreed to lead our prayer meeting. After the meeting another couple walked up to us and Lorena said, "Nan, Wright, I'd like you to meet Marge and Mike O'Halloran."

We found out that the O'Hallorans had started the Arlington Wednesday night prayer group in their home the previous November. Then Marge said, "And your son had something to do with it."

"Oh?" I questioned.

"Yes," Marge answered. "You see, way back a year ago last February my mother called me from Phoenix to tell me about a new prayer group she was attending. Well, I didn't like the sound of it one bit. It sure didn't sound very Episcopalian to me. Then last July when Mike was on vacation we decided it was time to fly to Phoenix. My mother was becoming a religious fanatic and we were going to save her—so to speak."

We all laughed at that remark. "Well, to make a long story short," Marge continued, "it worked just the other way. We returned to Arlington very much the charismatics. We didn't tell a soul except the rector. But we did start to attend an Episcopalian charismatic prayer group in Burleson. The rector knew this and after every meeting he'd quiz us. Then, early last fall, he said, 'I wish it were time to have such a prayer meeting in this parish.' This went on until the last of November when he called me one day, 'Marge, I've just visited a couple from our parish in a hospital in Dallas. They have a very sick little boy and while I was there an Air Force officer and a businessman prayed for him. Later, I found out they were charismatics. Marge, I tell you I've seen the power of these people and I think it's time we had our own prayer meeting. I want you and Mike to start it at your house.' "

Wright and I just looked at each other. There it was again; the Lord was using Wrightsie's condition to awaken His people to the power of the Holy Spirit.

Then Marge said, "I hope you and Wright will come over to our house. We had the prayer meeting here tonight so there'd be room for all the people that came up from Burleson. It'll be back at our house next Wednesday."

Mike and Marge O'Halloran became our close friends and later they and the Wednesday night prayer group would minister to us in a powerful way.

After Wrightsie finished his physiotherapy, the next afternoon, he clutched a brown paper sack underneath his arm trying to hide it from my view. But when we got to the car he said, "Mom, please put this in the back seat. And don't look at it, don't even feel it. It's your Mother's Day present."

I did as he asked and then we headed for the hospital and Kimmy. When we walked into her room Wrightsie carried her gift under his right arm, while behind his back—with his left arm, he hid his own Snoopy.

Kimmy was delighted to see Wrightsie again and her pretty face beamed like the smile faces on the gift paper when she saw the large package. Beverly unwrapped the gift and when its contents came into view, Kimmy exclaimed, "Oh, look, mom! A Snoopy!" She wrapped her arms around the large stuffed dog and buried her cheek into his soft furry neck.

Then Wrightsie said, "See, I brought mine too!" He flipped his Snoopy from behind his back and they both laughed with delightful abandon. Wrightsie put his dog beside hers and they laughed again when he said, "I guess I've loved and hugged mine too much—he's not as white as yours."

"I've got something else for you too. Hold up your hand." Wrightsie reached into his pocket and pulled out a ring and placed it on Kimmy's little finger saying, "I got this from a Cracker Jack box."

Their carefree laughter rang out again. Then Kimmy said, "Oh, Wrightsie, thank you. Thank you very much."

Beverly was very touched and she also thanked Wrightsie. Then she asked, "How's the physiotherapy coming along?"

"Fine," I replied. "Those therapists are so kind and patient."

"Yeah," Wrightsie agreed. "Even Killer," he said with an impish grin.

"Wrightsie!" I scolded. "Don't call her that. She's sweet and you know it."

"Aw, I know, mom. But that's what the rest of the guys call her."

"Well, those guys, as you call them, are Vietnam veterans, not eight-year-old boys."

Then Kimmy asked, "What do you do there, Wrightsie?"

"I have to crawl around on a mat and do exercises—stuff like that. Then I go to another room and do occua—occua—what's it called, mom?"

"Occupational therapy."

"Yeah, occupational therapy. I make things—that's for my hand. I'm making place mats. And today I finished a secret for my mom—for Mother's Day."

"Oh, Wrightsie," Kimmy said wistfully, "I wish I could go with you. I want to walk again."

A look of anger flashed across his face. "If your doctor told you you couldn't walk right again, don't believe him! Look at me!" Then, to encourage Kimmy, Wrightsie strutted around the hospital room as best as his limp would permit. Kimmy looked on with an approving smile.

After that the children compared their Snoopys while Beverly and I chatted. "What does the doctor say about

Kimmy?" I asked.

"The pneumonia seems to be clearing up. She should be able to go home in a few days."

"That's wonderful!" I replied. We talked awhile longer and then, before leaving, Wrightsie laid hands on Kimmy and prayed for her recovery.

Wrightsie and I left her room and headed for the emergency room entrance, then to the parking lot. We'd just exited the door when we met Wrightsie's radiologist—we hadn't seen him since Wrightsie had completed his radiation therapy back in February. As the doctor approached us a hint of recognition crossed his face and he nodded a polite, "Hello." Then he did a double take—I'll never forget the expression on his face. "Wrightsie!" he blurted out. "It's good to see you," he said, rushing up to Wrightsie and shaking his hand. Then he turned to me and in an excited voice asked, "What do the doctors in Boston say?"

I was so thrilled with his reaction I can't remember how I answered his question. But I'm sure I must have told him we hadn't called Boston, for as we talked, all I could think was, "I've got to get home and call Dr. Shaw at Children's Hospital."

I waited until Wright came home from work and then we placed the call to Boston. Dr. Shaw was in late surgery so we asked if he might call Wright at work the next day. The next day the phone rang about mid-afternoon. I just knew it was Wright and without even a hello, I said, "What'd he say?"

Wright laughed and answered, "Well, the first thing he said was, 'How's my little friend?' Then I told him about Wrightsie's condition. Then he asked if Wrightsie had had any vomiting or nausea or intracranial pressure. I said, 'No.' He was silent for a few seconds and then he said, 'Tremendous! You have six months under your belt; keep up what you're doing.' "

# 27

## *Lord, Forgive Us Our Impatience*

The phone rang again while I was still thrilling over Dr. Shaw's words. It was Mary Bingaman, the woman who'd given us Father Dennis Bennett's book, *Nine O'clock in the Morning.*

She called to remind me about the Kathryn Kuhlman services in Fort Worth, scheduled for the next weekend. I had forgotten to tell Wright about the meetings, but I felt sure we would be able to go on Saturday.

Since Mary and her daughter planned to go on Saturday also, we decided to drive over together. I told her we would pick them up.

I called Wright and told him about the plans. "Hey, I've got an idea," Wright said. "I'm going to see Kimmy at the hospital over my lunch hour. I'm going to tell her I'll sit in proxy for her at the healing service."

When Wright returned from lunch he called me. "Nan," Wright said, his voice almost breaking. "I really love that little Kimmy. It just breaks my heart to see her in bed. And there's something different about her—like a glow—I don't know, I can't describe it."

"I know what you mean," I answered. "These two kids sure have something wonderful."

The next day we picked up Mary Bingaman and her daughter

and headed for Fort Worth. We arrived at the convention center at least two hours before the service started. People were already beginning to gather around the entrance so Wright let us out to get in line while he parked the car. He got Wrightsie's wheelchair from the trunk.

I pushed Wrightsie up to the entrance and even before Wright had returned from parking the car an usher appeared on the other side of the glass doors. He opened a door, motioned to me and said, "You and your son can wait inside if you like. But I'm sorry; the rest of the family will have to wait outside."

"Thank you," I replied, accepting his invitation. The welcomed coolness of the air conditioning greeted me as I pushed Wrightsie into the convention center.

The usher tagged Wrightsie's wheelchair, placed it in a storage area and led us into the auditorium saying, "You can sit over there. It's a special section for the sick."

Wrightsie and I made our way into a row of seats and I sat down beside a man who was sitting with his son—a boy about Wrightsie's age. We started to chat and in a few minutes I found out his son had muscular dystrophy. And worse yet, his wife was waiting outside the auditorium with their two older sons who also had the same disease. I was shocked and I thought, "Oh! How terrible! I don't know how they stand it!"

When the doors finally opened, I watched for Beth and Wright. When I spotted them, I stood up and waved my hand. Wright caught sight of me, grabbed Beth's hand and hurried down the aisle. There were enough seats for all of us—Beth and Wrightsie sat between Wright and me while Mary Bingaman and her daughter found two seats a couple of rows behind us.

Just before the service began Wright leaned over in front of Wrightsie and said, "Now remember, Wrightsie's healed, so we're asking the Lord for a quick and complete recovery."

Beth and I nodded. "And I'm sitting in for Kimmy's healing," he reminded us.

Then the service began. At first Miss Kuhlman seemed too theatrical for my New England tastes. But as she preached the love of Jesus and the healing power of the Holy Spirit my sensitivities disappeared.

There were many beautiful healings testified to that day, but when the service came to a close we were a disappointed, dejected family. Wrightsie hadn't received his recovery. And my heart went out to the man who had been sitting beside us, as I watched him help his handicapped son from the auditorium.

Our spirits lifted a little on the trip back to Arlington. We returned home just long enough for Wrightsie to change into his Cub Scout uniform. Within minutes we were back on the road to Fort Worth and the Scoutarama.

Our disappointment was completely forgotten as we joined in the fun. We ate cotton candy followed by corn on the cob. Then, to wash it all down we drank root beer. We were strolling the midway when Wrightsie said, "Hey, wait for me. I'm getting tired."

"I'm sorry, best buddy," his dad answered. "How about a ride on my shoulders?"

"Yeah," Wrightsie said, his face brightening.

Wright hoisted him to his shoulders and we continued our tour. We checked out all the exhibits—at least twice—with Wrightsie joyfully riding high above the heads of the crowd. It was a fun family evening.

Late that night when we said our evening prayers, we praised the Lord for the healings we'd seen, asked Him to forgive us our disappointments and thanked Him for a wonderful evening. Then we said a special prayer for the three brothers who had muscular dystrophy.

Sunday was Mother's Day. Mary Bingaman joined me after church services as we made our way to the door. An Episcopal monk had visited Saint Alban's that Sunday and he chatted a few seconds with each parishioner as they left the church. Mary and I discussed the Kathryn Kuhlman service while we waited in line to greet the monk. When it was Mary's turn, the monk asked, "And what do you have planned for Mother's Day?"

"Why, I'm taking a friend of mine to the Kathryn Kuhlman services in Fort Worth."

The monk smiled and nodded. Mary explained, "She's had a great many problems and I hope the meeting will help her."

As I overheard the conversation, I thought, "Gee, I'd like to go to the meeting too. But I'm sure Wright and the kids already have something planned."

On the drive home Wright turned to Beth and in a teasing tone of voice said, "Gee, Beth, what do you think we should do this afternoon?"

"I don't know," Beth answered, going along with her father.

Then in a matter-of-fact tone, Beth asked, "Mom, is there anything special you want to do?"

"All right, you two," I laughed. "Quit the kidding, because there is something I'd like to do; I want to go back to the Kathryn Kuhlman services."

"You mean it?" Wright asked.

"Yes," I nodded my head.

"Okay," Wright answered. "We had something else planned, but it's your day. And we'd better hurry or we'll be late."

We hurried home, ate a quick lunch and rushed off to Fort Worth. We were almost late so, rather than using the wheelchair, Wright carried Wrightsie into the convention center. The service was even more moving than the day before and I was greatly impressed with Miss Kuhlman's sermon. She stressed two points. First, she did not know why some people were healed and many were not. And second, she emphatically insisted that it was the Lord Jesus who healed—not she. She repeated this fact again and again.

Many people also walked forward that day to tell of the healings they'd received. Towards the end of the service Wrightsie stood up and said, "Mom, I want to go too."

I looked over at Wright, wondering how to answer Wrightsie, and asked, "What do you think?"

"Wrightsie," his father asked, "do you feel something? Do you feel you can walk without a limp?"

Wrightsie shook his head sadly and I thought I saw tears in his eyes. He answered, "No, but I want to go up on the stage; maybe she'll pray for me."

With great difficulty Wright said, "No, I'm sorry Wrightsie."

Wrightsie sat back down in his seat and lowered his head. Shortly after that, as the service was coming to a close, Wright said, "I'm going to get the car before this crowd starts to leave. Look for me along the curb when you come out."

No sooner had Wright left the convention center when the closing hymn started, and people from all over the auditorium started to make their way to the stage. Then Beth suggested excitedly, "Mom, why don't we go get daddy so he can take Wrightsie up on the stage? Maybe she'll pray for Wrightsie!"

We hurried from the auditorium with Beth running ahead of Wrightsie and me as we struggled to keep up with her. She spotted our car, threw open the door and told her father what was happening. Wright jumped from the car and ran towards us.

He scooped Wrightsie up into his arms on the run, saying, "Come on, best buddy, let's go!"

Beth and I waited in the car for almost thirty minutes before they returned. As they neared the car I could see they were both dejected. "Did she pray for you, Wrightsie?" Beth asked hopefully.

Wrightsie didn't answer—he looked like he may have cried. So Wright said, "No," as he lifted Wrightsie into the back seat of the car. "No, there were too many people. We couldn't get near—" His voice trailed off and he never completed his explanation.

Very little was said on the drive home—each of us were lost in our thoughts. We'd seen many beautiful healings in the past two days but we were very disappointed that Wrightsie had not been included in the miracles.

Although the healing power of the Holy Spirit had not been with us, the Holy Spirit as the Comforter was. When we returned home, we immediately forgot our disappointment as Beth and Wrightsie disappeared to prepare their Mother's Day gifts.

The ceremony began when Beth and Wrightsie walked into the den carrying their gifts. "Happy Mother's Day," Beth said handing me a prettily wrapped package and a gift card.

I opened the package and exclaimed, "Oh, Wright! Look at the darling note paper. They remind me of New England. Look! They've got old-fashioned cooking utensils on the front," I said, holding up the card for Wright to see, "and a recipe on the back. Oh, thank you, Beth."

Then it was Wrightsie's turn. For preliminaries there was a bird house made from milk cartons and a recipe holder constructed from a plastic fork, a Styrofoam base and little plastic flowers. Both were Cub Scout projects. Next, came the really big present. "Don't drop it," Wrightsie warned me as I carefully unwrapped his gift.

"Oh, Wrightsie, it's beautiful!"

Then I held it up so Beth and Wright could see it. It was a hot plate made from little squares of ceramic tile.

"Wrightsie, did you make that all by yourself?" Beth asked.

"Yep," Wrightsie answered with a broad smile. "I made it at therapy—finished it last Thursday."

"Look, mom," Beth said, "the colors are perfect. The oranges, golds and greens match up with everything we have."

I was delighted with the gifts. Beth's had stirred pleasant

memories of my New England home. And with Wrightsie's—more important than the gift was the fact that he could do such intricate work with his previously bad right arm and hand.

I gave them both a big hug and kiss, and said, "Oh, thank you. What a special Mother's Day."

Then Wright gave me a Mother's Day card saying, "Thanks, Nan, for giving us two wonderful children. I love you."

Next on the agenda were phone calls to Grandma Harkins in Connecticut and Grandma Flossy in upstate New York. When the calls were completed, I asked, "Who wants to help me make ice cream?"

A chorus of "Me!" echoed from the den.

"What's the occasion?" Wright asked.

"It's for the Navy wives' party I'm having Wednesday," I answered. "Evelyn Fox said I could borrow her ice cream maker, and she's got a recipe for me too. Would you mind running over to her house to get them now?"

"Okay, be right back," Wright answered.

Very slowly and sometimes hesitantly, Wright and I had started to involve ourselves in a few social activities. But the party Wednesday, given in honor of the wife of Wright's commanding officer, was a special treat for me. She'd really helped me through the many months of Wrightsie's illness. She always seemed to arrive on the scene—either by phone or her bicycle—just when my morale was the lowest. Her light humorous conversation never failed to act as a pick-me-up.

"Here's the ice cream maker," Wright said, walking into the kitchen. "Are you going to let us workers test the finished product?"

"I think that can be arranged," I answered. "But you can't have very much; I've got thirty-five girls coming to the party. Even Joy Jeffrey's coming in from Dallas."

"Say," Wright asked, "has she gotten any letters from her husband recently?"

"Yes," I answered. "She's bringing the latest one to show Wrightsie. You know, I think that letter campaign to Hanoi we all worked on is paying off. The POW families seem to be getting more letters from their husbands."

Wright took the ice-cream maker to the garage to pack it with ice and rock salt and I was preparing the ingredients when the phone rang.

"Nancy, this is Mrs. Lane. Kim was released from the hospital Saturday. Thought you'd want to know."

"Oh, praise the Lord!" I exclaimed. "Wonderful!"

We continued to chat as I cradled the phone to my ear, freeing my hands so I could do my kitchen work.

By the time we had our supper and the workers had tested the finished product it was late. Even so we had a long prayer list that night. We praised the Lord for our blessings, thanked Him for the healings we'd seen and for Kimmy, then we asked Him to heal those who were still sick. Then I said, "Lord, forgive us our impatience, forgive us for wanting more and more, and forgive us for being disappointed that Wrightsie didn't receive an immediate recovery. In Jesus' name. Amen."

## 28
## *And Pray for Their Healings*

All in all, that Mother's Day weekend was glorious. But on Monday morning mother's work began again. I spent a good share of the day cleaning and that lasted over into Tuesday morning. I was pretty well satisfied and inspecting the house when Mary Bingaman phoned. "Hi, Nan. Do you have your coffeepot on? I'd like you to meet a miracle.

"If you have time," Mary explained, "I'd really like you to meet this woman I took to the Kathryn Kuhlman service Sunday. She's had an inner healing."

"Sure, come on over, Mary," I answered. "I'd love to see you and meet your miracle. I'll have the coffee ready when you arrive." As I hung up the phone, I thought how nice it would be to have a relaxing visit with Mary and her miracle.

I put the coffee on, made up a couple of sandwiches for lunch and put them in the refrigerator. Just as I put out the coffee cups the doorbell rang. Mary introduced her friend and we sat down to a pleasant talk.

Wrightsie's teacher arrived. And while she helped him with his lesson in the dining room, Mary, her friend and I continued our chat in the den. It was very obvious that Mary's friend had received a healing. Just before they left, Wrightsie completed his lessons and I introduced him to Mary's friend. I could see they immediately developed a close rapport.

The ice cream party Wednesday was a huge success. I hadn't been with many of the girls for months and it was great to see them again. When Joy Jeffrey arrived, her first question was, "Where's Wrightsie?"

"In his bedroom," I answered. "I've set the TV up for him."

"I want to show him this," she said, waving her husband's letter in her hand.

I took her back to the bedroom and left her with Wrightsie—they had a good visit together.

Thursday I spent the day cleaning up after the party, Friday night we attended the Resurrection. Then Saturday another first occurred on Wrightsie's road to recovery.

It was a warm day and he and Wright had finished mowing the lawn. They were drinking a glass of ice water in the kitchen when Wrightsie surprised us by asking, "Mom, dad, can I go swimming?"

Wright and I looked at each other for a moment or two, then he said, "Why not—let's go."

"Hey, Beth," I called, "want to go swimming with us?"

"You mean Wrightsie too?" she asked in a tone of disbelief.

"Sure!" Wrightsie answered with happy bravado. "Me too."

Within minutes we'd all changed into our swimsuits. We walked out to the back yard, ducked under the weeping willow boughs and stepped down onto the patio bordering the canal. I tied a bright orange life vest around Wrightsie and, remembering the doctor's caution about the hot Texas sun, I made him wear his white tennis hat over his bald head.

Then Wright slowly lowered him into the water. At first, he sat—waist deep in the water—on a step leading into the canal. Later, with uncharacteristic timidity, he pushed into deeper water and let the life vest support him. I felt a twinge of heartache as I watched his cautious, careful efforts. He'd been such a strong, confident swimmer the previous year. My mind retreated to our last summer's vacation. Again I saw him, lean and tanned, running along the white sands of Pensacola beach, then he plunged fearlessly into the blue water. The sun flashed off his full head of hair as he bobbed in the sparkling waves.

Wrightsie's voice brought me back to the moment. "Mom, mom," he called, "I think I'll get out now."

With a great deal of effort he dog-paddled his way back to the edge of the patio and I lifted him from the water. "I'm proud of you, Wrightsie," I said. "You'll be swimming across the canal in no time."

For my sake, he forced a little smile.

On Pentecost Sunday we attended the Church of the Resurrection. After church we ate brunch in Dallas, then we hurried home to prepare for company.

Captain Muery, the commanding officer of Dallas Naval Air Station, and Mary Lou, his wife, arrived first. Captain Muery was going to retire from the Navy the last of June and they would be leaving the area. We wanted to give them our personal farewells and thank them again for their support. We'd never forget the gift Captain Muery had presented to Wrightsie the day he flew out of the air station for Boston. The sailor's white hat, with the Navy wings and officer's shield pinned to it, rested in a place of honor on Wrightsie's nautical-looking dresser. And Mary Lou had been a real source of encouragement for me through the months.

We had a lovely evening. Before leaving, Captain Muery asked us to his change of command and retirement ceremony. And Mary Lou invited us to the reception that would follow afterwards.

That night, after the house was straightened up, prayers said and the children asleep, Wright and I discussed the evening around the kitchen table. "I'm going to miss Mary Lou," I said. "She's really helped me."

"I know it," Wright replied. "I guess you have to lose a child, like they did, to really understand what other people in similar circumstances are going through."

"I think you're right," I answered. "Did Captain Muery have any advice for you?"

"No, not really," Wright answered, but a troubled look on his face told me a different story.

"What's the matter?" I asked. "What'd he say?"

"Well, I can't remember exactly what he said," Wright answered, "but he hoped I wouldn't come down too hard if Wrightsie doesn't make it."

Nothing more was said for a few moments, then Wright broke the silence saying, "Well, it's late; we'd better get some sleep."

Monday night our family attended a special Cub Scout awards meeting at J.L. Hill. Wrightsie was awarded one gold and one silver arrow point for his scout work, a one-year pin and an award for selling twenty Scoutarama tickets. He was proud; we were proud—he'd put in a great deal of work on his scouting projects.

The next day Wrightsie worked with his home-bound teacher between 10:00 A.M. and noon. After a fast lunch, we were on our way to Dallas for physiotherapy. This was followed by a Cub Scout den meeting later that afternoon.

Wednesday evening we attended the prayer meeting at Marge and Mike O'Halloran's home. Wright and I did a great deal of sharing that night on how the Lord had entered our lives. The meeting closed with many prayers for the sick, the needy and the troubled. And Wrightsie was lifted up to the Lord by the group for a complete recovery.

On the following day Wrightsie had his therapy.

On the drive home Wrightsie exclaimed, "Hey, mom! Look!

They've got the sign up!" He was referring to a building that was under construction beside the turnpike. Twice a week—to and from Dallas—we'd questioned each other as to what the building would be used for.

"It's going to be a wax museum!" he said, jumping up and down on the seat with excitement. "Oh, mom, can we go see it?"

"Just as soon as it's completed," I answered.

When we arrived home, Wrightsie donned his swimsuit. I helped him put on his life vest and then he swam in the canal. He seemed more confident in the water and it warmed my heart to see this change.

My busy week continued Friday. Wrightsie and I shopped most of the morning and into early afternoon. After we returned home and I'd put everything away, I decided to call a Navy wife whose husband worked with Wright. He'd received orders to Washington and I'd promised to tell her about the area. I ended our phone call by saying, "Louise, I know you'll love northern Virginia and Washington—we did. And I really recommend you look for a home in Fairfax where we lived."

Louise said they'd look the area over and thanked me for the advice.

Friday night we all attended the Resurrection, and Saturday I cleaned the house while Wright worked in the yard. That night we ate a late supper around the coffee table in the den while we watched a movie about an airliner with a sick boy aboard. It was a pretty good movie, and I noticed Wrightsie lowered his head in prayer every time a dramatic scene took place. After prayers that night, Wrightsie must have been thinking about the movie, for he said, "Dad, does the Navy have hospital airplanes like the Air Force? You know, like the one I flew in to Boston?"

"No," Wright answered. "The Air Force does that job for all the services."

"Well, then, I hope you don't mind, dad, if I'm not a Navy

pilot. I want to be an Air Force pilot so I can fly hospital airplanes. Then before each takeoff, I'm going to lay hands on all the sick passengers and pray for their healing."

Wright swallowed a lump in his throat before he answered. Then he said, "Best buddy, you go right ahead and become an Air Force pilot."

# 29
## Welcome to the Order of the Silly Grin

The rush of activities continued. I added to the many scheduled events by enrolling Wrightsie in a special swimming class for handicapped children. This program, sponsored by the City of Arlington, had a wonderful group of devoted and compassionate instructors.

The unscheduled events also kept us busy. We visited the special school for the handicapped as recommended by Wrightsie's home-bound teacher; the Harston boys next door—Gary and Mike—took Wrightsie to a couple of Texas Ranger baseball games and to see the Harlem Globetrotters; and they frequently challenged him to games of checkers. Wrightsie enjoyed it all.

The next few weeks were also filled with many spiritual blessings and experiences. Nevertheless, I had my weary moments. One night after supper—during the first week of June—I felt unusually tired. I laid down on the couch in the den while we all watched TV. When bedtime approached I commented, "I'm so tired I could sleep here all night."

Wrightsie walked over to the couch, put his hand on my arm and said, "You took good care of me, mom, when I was sick, now I'm going to take care of you." Then he walked into our master bedroom.

In a few minutes he returned to the den. "Okay, mom," he

said, and he helped me to the bedroom. The drapes were pulled, my bedside light was glowing, there were two pillows at the head of my side of the bed, the covers were pulled down and he'd put my nightgown out on the foot of the bed. "Oh, Wrightsie, you're too much," I said. "Thank you."

Then leaving the room, he said, "Call me when you're ready for bed."

In a few minutes, I called, "Ready!"

He returned to the bedroom. I climbed into bed and he put the covers over me. Then he picked up a plastic bottle of lotion from my bedside table and said, "I'm going to massage your hands and arms."

"Oh, Wrightsie—" I started to protest.

"No. You did it for me and I'm going to do it for you. I'm going to be your 'mouser,' " he laughed.

I relaxed my head on the pillow and closed my eyes. I relished the feeling of love as his little hands gently rubbed the lotion into my arm. Then I turned my head, looked at him and said, "Wrightsie, I'm the luckiest mom in the world. I love you so very much."

He smiled, then looking into my eyes he said, "Mom, I think you're special—cause you had me."

I closed my eyes and dropped off into a peaceful sleep.

The next day was the last day of school at J.L. Hill. Earlier in the week I'd called the principal to ask if Wrightsie could join his classmates on the special occasion. And he gave permission for us to attend the last hour of classes.

His school chums greeted him warmly and after saying hello to his teacher Wrightsie joined his classmates in their final activities: cleaning desks, stacking textbooks and washing blackboards. I noticed Wrightsie washing a blackboard with a great deal of vigor. I knew he was trying to prove to everyone that he could return to school next fall. Then I realized he thought the other school was all right but he really wanted to return to J.L. Hill.

All too soon class was dismissed and it was time to go. "Mrs. Brunson," I heard my name called. I turned around and saw a neighborhood boy—a friend of Wrightsie's—who lived across the canal. "Mrs. Brunson, can Wrightsie come home with me?"

"Oh, mom," Wrightsie joined in, "can I go home with Stevey? Can I? Can I?"

"Yes, go ahead," I smiled.

"Oh, boy," they chimed in together.

As the two boys left the school Stevey spotted his older brother. "Come on, Davey," he shouted. "Wrightsie's coming home with us!"

Arm in arm, the three boys walked down the sidewalk. Wrightsie was in the center with a brother on each side helping him along. I watched them until they were almost out of sight. Then I walked home.

Every once in a while, I couldn't help but glance out the den door to the neighbor's back yard across the canal. I watched the three boys having the time of their lives. And each time I looked I said out loud, "Praise the Lord," as my heart thrilled when I saw my Wrightsie enjoying himself.

That evening we attended the Resurrection. I was still thrilled by the afternoon's events. Although the church was packed with people, I felt strongly led to give my witness—in the past I'd hated to speak publicly, even before a small group. I felt no hesitation whatsoever as I raised my hand to speak.

Father Ted knew of my past shyness, and when he spotted me in the crowd with my hand raised, he boomed, "I wondered when the Holy Spirit was going to tell Nancy to speak up. Stand up, Nan. Folks, I tell you this is a small miracle in itself that Nancy Brunson wants to stand up before this crowd and tell her story. Go ahead, Nan."

I don't remember how long I talked. But I do know that, as I told my story, I reminded myself again of how the Lord came to me and comforted me all through Wrightsie's illness.

Shortly after I witnessed, the prayer meeting ended with Communion. Wrightsie, who had been playing outside with Father Ted's son, Mark, joined us and we slowly worked our way to the altar rail. Beth and I became separated from Wright and Wrightsie in the large crowd. The next time I saw them they were kneeling side by side at the rail. After they'd drunk from the cup, Wright stood up but Wrightsie continued to pray. Wright tugged gently on his son's shoulder, then with an apologetic smile he looked at the people waiting to take their place at the rail. But still Wrightsie remained deep in prayer. Finally, he stood up and as his dad tried to lead him away he wouldn't move—he wanted to tell his dad something. Wright bent over and Wrightsie whispered in his father's ear. Wright smiled a wide grin, hugged Wrightsie, picked him up in his arms and carried him through the crowd to the back of the church.

After Beth and I took Communion, we joined them and I asked, "What did Wrightsie whisper?"

Wright smiled again and answered, "He said, 'Know what I was praying for, dad?' " Then Wright stopped and said, "You tell 'em, Wrightsie."

"Well," Wrightsie smiled, "I was thanking Jesus for dying on the cross for me and all the other people in this world."

"Oh, Wrightsie, that's so beautiful," I said as I hugged him.

Just then Lorena Hamilton walked up and said, "Nan, your witness was wonderful; it gave me chills."

"Hi, Lorena," I said. "Thank you. It really had to be the Lord. I could never have gotten up there without Him."

"Where's Wingo?" Wright asked.

"That's why I came to get you," Lorena said excitedly, "he's waiting up front. He's going to ask for the baptism in the Holy Spirit. And he wants the Brunson family to pray with him."

We returned to the altar rail and Wingo was already kneeling. We all stepped up to the rail. Beth and Wrightsie stood on each side of Wingo, while Lorena, Wright and I stood behind him. Some other Arlington prayer group friends joined us as Father Ted knelt in front of Wingo on the altar side of the rail. After giving him a few words of instruction Father Ted laid hands on Wingo's head and asked Jesus to baptize him with the Holy Spirit.

When Wingo stood up, he turned around, put his arms around Beth's and Wrightsie's shoulders and looked at us. His face was glowing with a great peace.

On the drive home Beth said, "Mom, I love Dr. Hamilton and I can't get over how much he looks like Feef."

"Yes, I know," I agreed. The similarity between Wingo and my father was amazing—not only in their looks but also in their actions.

"Mom," Beth asked, "do you think Feef will ever ask for the baptism?"

"Yeah," Wrightsie chimed in, "and Gramma too?"

"I don't know," I answered. "But I hope so. We'll have to pray about that. You know, I'm sending Feef a copy of *Nine O'clock in the Morning* as a Father's Day gift. Maybe it'll start them both thinking."

During our bedtime prayers that night we asked Jesus to reveal the Holy Spirit to Grandma and Feef. Wright and I included all our families in the same prayer. Then Wright said, "Wrightsie, tell mom what else you prayed for tonight after Communion."

"Should I?" Wrightsie asked with an embarrassed smile.

"Sure," his dad encouraged him.

"Well, mom, I know that if I don't go to the bathroom tomorrow morning," Wrightsie explained almost as if he were apologizing, "I'll have to take one of those depositories. And you—"

"That's *sup*pository," I said, giving him the correct word for the rectal medicine that would help him.

"Oh, yeah, *suppository*," Wrightsie corrected himself.

"And you know how I hate that, mom," he continued. "So I asked Jesus to help me go to the bathroom tomorrow by myself so I won't have to take the depository."

"Wrightsie, you're wonderful," I said, giving him a big hug.

Wrightsie's prayers were answered on two separate occasions the next day.

"Call Father Ted and tell him Jesus answered my prayer!" Wrightsie insisted. "Call Father Ted!"

Father Ted was duly informed.

We didn't make it to Saint Alban's the following Sunday. But I did manage to bake a batch of cookies for our new rector's reception that followed the church service. Wright delivered them to the parish hall about 11:30 A.M.

When he returned, I asked, "How was the reception?"

"Great! There was a good turnout and you wouldn't believe how much food they had," he answered with a nibbler's smile.

"Did you get a chance to meet the new rector?"

"Yep. Father Dennis Smart," Wright answered. "In fact I had quite a talk with him."

"Well, what's he like?"

"A very gentle man," Wright said. "I like him. I told him about you and Beth and Wrightsie—he's looking forward to meeting the family. I know you'll like him."

The rest of the week seemed to fly by. Wright and I had planned a Navy party for the coming Saturday. It was to be a more or less official farewell party for Wright's commanding officer and a welcome aboard for his new one.

I'd bought some potted flowers from a local nursery to decorate our den patio for the occasion. They were delivered Thursday afternoon and, with Wrightsie's help, I was trying out different arrangements on the patio. All of a sudden we heard the fur-flying commotion of a dog fight erupt from

Evelyn Fox's back yard.

Through the staccato of mean barks, the vicious growls and snarls, I heard Evelyn yell, "Stop it! Stop it! Somebody, get that collie out of here!"

Then the fight ended with the heart-rending yowl that can only come from a severely wounded dog.

"Oh, no! Jacque! Jacque!" Evelyn exclaimed. (Jacque had been her father's—Bopo's—dog. But when Bopo died, the Foxes had taken him.)

Wrightsie and I looked at each other for a second, then we ran around our garage, over to the Foxes' house. Evelyn already had Jacque in the house. He was lying on their den rug. I could see the handsome silver-gray poodle was badly hurt. His chest heaved with each breath and his right foreleg was bent over at a sickening angle.

"Nan," Evelyn said, "I've got to get him to the vet."

"I'll take you," I volunteered. "Let me run home and get the car."

I ran home, turned off the stove—I had a few things cooking—grabbed my purse and headed for the car. Then, of all times, the phone rang. I explained the circumstances to the caller, hung up and again hurried for the car.

Just then Wrightsie walked into the den. "Come on, Wrightsie," I said.

"We don't have to go, mom," he explained in a somewhat breathless voice. "The lady who owned the collie has already taken them to the vet. And don't worry; Jacque's going to be all right."

"What do you mean, all right? How do you know?"

With simple, honest confidence Wrightsie answered, "Oh, I laid hands on him and prayed for his healing."

Evelyn called when she returned from the vet's. He'd put a cast on Jacque's leg and said it would be six to eight weeks before they knew if the leg would heal. But that didn't make any difference to Wrightsie—he knew no "if" was involved.

The next morning Mary Bingaman's friend called me. We talked awhile and I had an idea. "Say," I said, "we go to the Church of the Resurrection every Friday night. Would you like to go with us tonight?"

"Oh, yes," she answered.

"Okay. We'll pick you up."

After Communion that night, Mary's friend decided to ask for the baptism. She also requested that we all pray for her. As she knelt at the altar rail we gathered around her and waited for Father Ted who was ministering to another woman. But before he got to us a layman came up and asked her if he might pray for her.

He started to pray in a loud voice and I thought, "Oh, no. He's really going to upset her." But Mary's friend received the baptism and when she stood up and turned around I was amazed. She looked ten years younger. She had a glow.

On the drive home, she told us of her experience at the rail. She started by asking, "Who was the man who prayed with me?"

"I don't know," I answered. "But I sure was worried for you. He had an awfully loud voice."

"Yes, I know," she answered. "And it really shocked me when he started to pray. But then I felt Wrightsie's hand on my arm and I realized I couldn't hear that booming voice any more, it was shut right out of my mind. Then I felt a warmth from Wrightsie's hands and it flowed through my arm and all over me. The next thing I knew I was praying in my new prayer language. Praise the Lord!"

And a sense of wonderment and awe came over me as I realized how the Lord was using Wrightsie.

As we neared Arlington, she asked, "Say, I wonder if Wrightsie would pray for a woman who's dying of cancer."

"Would you, Wrightsie?" I asked.

"Yes," he answered with a serious look on his face.

"Would Sunday after church be all right?" I suggested.

"I'm sure it would," she answered.

Sunday afternoon we all rode together to visit the sick woman. We were greeted warmly and shown to the bedroom. After a brief exchange of pleasantries Wright said, "Wrightsie would like to pray for you. Would that be all right?"

The woman smiled and answered, "Yes, please."

Wrightsie walked up to the bed and gently placed his hands on each side of the woman's head. Then he closed his eyes, lowered his head and prayed silently.

There was complete silence in the room until he lowered his hands and raised his head. "Thank you, Wrightsie. Thank you," the woman said taking his hand.

"You're welcome," Wrightsie answered with a little boy smile.

The woman died a few weeks later. We heard that her family said that although she'd had a painful type of cancer, she died in peace with a radiant look on her face. I can't help but think the Lord in his mercy used the faith of a young boy to ease her journey into everlasting life.

I accomplished a great deal the next week. Beth, Wrightsie and I shopped for Father's Day which was coming up on the next Sunday. I'd caught up on my thank you notes and was looking forward to a relaxing family weekend. Then late Friday morning, Lorena Hamilton called. "Nan, there's a Roman Catholic nun speaking in Arlington at a luncheon today," she said. "She's a charismatic and I'd like to hear her witness. How about going with me?"

"Oh, Lorena, I'm sorry, I can't. I've been in such a rat race. And I've promised myself I'm going to spend more time with the kids."

Beth overheard my conversation as she walked into the kitchen. "Go, go," she said silently, forming the words with her mouth.

"Just a minute, Lorena," I said taking the phone from my ear.

"Go ahead, mom," Beth said. "You can relax with Mrs. Hamilton. And besides I want to baby-sit with Wrightsie. We can work on a puzzle and play some of our favorite games. We'll have fun."

"Are you sure?"

"Yes, mom. Please go."

"Okay, Lorena," I said. "Beth wants to sit with Wrightsie."

"All right," Lorena said. "I'll pick you up in an hour."

We had a wonderful time at the luncheon and on the drive home Lorena and I discussed the nun's witness; it was a beautiful story. As we neared our house she said, "I don't want this spiritual day to end. Are you folks going to the Resurrection tonight?"

"Yes," I answered. "Why don't you and Wingo go with us?"

"No," she answered. "Thanks. I know you leave home early and stop for hamburgers and Wingo's getting home late this afternoon. We'll meet you over there instead."

"Okay," I said, as she drove up to our house. "See you later."

There was a guest speaker at the Resurrection that night. A black minister from the West Coast was attending a church convention in Dallas. And before he left Seattle, Washington, his good friend, Father Dennis Bennett, had encouaged him to visit the Church of the Resurrection.

After the prayer meeting, Lorena walked up to us with a sparkling smile and said, "I want to ask for the baptism. Will you all come and pray for me?"

"Let's go," Wright said.

Lorena knelt at the rail. Wrightsie put one hand on her shoulder, Beth stood on her other side while Wingo, Wright and I stood behind her. Just as we started to pray the guest speaker came over, smiled and said to Lorena, "May I help you?"

Lorena raised her head and said, "Yes, I want to receive the baptism in the Holy Spirit."

The minister broke into another wide smile, Lorena lowered her head and in a deep, gentle bass voice the black minister asked Jesus to baptize Lorena in His Holy Spirit. Lorena received her prayer language and when she stood up I again witnessed a Christian who had experienced "the peace that passes all understanding."

On the way home we all stopped for donuts and coffee to celebrate the occasion. Some other couples from Arlington joined us and we had a happy time. Wright raised his coffee cup in a toast and said, "Well, Lorena, welcome to the Order of the Silly Grin as Father Ted says."

Lorena smiled, her eyes sparkled and then she was serious for a moment. "I know the Lord arranged all of this. I know He put the Brunson family in my life, for if He hadn't I wouldn't be as happy as I am now.

"And I know the Lord had that black minister come to the Resurrection tonight just for me too," Lorena continued. "You know, when he walked up and said, 'May I help you?' I looked up into one of the most beautiful faces I've ever seen in my life. Praise the Lord!"

We all laughed and raised our coffee cups in agreement.

# 30
## *Mom, I Love Jesus So Much*

The following Sunday we saw Lorena after the Saint Alban's church services. She was still wearing a smile from ear to ear. When we arrived home from church we ate a quick lunch, then placed a Father's Day call to my dad in Connecticut. Beth was on the extension in the master bedroom and I was on the kitchen phone.

"Hi, Feef," Beth said when he answered. "How are you?"

"Hi, dad," I said. "Happy Father's Day!"

"Hi, Nan. Hi, Beth. Oh, I'm fine," he answered. "Thanks for *Nine O'clock in the Morning.* I opened it early this morning and I'm already halfway through it. I was reading it when you called. I can't put it down."

"Wonderful!" I exclaimed. "We'd hoped you'd like it. Be sure and have mom read it when you're through."

My mother picked up their extension. "Nan," she said, "Dad loved your Father's Day card. It made him cry."

"Oh," dad said, trying to cover up, "I just got to thinking about the tough time you're having and I got all choked up. You know, you're still my little girl."

"Oh, dad, now you've got me choked up," I answered. "Please don't worry about me; I'm fine." Then I brought them up-to-date on our lives since we'd last talked. And I told them

223

my strength was coming from the Lord.

When I mentioned the Hamiltons, Beth interrupted and said, "Feef, Dr. Hamilton looks just like you!"

"I've got to meet that man someday," Feef laughed.

"That reminds me," I said, "are you folks still coming down here the last of July?"

"Oh, yes," my mother assured me.

"Good," I answered. "'Cause I got a letter from Kathy the other day and—"

"Hi, in-laws," Wright interrupted—I didn't know he'd taken Beth's place on the extension. "Nan, I didn't know you'd gotten a letter from your sister."

"I'm sorry, Wright," I apologized. "I just haven't had time to tell you."

"Hi, Wright," Mother said.

"Hi, Wright," Feef spoke up.

"Hey, you three," I laughed, "let me tell you about Kathy's letter. She's made arrangements with the other nurse in the office, so she can get off the last of July too—she'll be here when you are."

"Wonderful!" mom said.

"Hi, Gramma. Hi, Feef." Wrightsie had replaced his dad on the extension. "Happy Father's Day, Feef."

"Oh, thank you, Wrightsie," Feef answered. "How are you?"

"Fine," Wrightsie answered in a happy voice. "We're taking my dad to a special place today. It's a—"

"Wrightsie," I cautioned, "don't let daddy hear you."

"Yeah, I almost forgot," Wrightsie laughed. "It's a surprise."

We talked five or ten minutes longer then said our goodbyes. After the call, Wrightsie hurried into the kitchen. "Mom, when can I tell dad where we're taking him?" he asked, fairly bursting with excitement.

"Let's wait 'til the very last second," I suggested. "I know;

you can tell him when we see it from the turnpike."

"Yeah!" Wrightsie agreed. "Oh, boy! Can we go now?"

"In a little minute," I laughed.

Soon we were driving down the turnpike headed for Dallas. We sped over a rise—about three miles from the Grand Prairie exit—and Wrightsie blurted out, "There it is, dad! There it is!"

"What? Where?" his dad asked.

"Way down there," Wrightsie said, pointing down the highway. "Read the sign, dad. Read the sign."

"Now I see," Wright said. Then he read the sign, "Wax Museum."

"Yeah!" Wrightsie fairly shouted. "Mom and I have been watching 'em work on it for a long time. They just finished it."

"How about that," Wright said with a smile. "Just in time for Father's Day."

Wrightsie was so excited he could hardly wait until his dad parked the car. Then he hopped out saying, "Come on, everybody, hurry!" But during and after the tour he said very little. I think the many weeks of anticipation were more exciting than the real event.

We climbed back into the car and Wright asked, "Where to now?"

"You tell your dad, Beth," I said.

"Okay," Beth answered. "Dad, we're going to take you to a special restaurant where you can eat all you want."

"Oh, boy!" Wright's response was genuine.

"But mom will have to show you the way," Beth said. "I can't remember how to get there."

Back on the turnpike, we continued on towards Dallas. "You know, it's still a little early to eat," I said. "Let's do something else first. Anybody have a suggestion?"

"Can we go to the Brunsons' in Dallas?" Beth asked.

"Yeah!" Wrightsie agreed.

We drove up to Wright's cousin's house in North Dallas.

Chuck answered the door and, with a surprised look, said, "Wrightsie, you're looking great! Come on in. Come on in."

Wrightsie responded with his impish smile and gave a cheery, "Hi, cousin Chuck."

Beth and Wrightsie ran off to find Jackie and Doug—Chuck's two teen-age children—while Chuck, Wright and I talked in the den. "I can't get over it," Chuck said, "Wrightsie's recovery is unbelievable. It's a miracle."

"We think so too," Wright answered. "And we think we know why." Then Wright and I described how the Lord was using Wrightsie.

"You know, there's been something different about Wrightsie ever since he came back to Dallas," Chuck said. "I'll never forget how sick he looked that day at the Naval Air Station—just before you flew to Boston. Then the night you returned—I met you at the hospital—I saw the difference immediately. In fact I mentioned it to Jackie and Doug as soon as I got home that night. I can't describe the difference. Maybe it's the look in his eyes or a certain peace about him—I don't know, I can't explain it."

"Well, Chuck, I was talking to him one night just before his bedtime. And he said, 'I've been happier than ever since I left Boston; the Holy Spirit leaped in my brain during surgery and I have the gift of healing.' "

For a moment Chuck didn't respond, then he said, "I'd like the people at our church to see him. He's been on the Saint Thomas' prayer list. Could you come over two weeks from today? I'll be out of town next week."

"Sure," I agreed. "Why don't we meet you at Saint Thomas's?"

"Good," Chuck said, "then we'll go someplace for lunch afterwards."

We gathered up the kids, said goodbye to Jackie and Doug, then drove to the special restaurant. "Oh, no," Beth said as we pulled into the parking lot. "Mom, look at the line."

By the time we'd waited in line, taken full advantage of the "all you can eat" provision and driven back home to Arlington, it was late. We all got ready for bed, then we put on robes and returned to the den for the final Father's Day event.

First, the cards. Wright read each verse and when he got to Wrightsie's card there was an extra hand-printed invitation. Wrightsie had worked on it for hours since he still lacked some dexterity with his right hand. Wright read the note: "Dear dad, This is to invite you to a Texas Ranger baseball game with me at 7:00 o'clock in the night. Happy Father's Day, Wrightsie."

Then Beth said, "Close your eyes, dad."

We'd rehearsed it well; Beth and Wrightsie pulled three long, white metal poles from their hiding place underneath the den couch. I took a gift-wrapped box from the desk beside the fireplace and handed it to Wrightsie—he put it on his father's lap. "Okay," I said, "this is your big gift from the three of us. Open your eyes."

For a few seconds a questioning look came over Wright's face, then he exclaimed, "A flag pole for the back yard! And I know what *this* is," he said unwrapping the gift in his lap.

Beth and Wrightsie stood on each side of their dad, as the paper came off. "Aha," he said. "Just as I thought—an American flag and a nylon one at that."

Wright reached out both arms and hugged the kids. "This is wonderful! I've always wanted a flag pole." Then he stood up, kissed me and said, "Thanks, Nan, for a wonderful day." He hugged the kids again saying, "This has been the happiest Father's Day in my life. Thank you all."

Monday morning after Wright left for work, I was cleaning up the breakfast dishes when Mrs. Lane called. I could tell from the sound of her voice that she had good news. "How's Kimmy doing?" I asked.

"Oh, Nan, we're so excited," she answered. "She's so much

better. Yesterday, she was sitting in the den watching TV and I was cleaning up the kitchen. I took the garbage out and when I came back in the house I decided to check on her. But she startled me. She was sitting on the floor in the hallway that leads to the den. 'Kim,' I said, 'how'd you do that?' And she laughed and laughed."

"You mean she walked?" I asked, excited.

"No," Mrs. Lane answered. "She scoots herself around on her hands and derriere. But she'd never traveled that far before and so fast. And I won't be surprised if she starts walking soon. Oh, how she wants to take physiotherapy."

"She's a brave girl," I said.

"Yes," Mrs. Lane answered. "We're so proud of her. The other day she was sitting on my lap while her two younger sisters were playing outdoors with some neighborhood children. We could hear them laughing and Kim turned to me and said, "Grandma, I wish I could run and play with the other kids. But if Jesus wants to use me this way it's all right with me. He has a plan for everyone!"

"Mrs. Lane," I said, "that makes me cry."

"I cried too," she answered. "These kids are so courageous."

When I told Wrightsie how much Kimmy had improved he beamed.

Tuesday afternoon after therapy, Beth, Wrightsie and I stopped in to see Mary Lou Muery at the Naval Air Station—she'd invited us to their quarters for a little party. Her ice cream floats were delicious and so were the candies and nuts that overflowed from several little silver dishes on the table. Captain Muery even managed to drop by for a few minutes. "Beth, Wrightsie," he invited. "Let's go down and feed the ducks."

Mary Lou and I followed them down to a pond at the back of their quarters. They fed bread crumbs to the wild ducks. "Mallards, I think," Captain Muery said. When we returned to the house, Mary Lou asked Beth, "Would you like to see the rest of the house?"

"Oh, yes," Beth answered, delighted.

They returned from the tour and Beth said, "Mom, Mrs. Muery has hand-decorated eggs sitting all around! They're beautiful!"

Mrs. Muery handed Beth some plain white empty eggs and trimmings and said, "You take these home, Beth, and see what you can do with them."

"Thank you!" Beth exclaimed.

Then I took a book from my purse, handed it to Beth and nodded towards Mary Lou.

Beth said, "Mrs. Muery, this is for you."

Mary Lou leafed through the pages and I explained, "Mary Lou, that's the book I've been telling you about—*Nine O'clock in the Morning*. The author, Father Dennis Bennett, is the priest Wright called last December. He's the one who told us to go to the Church of the Resurrection."

"Thank you, Beth, Nan," she said.

"When you read it, you'll see what our prayer meetings are all about," I said. "Maybe you'd like to go with us some Friday night. Give me a call if you do."

"All right," Mary Lou answered. "Thank you."

The very next Friday she called, "Nan, we'd like to go to the Resurrection with you and Wright. Are you going tonight?"

"Yes. Wonderful," I answered. "We'll pick you up."

"No, thanks," she said. "We thought we'd take another couple with us. Can we meet at the church?"

"Fine," I agreed. "We'll wait in the parking lot for you. We try to get there by seven o'clock so we can reserve a seat."

For all my advice, we ran late that evening and it was close to seven-thirty as we pulled into the parking lot. Fortunately, the Muerys drove in right behind us. After they'd introduced us to their friends we hurried into the church. The singing had already started but we did manage to find eight empty seats together.

We'd just sat down when I noticed a handsome couple on the other side of the church. The husband and wife were trying to find four empty chairs side by side. Their two sons followed them: one about twelve years old and the second looked to be Wrightsie's age. "Look, Wright," I whispered. "That family over there. Their son is bald like Wrightsie."

"Oh, no," Wright said. "The poor kid. I'll bet he's had radiation or chemotherapy."

The family sat down and I lost sight of them. The singing ended and Father Ted opened the meeting with a prayer. Then he said, "I think I'll be giving a teaching tonight—but I'm not sure. We'll just let the Holy Spirit lead us. Now, would anyone like to tell us what Jesus did for them this last week?"

A woman jumped up with her hand in the air. "Yes," Father Ted invited. "Go ahead, Crystal."

"I don't have a witness, Father Ted. But I'd like prayers for a very sick friend of mine." She described the illness, then somebody else made a similar request. And from all over the church, people asked that prayers be said for sick relatives, friends and loved ones.

Father Ted raised his hands. "Okay, okay," he said with a surrendering smile. "It's obvious the Holy Spirit isn't going to put up with any of my—shall we say profound—teachings tonight; He wants a healing service. Somebody find me an empty chair and let's get started."

The empty chair was placed up front and near the center of the church. The person needing prayer for himself or for a loved one sat in the chair. Gentle hands were placed on his shoulders and Father Ted started the prayers. Then, as led by the Holy Spirit, others added their prayers. One after another were prayed for, then I noticed the handsome husband and wife making their way to the chair. As their bald son sat down, his mother seemed to whisper her son's illness into Father Ted's ear. He looked up, scanned the room, spotted me and boomed out, "Where's Wrightsie? I want him to pray for this boy! Beth, go get Wrightsie!" he commanded.

Beth ran out the door. Wrightsie had left earlier to play with Father Ted's son, Mark. In a few seconds she returned with Wrightsie in tow. They knocked a couple of folding chairs sideways in their rush to the prayer chair.

"Wrightsie," Father Ted said, "this is Hill and he's got a little problem—something like you had. Right now he's got trouble here," and Father Ted pointed to the area of a lymph node on the inside of Hill's thigh.

Wrightsie nodded and Father Ted continued, "Now, I'd like you to lay hands on Hill's leg and pray for his healing. We'll all join you."

Wrightsie looked Father Ted squarely in the eye and said, "But, Father Ted, I have to lay hands on his head," and he placed his hands on each side of Hill's head. Father Ted gave an it's-up-to-you-Lord shrug, smiled and lowered his head as Wrightsie began his silent prayer.

For a minute or two the church was silent, then Wrightsie raised his head and lowered his hands. Father Ted stepped forward and anointed Hill's forehead with oil with the sign of the cross in the name of the Father, the Son and the Holy Spirit.

It was a beautiful, touching scene. But more important, Hill was healed. The last I heard he's a very happy and healthy young man. And later, Mary Lou Muery was to tell me she had an inner healing as she'd watched Wrightsie pray for Hill.

Wrightsie stayed in the church with us, and after the healing prayers were completed Father Ted did get a chance to do a little teaching. He began to tell us how the Lord loves each and every one of us personally. "Remember," he said, "the Scriptures tell us that Jesus said, the Father knows every hair on our heads."

At that moment I felt a tap on my shoulder and I turned around. It was Lorena Hamilton; she was pointing at Wrightsie. I looked and Wrightsie was feeling the little wisps of hair that had started to grow at the nape of his neck.

That night when we'd returned home, Wrightsie ended our bedtime prayers with, "Lord, please let my hair grow back. Amen."

The next six or seven days passed swiftly and we were looking forward to a long Fourth of July weekend. It was to begin with Captain Muery's ceremony on Friday at the Naval Air Station and end with the fourth on the following Tuesday.

On Thursday, the twenty-ninth, I was talking with Lorena on the phone when Wrightsie walked into the kitchen. "Mom," he said with a hurt look on his face and a hand on his stomach, "I don't feel good."

Before I could do a thing he vomited. I quickly said goodbye to Lorena, cleaned up Wrightsie and had him rest in bed. Within the hour he came out of his bedroom and asked, "Can I go out and play?"

"How do you feel?"

"Fine, mom," he answered and out he went.

That evening when I told Wright about the incident at the supper table he said, "It doesn't surprise me. When he was swimming the other day he got a mouth full of water and I'm sure he's picked up a bug."

Friday afternoon we attended Captain Muery's retirement and change of command. It was stirring event—but also sad. Again I was reminded how I would miss Mary Lou. After the military ceremony, held in a large hangar, we drove several blocks to the Officer's Club for the reception. Beth and Wrightsie joined Lisa and Mary Swor in the lounge outside the reception hall. Wright and I joined Val and Jerry Swor in the reception line to bid a final farewell to Captain Muery and

Mary Lou.

The following Sunday morning we were preparing to attend Saint Thomas' Episcopal Church in Dallas with Cousin Chuck when Wrightsie vomited again. After the incident Beth, Wright and I laid hands on him and prayed. He was fine for the rest of the day.

Nevertheless, after we'd returned home and were getting ready to swim in the canal, Wright cautioned him, "Now, be careful; don't swallow any more canal water."

Monday we took Beth and Wrightsie to Dallas to see two children's movies and Tuesday we had a great Fourth of July. It started out with a parade in downtown Arlington, followed by swimming and boating at home, and ended with fireworks at Randol Mill Park. Late that night, after our bedtime prayers, I reminded Wrightsie, "Since you didn't have therapy today, you've got it tomorrow. Then your regular session the next day—Thursday. So sleep in tomorrow morning. You're going to need all the rest you can get. Okay?"

"Okay, mom," he smiled. "Night."

The next day he was tired and I thought of canceling his therapy but he insisted he wanted to go. After he'd finished his physical exercise he started his occupational therapy. Beth and I were waiting for him when his physical therapist—the one he called Killer—walked up and said, "That's quite a boy you've got there."

"Oh, no," I said. "What's he done now? Come up with a new name for you or something like that? I'm afraid he gets too familiar sometimes," I apologized.

"No," she answered with a smile, "nothing like that. No, you see, I had him on his back and I was working his right leg—he was pushing against my hand. Well, all of a sudden he stopped pushing, looked me straight in the eye and said, 'Killer, do you know Jesus?' "

"Oh, no!" I laughed thinking, "that sounds like Wrightsie, all right."

"Well, I'm a Christian," she continued, "but that set me back for a few seconds. Then I answered, 'Well, yes, Wrightsie, I do.' But I guess my answer didn't satisfy him because a few minutes later, again without warning, he said, 'Well, do you really know Him?' "

"I'm sorry," I apologized.

"That's all right," she smiled. "I mean, he wasn't kidding around—he was serious. He's a wonderful boy, Mrs. Brunson. You don't find many like that; he can really make you stop and think."

And the next day Wrightsie made me stop and think. That morning, right after he got out of bed, he was sick again. I freshened him up and put him back to bed saying, "Wrightsie, I'm canceling your therapy today. I want you to stay in bed and rest. You may have a little bug."

But for the first time, I was really worried that it could be more than a bug. After I'd canceled his therapy I called Wright at work. "Honey, I'm scared," I admitted. "A brain tumor could cause this vomiting."

"Now, Nancy," Wright answered, trying to calm me down. "I'm sure it's nothing serious. We've been keeping a pretty fast pace the last few weeks. I'm sure he's just run down and caught something. If he's not better tomorrow we'll take him to a doctor. Now, don't worry."

I felt better after talking with Wright, and Wrightsie did improve. But even so, off and on during the day I felt a nagging fear tug at my heart. Then that afternoon Beth needed a ride to her sewing class. I'd thought about canceling it too, but by that time Wrightsie was much improved so I drove Beth to her appointment. On the way we stopped at a shopping mall to buy a spool of thread. As I was driving out of the parking lot towards Division Street, Wrightsie spoke up from the back seat and said, "Mom, I love Jesus so much that if He calls me I'm going to go."

I jammed on the brakes, brought the car to a halt, whirled my head around, looked at Wrightsie and in a startled voice exclaimed, "Wrightsie! What did you say?"

He looked at me, his eyes honest and serious, and repeated, "I love Jesus so much that if He calls me I'm going to go."

For a moment I looked at him dumbfounded and speechless. Then, in a resigned voice, I managed to sigh, "Oh, Wrightsie, we'd miss you. But I think I understand."

# 31
## That, Doctor, Is Our Decision, Not Yours!

When Wright came home from work that evening, I told him about Wrightsie's pronouncement in the parking lot.

"Whew!" Wright reacted. "For an eight-year-old he sure can come out with some profound thoughts."

"I know," I answered. "But I've never had one of his thoughts hit me like that before."

"Were you talking about Jesus or heaven before he said it?" Wright asked.

"Not a word," I answered. "He spoke right out of a clear blue sky."

We were both lost in our thoughts a few moments, then I said, "Oh, Wright, do you think Jesus will take him to heaven?"

"Well, I'm sure he will sometime," Wright answered trying to make light of my question, but then his mood changed. With a serious frown, he said, "I don't know, Nan. I hope not."

The next morning Wrightsie was sick again. I called his specialist in Dallas and he said, "Let's see how he does over the weekend. If there's no improvement, call me Monday."

Next, I called Wright at work and relayed the information. "Well, I think we should take it easy over the weekend," Wright said. "I don't even think we should go to the Resurrection tonight."

"You're right," I agreed. "But, I do have to go grocery shopping tomorrow. We're out of everything."

"Nan," Wright protested. "I'll go; you need the rest too."

"No," I insisted, "I'll go. It'll give you a chance to be alone with your best buddy."

"Okay," Wright relented with a little laugh. "I'll let you go."

Beth went shopping with me and when we returned late Saturday morning, Wright said, "The news travels fast."

"Why, what happened?" I asked.

"Wrightsie's earthly guardian angel just left," Wright answered.

"Gordon Bell? Oh, I wish I'd been here."

"Yes," Wright said. "And he brought along the Roman Catholic nun that you and Lorena heard speak."

"Oh," I said, upset that I'd missed them.

"They talked with Wrightsie for a long time. Then we all prayed over him," Wright said.

"How's he doing?"

"Asleep, right now," Wright answered.

Wrightsie slept a great deal over the weekend and it worried me. Yet I was also hopeful because he didn't vomit. Then, Monday morning as soon as he woke up he was sick. I called the specialist in Dallas and he set up an appointment for Tuesday afternoon.

Wright took off from work and we all traveled to Dallas, including Beth. As we sat in the waiting room I began to relive our last visit back in February. I shuddered involuntarily as I inwardly heard the specialist say, "I'm going to tell it like it is, you'll never walk right again."

Then I thought, "I can't let him hurt Wrightsie again."

I turned to Wright and whispered, "I've got to talk to you—alone!"

"All right. Let's go out in the hall," he answered.

"Beth, will you watch Wrightsie a minute?" I asked. "Daddy

and I will be right back."

As soon as the door closed behind us, I said, "Wright, we can't let the doctor devastate Wrightsie again."

Wright's eyes flashed with anger. "I've been thinking about that too," he said. "Look, when we take Wrightsie back to the examining room, you stay with him. Then, I'll go down to the doctor's office and have a talk with him before he examines Wrightsie."

"All right," I agreed. "But, please, don't get angry."

We returned to the waiting room and shortly Wrightsie's name was called. Wright carried him into the examining room, sat him gently on the examining table and left immediately for the doctor's office.

I'd just finished undressing Wrightsie to the waist, when the doctor entered the room and displayed a slightly forced yet courteous, "Hello, Mrs. Brunson." And a genuine pleasant look of surprise crossed his face when he saw how much hair had grown back on Wrightsie's head.

When the doctor finished the examination, he looked up and started to say something. But he stopped himself. Then he smiled and said, "I'll see you alone after you get him dressed."

I dressed Wrightsie and Wright carried him back to the waiting room where Beth looked after him. Wright returned to the examining room and shortly the doctor appeared. "Well, he looks about as I would expect," the doctor said. "There's no indication of intracranial pressure. If there were, it would explain the vomiting. But I still don't like it. We'll just have to wait and see how things go for a few days."

Wright and I nodded our heads. Then he said, sincerely, "Please give us a call if you have any questions."

"Thank you, doctor," I replied. "We will."

We left the office and took the elevator down to the first floor. The elevator stopped and as the doors opened, Wrightsie said in a weak voice, "I'm gonna be sick."

I hurried him off the elevator, into a corner, and Beth said, "Here, mom," handing me the gaily colored peanut butter bucket we carried for such an emergency.

I grabbed the little wire handle, pulled the damp washcloth from the bucket and thrust it underneath Wrightsie's chin just in the nick of time. Then I took him into a rest room, freshened him up and we drove home.

Wright returned to work. Later he called me to see how Wrightsie was doing.

"He's napping right now," I answered. "He hasn't had any problems since the elevator."

Then, changing the subject, I said, "That reminds me, what did you say to the doctor?"

"Nothing much," Wright answered in an evasive and slightly embarrassed tone of voice.

Wright was silent a moment and then reluctantly he continued, "He was coming out of his office when I walked up. And I said, 'I'd like to talk to you before you examine my son. Doctor, you hit my son pretty hard when you talked to him last time about his walking. Now, if you have any derogatory comments after his examination today, I'd appreciate it if you not say them in front of him.'"

"What happened then?" I asked.

"He came back with, 'If you think this business is easy for me, you're mistaken!' Then he started to say, 'I believe in telling it like—' I'd heard that expression one too many times," Wright said, "and I jumped up, put my hands on his desk, leaned over him and said, 'Doctor! You're not going to tell my son like it is today! If you have anything to say today, you'll tell it to me or my wife! Alone!' Then, I walked out of his office and waited for him in the hallway."

"Wright, you shouldn't have," I said.

"Nan, I'm sorry," Wright said. "I guess one of the reasons I got angry is because I was a little frightened. I'm sure he is in a tough business. I'm certain his heart goes out to his patients or he couldn't stand to be in such a demanding profession. In fact I'm sure he's put on a hard shell to cover up his heartache. But, Nan, I couldn't stand to see Wrightsie hurt again.

"I'm sorry, Nan. I was right in saying something but wrong in the way I said it."

"Don't worry," I replied. "Maybe we've all learned something."

While Wrightsie napped, I also tried to rest, but I couldn't turn my mind off. I tried to pray but that didn't help, so finally I decided to call the radiologist—the one who'd been so surprised by Wrightsie's rapid recovery. After I'd described Wrightsie's symptoms the radiologist said, "I wish I could give you some encouragement, but we could be in trouble."

We talked awhile longer, then he closed the conversation saying, "Please call if I can help you."

After the call I went into my bedroom and prayed. I was asking the Lord again to heal my son. I was interrupted by, "Mom. Mom?"

I opened the door to Wrightsie's room, opened his drapes, and looked down at him in bed. "Wrightsie!" I said. "I swear your hair's grown half an inch since you went to sleep! I can't believe it!"

Wrightsie smiled and ran his hand through his new growth of hair.

And yet his condition worsened on through Wednesday and into Thursday. So Thursday morning I called the specialist's office in Dallas but the secretary said, "I'm sorry he's on vacation. Would you like to speak to his associate?"

"Yes," I answered. "Please."

After I'd described the situation, the associate said, "I'm sorry, Mrs. Brunson. All we can do now is hold your hand. What you need is a good pediatrician."

Frustration and anger welled up within me—I don't even

remember how I responded to the doctor's advice.

Nevertheless, over the weekend, Wright and I decided to take the associate's advice and we made an appointment with a pediatrician at Carswell Air Force Base hospital for Monday. We fixed up the back seat of the car as a bed. Wrightsie's cowboy sleeping bag was again his constant companion as was Snoopy. And I put a fresh pillowcase—decorated with Yogi Bear—on his pillow. Up front, I carried the happily colored peanut butter bucket containing a damp washcloth.

When we arrived at the air base Wright carried Wrightsie into the pediatric clinic. We sat down and Wright cradled Wrightsie lovingly in his arms. What we hoped would be a short wait turned into an hour. Finally a medic announced, "Brunson," and motioned to an examining room. As Wright carried Wrightsie towards the room the medic looked down and said, almost to himself, in a surprised tone of voice, "This boy is sick."

Wright carefully lowered Wrightsie to the examining table set at one side of the small room. On the other side of the room—never acknowledging our presence—the pediatrician sat at a desk studying Wrightsie's records. Wright and I looked at each other with a questioning look but we remained silent. After perhaps three or four minutes, the doctor spun around in his chair, looked up at us and shouted in anger, "What do you want me to do about it?"

His attack was totally unexpected and for a few seconds Wright and I were speechless. Then simultaneously we shot back, "Examine him, doctor! Examine him!"

The pediatrician stormed over to the examining table, made a perfunctory examination, jabbing and poking Wrightsie here and there. Then he looked up and in a piercing, condescending voice said, "It's obvious the brain tu—"

"DOCTOR!" Wright commanded. "That's enough! Step outside!"

When the door to the examining room was closed, Wright said, "Doctor, we haven't told our son he has a brain tumor. We know it and we're pretty sure he knows it, but it's a horrible secret we are keeping from each other—out of love."

With a still angry and somewhat defensive voice the doctor said, "Well, I think an eight-year-old child can be told he's going to die!"

"That, doctor, is *our* decision, not *yours!*" Wright fired back. "He's already told his mother he's ready to go if the Lord calls him."

The confrontation ended, Wright gathered his son in his arms and we marched out of the clinic. Then Wright said, "Nan, let's take him up to the neurologist on the fifth floor. Maybe he'll see him."

"That's a good idea," I agreed.

It was the same Air Force neurologist who'd seen Wrightsie when he was first sick way back the previous October. When he heard we were waiting he promptly called us into his office. He gave us a warm, sympathetic greeting, examined Wrightsie, then put him in the care of a medic outside his office. Then he closed the door and asked, "What did the pediatrician say?"

Controlling his anger, Wright answered, "About all he said was that we should tell Wrightsie he's going to die. Do you think that's necessary, doctor?"

"No," the Air Force neurologist said slowly. "Wrightsie's a bright young boy; I'm sure he knows much, much more than we'll ever realize."

"Thank you, doctor," Wright said with real relief. "Thank you."

Then I asked, "Doctor, my parents and sister are planning to arrive for a visit this coming Saturday. Do you think they should come earlier?"

"Yes," he answered gently. "If they can get here

earlier—without too much trouble—I think they should."

"Thank you, doctor," I said sincerely. "You've really helped us. Thank you."

That evening I called Kathy and mom and dad. They were shocked by the news and later they called back to say they would all arrive Wednesday.

# 32

## *I Never Believed So Many People Could Express So Much Love*

After the kids were in bed that night, Wright and I talked over the recent experiences we'd had with doctors. Wright's anger returned and he said, "Not one of those objective, highly trained scientists has really given Wrightsie a thorough examination. Of course, this vomiting could be caused by a brain tumor. We both know that. But it could be something he got from the canal too. Don't they take stool specimens anymore? Why, they haven't even taken his temperature."

"But, Wright," I said, "I've taken his temperature. He isn't running a fever."

"I know, Nan," he said in a resigned voice. "But, we've got to do something. Why don't you call the neurologist in Dallas tomorrow morning? Maybe he can recommend a pediatrician here in Arlington."

"I'd already planned to do that," I smiled. "Now, let's get some sleep. It's been a frustrating day."

I called the neurologist the next morning. After I'd brought him up-to-date on the situation and I'm sure he sensed my frustration, I asked, "Can you recommend a good pediatrician here in Arlington?"

"Yes," he replied. "I know a pediatrician at the Arlington Children's Clinic." Then he gave me the doctor's name.

Immediately, I called the Arlington Children's Clinic and asked the secretary for an appointment with the recommended pediatrician.

"I'm sorry," the secretary apologized, "he's booked up. May I recommend Dr. Mark Welch? He has an appointment open at 4:00 P.M. this Friday."

"Fine, we'll take it." I was relieved to get any doctor.

Next, I called Wright at work to tell him about the appointment. Then he said, "I was just about to call you; I called Dr. Shaw in Boston."

"What did he say?"

"He was disappointed to hear about his little friend. And he was very understanding—wanted to know how you were holding up."

My heart was warmed by his concern. "Did he say anything else?"

"Only to call him anytime we thought he could help us."

For a moment, tears of thankfulness came to my eyes, and I thought, "Thank you, Lord, for Dr. Shaw."

Then Wright said, "The boss asked me about Wrightsie this morning and when I told him, he ordered me to take emergency leave. He said, 'Get home and take care of your family.' "

"Wright, how thoughtful."

"Yes," Wright said. "I didn't know it 'til today, but he lost his first wife after a long illness. He really understands."

"Wright, the Lord's bringing a lot of people to us. I don't know what I'd do without them."

Wright agreed and he said, "You know, there may be a few doctors of the scientific world who are defeated by things like this—and I'm sure their heartache has something to do with it. And in their defeat they can't help us or themselves. But the Lord sure seems to be rushing in reinforcements from the body of Christ."

More reinforcements arrived later that day. Gordon Bell and his wife Phyllis drove all the way from Dallas to pray for Wrightsie. Next, Father Ted called long distance. He and his family were on vacation in the Northeast and evidently someone in his parish had called and told him of Wrightsie's condition. "Nan," he said, "we're not going to accept this. I want you to know Lee Ann and I are praying and fasting." (Lee Ann, Father Ted's beautiful wife, was a vital part of the Nelson family's ministry to us.)

Then Father Ted asked, "Nan, are you all right? Do you want us to come home?"

"No. Please," I answered. "I'm fine—we're fine."

"I mean it," Father Ted said. "Just say the word and we'll be there."

"Thanks, father, but no. The Lord is sending many people to us," I explained. "You stay there and relax. You need a vacation. We'll see you when you get back."

Soon after Father Ted's call, Father Smart, the new rector at Saint Alban's, came by the house. His sweet, gentle and patient spirit warmed our home. And before leaving he served Communion in Wrightsie's bedroom.

Then for good measure, the Lord sent Lorena and Wingo Hamilton to visit us that evening. They brought along their daughter and son-in-law who were visiting them. Their son-in-law was studying for the ministry—and I believe the prayer of his parents-in-law for Wrightsie was a witness to him.

The next morning Wrightsie vomited again. Right after the incident—about eight o'clock—Wingo called and said in an apologetic voice, "I don't want to bother you, but I've been praying in my prayer language since I got up this morning, and I feel the Holy Spirit wants me to come over and pray for Wrightsie again."

"Please come over, Wingo," I answered. "We all need your prayers."

When he arrived we prayed over Wrightsie in his bedroom. I'm sure Wingo's beautiful prayer was inspired by the Holy Spirit.

Wrightsie dropped off to sleep soon after Wingo left. Wright and I were having a cup of coffee in the kitchen about an hour later when we heard over the intercom, "Mom? Mom, are they here yet?"

I walked into his room and explained, "Wrightsie, Grandma, Feef and Kathy won't be here 'til later this afternoon."

"I forgot," he said in a disappointed voice.

"How do you feel?" I asked.

"Better," he answered.

He seemed to perk up and soon he and Beth were listening to a tape cassette in his room. Early in the afternoon I said, "Wrightsie, I want you to try to get some more rest before Grandma, Feef and Kathy get here. Okay?"

"Okay," he said, good-naturedly.

"Give me a call when you wake up."

"Okay, mom," he answered and he put his arm around Snoopy, rolled over and faced the wall. In a few minutes I checked him and he was asleep.

Then the Lord surprised us by sending another Christian warrior into the fray. The Episcopal priest who baptized Beth and Wrightsie some seven years before dropped in for a visit. He and his family were passing through Texas on their way to a vacation.

I explained that my family was coming in and asked, "Please stay for supper. I'd really like you to meet my folks again. Isn't this ironic, you haven't seen them since you baptized Beth and Wrightsie."

After some persuasion he and his wife accepted my supper invitation, then it was time for Wright to head for Love Field in Dallas. Right after he left I heard, "Mom, are they here yet?"

"Not yet," I answered, "but daddy's left for the airport."

"Oh, boy!" he answered. I could see he was feeling much better.

"Let me wash your face," I said, helping him to the bathroom. "Then I want you to meet somebody."

Wrightsie was thrilled to meet the priest who had baptized him. I left the priest with Wrightsie in the bedroom for a while. When he returned to the den, the priest said, "I really felt the Spirit of the Lord in his room."

"Isn't it wonderful!" I exclaimed. "Many people have said the same thing."

Wright returned with my family and they had a touching reunion with Wrightsie. He ate supper with us on the den couch and seemed much improved. The priest and his family left after supper—he said a final prayer for Wrightsie before departing.

We did a great deal of talking that night—we had much to catch up on. After late bedtime prayers in Wrightsie's bedroom, Grandma said, "Wrightsie, I got a little something for you." And she handed him a small pencil flashlight.

"Thanks, Gramma!" Wrightsie exclaimed.

About fifteen minutes later, I heard Wrightsie happily call over the intercom, "Mom! Mom!"

"What is it?" I asked, opening his door.

"Look," he said and he threw the beam of his new flashlight around the room. The back glow from the flashlight revealed his laughing, happy face.

Wrightsie was even better Thursday. He sat in his wheelchair for part of the day and, when he woke up from his afternoon nap, his dad asked, "Wrightsie, would you like to go for a ride with Feef and me? I want to show him around the neighborhood."

I was thrilled when Wrightsie said, "Sure!"

Wright made up the back seat of the car into a bed and off they went. Then, that night Wrightsie fairly demanded that he be permitted to eat tacos. I relented and was rewarded with his smacking lips as he ate two tacos.

But Friday, although he didn't complain, he was very listless and slept a great deal. Nevertheless he said, "Mom, can we go to the Resurrection tonight?"

"Wrightsie, are you sure you feel good enough?"

He firmed his lips and emphatically nodded his head.

"Well, we'll see how you feel after your doctor's appointment this afternoon."

Wright drove us to the doctor. My sister Kathy rode in the front seat and I cradled Wrightsie in my arms in the back seat. Wright carried him up to the receptionist's desk and she immediately directed us to a small examining room down a corridor. I couldn't help but notice the tasteful color schemes of the office and the cheery decor of the examining room. Everything was coordinated to please a child.

Wright gently lowered Wrightsie to the examining table and pulled the cowboy sleeping bag up around his shoulders. Then Wright said, "I'm going to turn that overhead light off 'til the doctor gets here; it's too bright."

Ordinarily Wrightsie would have taken in every picture, every color and every piece of equipment in the room. But he laid on his side and dozed while Kathy, Wright and I talked in low voices so as not to disturb him.

As the minutes ticked by Wright began to do a slow burn. About four-thirty he said in a disgusted voice, "I wonder what time our four o'clock appointment's going to be—five o'clock? It's just like Carswell the other day!"

Then half prayerfully and half humorously—in an effort to calm Wright—I said, "Yes, doesn't he know we've got a date with the Lord tonight at the Resurrection."

"I'm going out and ask the receptionist where he is," Wright said.

"Well, I'm going with you. Now be nice," I pleaded.

With great control, Wright asked in a not unpleasant voice, "Do you know how long it will be before the doctor can see us?"

The receptionist looked up and said, "Oh, I'm sorry; he is running late. He should be through shortly with the patient he's seeing now. And you're next. Oh, there he is now," she said, nodding in the direction of the doctor.

We looked up and the doctor walked towards us, smiled and said pleasantly, "I'm Dr. Welch. Sorry I'm—"

Wright's self-control disappeared, "Doctor!" he said, stopping Dr. Welch in his tracks. "I want you to know we're not hysterical parents. If our son has a—"

"Wright! Wright!" I said. "You're coming on too strong! Give the doctor a chance."

"I'm sorry," Wright said sheepishly, "I'm sorry," he repeated and backed off.

The doctor put out his hand, smiled and said, "Sorry I'm running late."

"I'm Wright Brunson," Wright said apologetically, shaking the doctor's hand. "And this is my wife, Nancy."

"How do you do?" he smiled at me. "Well, let's go down to my office a minute before I look at your son. Is there someone with him?"

"Yes," I answered, "my sister."

"Fine," and he led the way to his office.

Wright apologized again and told him about our earlier experiences. Then he said, "Doctor, Nan and I know this is probably the tumor and we're prepared for that. But, we've been to numerous doctors recently and not one has given him a complete examination—no blood pressure, no temperature, no blood sample, no stool sample, no urine test. They just automatically assume it's the tumor."

Before we left Dr. Welch's office we'd given him a pretty good rundown, including the fact we'd never told Wrightsie he had a brain tumor. Then the doctor asked, "Do you have any other children?"

We told him about Beth and the close relationship she had with her brother. "How's she taking all this?" Dr. Welch asked.

I explained we'd told Beth everything almost from the start. I ended by saying, "We didn't want Beth to ever feel cheated or say something she might feel guilty about later."

Dr. Welch didn't respond directly, but I got the impression that, considering our circumstances, he approved of our actions.

"Well, let's take a look at him," the doctor suggested.

We followed him down the hall to the examining room and under my breath I said, "Thank you, Lord." I sensed he had sent another Christian to minister to Wrightsie and our whole family.

I introduced him to Kathy, and before he turned the bright, overhead fluorescent light back on he said, "Wrightsie, I'm sorry but I've got to turn this light on so I can get a good look at you."

Then he walked over to the table and said to Wrightsie, "Let's look at your tongue."

Wrightsie half-heartedly pushed out his tongue. Then Dr. Welch said, "Stick it out like you really mean it."

Wrightsie took a deep breath and thrust his tongue out with great emphasis and determination.

Dr. Welch gave an understanding laugh and said, "I don't blame you. I'm sure you don't feel well and you just told the whole world. That's all right."

Wrightsie pulled his tongue back and he couldn't stop the little boy smile that spread over the right side of his face.

After a very thorough examination Dr. Welch covered up Wrightsie with his sleeping bag and said, "Let me know how he does over the weekend. I'll give you some medicine for his nausea and vomiting. And then after these tests come back I'll want to see him again. Also I'd like you to keep track of his fluid intake and output."

"Thank you, doctor," I said. "Thank you very much."

"Do you have any questions?" he asked.

"No," I answered. "But I probably will later."

"I'm sure you will," he agreed. "Just give me a call when you do."

We bundled Wrightsie up and headed home. He still was determined to go to the Resurrection. We borrowed Evelyn Fox's large station wagon so there'd be room for everyone. We took a folding cot with us so Wrightsie could lay down at church. Soon we were on the road for Dallas and as usual we stopped at a drive-in for a hamburger. I fed Wrightsie his burger in very small bites but still he choked on a tiny piece. It frightened all of us. After the episode was over Wright and I looked at each other. We knew what was happening; Wrightsie had lost his gag reflex again.

I was emotionally drained and thankful we were headed for the Resurrection. When we drove into the parking lot, Wright said, "There's Gordon Bell."

He was standing on the steps leading into the church and facing Ferguson Road. His eyes tracked the strange station wagon we were riding in and I noticed a searching, worried look on his face. He started to glance back to the road, when he recognized Wright behind the wheel. His face broke into a grin and he waved an enthusiastic greeting.

He hurried over to the wagon and I introduced Wrightsie's earthly guardian angel to my family. Then, a troubled, hurt expression crossed his face when he saw Wrightsie's weakened condition. "Let me carry the cot," he said as we walked towards the church. "Let's set it up in the choir room off the back of the church."

"Okay," Wright said.

Gordon unfolded the cot next to one wall and Wright lowered Wrightsie onto it. Then he bundled the cowboy sleeping bag around him. The singing had already started and the harmony of over a hundred voices floated back to the choir room. Wrightsie lay on his side, his eyes closed—he didn't speak or move a muscle. But a look of absolute peace and contentment came over him, as if to say, "At last I'm in my home."

It wasn't long before people started coming into the choir room. Many had known Wrightsie since that New Year's Eve when we first carried him into the Church of the Resurrection. They came into the room singly, some in pairs, some in small groups. Some only looked at Wrightsie with compassion and heartache written all over their faces. Some laid hands on him and whispered a quiet prayer and some lined the walls around the room and prayed silently.

After ten or fifteen minutes Wright suggested in a whisper, "Why don't you take Beth, Kathy and your folks into the meeting? Gordon and I will stay with Wrightsie."

"All right," I answered, "I'll see you after the meeting."

When Communion was over, we returned to the choir room. It was overflowing with loving Christians, yet there was no jostling, no confusion. Instead a warm peace and serenity prevailed. Thoughtful people made room for us as we entered the room. Then I heard Gordon Bell say, "Mr. Harkins, may I pray for you?"

Feef lowered his head, Gordon placed his hand on my dad's shoulder and began his prayer, "Jesus, I ask you to comfort a broken-hearted grandfather."

On the drive home Feef said in wonderment, "I haven't seen anything like that in my life. I never believed so many people could express so much love, so much peace—yet, at the same time, so much heartache."

# 33
## Never Mind, Never Mind

When we returned to Arlington from the prayer meeting, it was very late. Everyone else went to bed, but Wright and I sat down at the kitchen table to discuss the night's events.

"I have to agree with what Feef said on the drive home tonight," Wright said, "about the peace and love at the Resurrection tonight. There was heartbreak too. I found myself feeling sorry for some of the people as I watched them pray over Wrightsie; they looked and acted as if they'd never see him again."

"I know," I answered.

We talked awhile longer, then went to bed ourselves. Saturday Wrightsie spent most of the day in his bed and Wright stayed in the bedroom with him. One time, when I walked back to the room to see them, as I neared the door, I heard Wright reading in a low voice. I opened the door and asked, "What are my men doing?"

Wright, sitting on the floor at the foot of the bed, lowered the Bible to his lap and answered, "Oh, I was reading to Wrightsie the first part of the Book of Acts."

Wrightsie was lying on his left side facing the wall. Wright got up, pulled the cowboy sleeping bag up over Wrightsie's shoulders, then he picked up Snoopy from the head of the bed and said, "Here, Wrightsie. I'm going to lean Snoopy against the wall so he can look after you. I think I'll have a quick cup of coffee with mom. Okay?"

Wrightsie didn't answer. Then Wright said, "I'll turn up the intercom; give me a call if you need me."

Wright poured two cups of coffee and sat down at the kitchen table with a sigh.

"You all right, honey?" I asked.

"Yes," he answered. "I was just thinking about Wrightsie and his bedroom; it's so quiet and peaceful in there. I read the Bible to him for a while, then if he drops off to sleep, I pray. You know, I can really feel the Holy Spirit in his room."

Then we heard, "Dad, dad," over the intercom in the kitchen.

Wright got up, pushed the talk button and said, "I'm on my way, best buddy." Then he picked up his coffee cup, smiled at me and hurried back to his loving duties.

Later in the afternoon, when Wrightsie again dropped off to sleep, Wright left his post for half an hour.

"Feef," he asked my dad, "this Navy friend of mine in Washington—Carl Wilgus—sent me a tape of a speech by a Roman Catholic priest named Father Joseph Orsini. I think he was speaking to a Catholic charismatic meeting in Washington. Would you like to hear it?"

"Certainly," Feef answered.

When the tape had played through, Wright handed Feef a book and said, "Feef, since you were raised a Roman Catholic, I decided to buy you this book the other day."

"Thanks, Wright," Feef said, accepting the gift.

"It's a book by Father Orsini entitled, *Hear My Confession*," Wright explained. "It's quite a story."

Then Wright returned to Wrightsie's bedroom and Feef started to read Father Orsini's book.

Early that evening we ate supper on the den patio. Wright

carried Wrightsie out and lowered him gently to the chaise lounge. Then he straightened Wrightsie's pajamas, placed the pillows just right to prop him into a sitting position and made sure everything was as comfortable as possible.

While the rest of us ate at the patio table Wright fed Wrightsie on the lounge. I took a moment and watched my husband feed our son. Wright was so patient and tender and loving.

"Now, Wrightsie," he said in a gentle voice, "I know you don't want to talk, so if I'm feeding you too fast just close your mouth when I put the fork up to it."

Wright fed him, tiny bite by tiny bite. "That's the way, best buddy," he encouraged. "That's a great appetite you've got tonight."

He raised another little fork full to Wrightsie's lips, but he kept his mouth closed. "I'm sorry," Wright said with a little laugh. "I'm feeding you too fast. Forgive me. But I love to see you eat."

They waited and I noticed a light breeze gently ruffle the furry new hair that covered Wrightsie's previous baldness.

We'd just finished our meal when the doorbell rang. "I'll get it," I said.

I opened the door and before I could say a word, I heard, "Nan, we don't want to bother you, we don't even want to come in, but John and I just baked some apple pies and we wanted to bring one over to Wrightsie—I know how he loves apple pie."

"Jackie," I said, "you and John are too much."

She handed me the pie saying, "Be careful; it's still hot."

"And you've got to come in," I said, taking the pie.

"Nan, are you sure it's all right? You're so busy."

"Yes," I insisted. "I'd like you to meet my folks and my sister."

"Just for a minute, then," she relented.

I set the pie on the kitchen counter and led them out to the patio. After I'd introduced Jackie and her husband to my family they walked over to the chaise lounge.

"Wrightsie," Jackie said in an exuberant yet gentle fashion, "you look so handsome."

Wrightsie responded with a small, shy grin.

Then John said, with sincere sympathy, "How you doing, big boy?" John's demeanor revealed a deep respect and great hurt for Wrightsie.

"Fine," Wrightsie managed to say in a little voice.

Wright walked back out to the patio with a tiny sliver of apple pie on a plate. And while the rest of us talked he fed the pie to Wrightsie who loved every morsel.

Jackie and John left after a short visit and I started to clean up the dishes. "Wrightsie's tired," Wright said, carrying him past me on the way into his bedroom. "I'll call you when he's ready for prayers."

We said bedtime prayers with Wrightsie. Then when I was putting the last of the dishes into the dishwasher Wright called, "Nan, come out and see the beautiful sunset."

I walked out on the patio and saw a sky painted with the most serene, subtle shades of blue, and rich, dark violets and the deepest purples I'd ever seen. A great sense of awe and spiritual peace filled my soul as I watched the slowly changing panorama.

"Let's pray," I said to everyone. "Let's all hold hands in a circle and pray for Wrightsie."

As each person said a prayer in turn, a thought came to my mind that I accepted with a great assurance and peace, "Wrightsie will join the Lord in heaven tonight."

I never mentioned the thought, even though the memory of it persisted on into the evening. Then late that night, after everyone else was asleep, I picked up a book from my bedside table entitled, *Voices from the Edge of Eternity*. I'd read some of the short stories it contained within the past few weeks or so—in fact, I'd read some of the more beautiful witnesses to Wrightsie.

I opened the book at random and felt a sense of fascination come over me as I read the true story of a young man who'd survived a death experience in a hospital. His story told of the events that had occurred to him during a nine-minute period when he'd been declared clinically dead.

First, he'd felt detached from his body and in this state he came before a brilliant light that caused him to believe he was in the presence of the Lord. His belief was confirmed when the Lord asked him what good he had accomplished in his life. The young man searched his memory and offered the comment that he had been a Boy Scout.

Next, he was asked if he'd ever told anyone about the Lord. The young man admitted he hadn't but mentioned he'd always intended to.

Towards the end of the experience, the man reminded the Lord that he was too young to die. In turn, the Lord told him that no one is too young to die.

Finally, the young man was reunited with his body; he survived the illness but he never forgot his encounter with the Lord. He became a dedicated Christian physician who told everyone he could about the Lord and how he longed to be in the presence of that bright light again.

I closed the book and put it back on my bedside table. Then I thought, "Wrightsie's a Cub Scout, but even though he's young he's told many people about Jesus and prayed for their healings."

Then the memory of my thought at sunset came to mind and I felt a great desire to pray for Wrightsie. I walked into his room, knelt beside his bed and gently placed one hand on his head, the other on his side and prayed, "Lord, please heal Wrightsie. I will try to guide him into the priesthood or into medical research or whatever work you have planned for him.

Jesus, I give Wrightsie up to you and your will—to be healed or to be in heaven."

I felt like I should pray even more but I knew my words were inadequate. Then without thinking I started speaking in my unknown prayer language—unknown to me but known to the Holy Spirit. At that moment I felt an actual spiritual and physical force press down on my arms and hands as they lay on Wrightsie. And I knew his future was truly in the hands of the Lord he loved so dearly.

Then I returned to my bed and settled into a peaceful, secure sleep. The Lord didn't take Wrightsie to heaven. He slept the night through and that Sunday morning I heard the heartwarming, "Mom, mom," come over the intercom in our bedroom.

As I looked back, I realized the Lord was trying to say something to those who were close to Wrightsie—for on Tuesday morning Wright woke me up as soon as he shut the alarm clock off.

"Nan, are you awake?" he asked in an urgent voice.

"What is it?" I asked.

"I've got to tell you about the dream I had last night."

"Let me get our coffee made first," I said.

"No," Wright argued. "I've got to tell you now. Oh, it was beautiful and I know the Lord is going to heal Wrightsie."

"Okay," I said with a smile. "But I didn't think you put much stock in dreams."

"This one was different," Wright said. "I've never had such a vivid dream in my life."

"Go ahead," I said.

"Well, I was lying down on a hillside," Wright began with a faraway look in his eyes, "and I was resting my head on my hands watching the clouds drifting across the beautiful blue sky. All around me were rolling hills covered with the greenest grass I've ever seen. There weren't any trees on the hills except for one large oak tree on a hill off to my left."

"How'd you know it was an oak tree?" I asked.

"I don't know," Wright answered, "by the branches and its shape, I guess—you know how I love oak trees—hey!" he exclaimed, "I just thought what that oak tree meant: it was the cross! Because right after I noticed the tree, I saw Jesus off to my right, walking up the hill towards me. I couldn't see His face, but I wasn't surprised because I knew it was Him.

"Anyway, He walked up to me, and without speaking a word He put out His hand. I took it and He helped me to my feet. Then He started to walk back down the hill—the way He'd come. I followed Him and then I noticed He held a ball cradled under His left arm.

"He stopped and when I caught up with Him He pointed down into a grassy valley at the foot of the hill. I looked down and there stood Wrightsie.

"Nan," Wright beamed, "Wrightsie was in perfect health. When he saw us he waved his hand and a perfect smile spread across his face—there was nothing wrong with the left side of his face.

"Then he started to run like the wind—across, in front of us. Jesus took the ball He'd been carrying under His arm and threw it to Wrightsie. He made a perfect catch on the dead run, then he stopped and threw the ball back to Jesus.

"Next, Jesus handed me the ball and I threw it to Wrightsie. He made another perfect catch. Then Wrightsie threw back his head and laughed with delight—oh, how he laughed. Then he ran off down the valley throwing the ball in the air and catching it again and again.

"It was beautiful," Wright said, beaming. "I know Wrightsie's going to be healed."

Without thinking, I replied, "But Wright, maybe your dream took place in heaven. And it means Wrightsie's going to be healed in heaven."

As soon as I said it, I was sorry. Wright's smile was replaced by a frown, and he shook his head, "No, I don't think so," he said. "Oh, Nan, I hope not."

I felt sorry for Wright, then for me, then for all of us.

It was during the following week that Wrightsie began to have attacks of severe stomach cramps. There was nothing we could do to prevent them or to ease the pain. Whenever they occurred I just did my best to comfort Wrightsie until they passed.

Then Thursday evening Wrightsie was on the den couch and Wright and I were with him—my family had taken Beth for a walk. Suddenly, Wrightsie doubled up with pain. Wright and I hurried over to the couch to comfort him, and then the phone rang.

"Oh," Wright said. "I'll get it!"

I heard him answer in a brusque, frustrated voice. He said, "She can't come to the phone; Wrightsie's got a painful stomach cramp and she's trying to help him."

In the next moment, Wright walked into the den, the long coiled extension cord taut behind him, handed me the phone and said, "Nan, it's Hazel, the woman who gave you that pamphlet about Satan. She said, 'Pain isn't from the Lord! You get over there and pray for your son. Get that pain out of him!' Here, you talk to her."

"What are you going to do?" I asked.

"Pray!" Wright answered.

I took the phone but I didn't really hear what Hazel said; I watched and listened to Wright. He quickly rolled Wrightsie onto his back, put one hand on his forehead and one hand on his bare tummy. Then in a loud, demanding voice he commanded the pain to leave Wrightsie.

Within seconds, Wrightsie lowered his doubled up legs and the look of pain on his face was replaced with relief. Then in a low, gentle voice Wright prayed, "O Lord Jesus, let the peace

261

and comfort of your Holy Spirit come over, around and into Wrightsie. Give him your priceless gift of sleep."

Wright continued his prayer for a few seconds and, in less than a minute, Wrightsie closed his eyes and dropped off to sleep.

"I'm sorry, Hazel," I said into the phone. "I was watching Wright; he prayed for Wrightsie. The pain's gone and Wrightsie's already sound asleep. I can't believe it. It's a miracle!"

"Praise the Lord," Hazel said. "I'll call you tomorrow."

Wright carried Wrightsie to his room, I rolled down the covers and we tucked him into bed.

When we returned to the den, I said, "I've never heard you pray like that before."

Wright was pleasantly amazed with the power of his prayer and he grinned and said, "I never have prayed like that before. To tell you the truth, I was a little scared."

The next Friday afternoon we took Wrightsie to see Dr. Welch, and then that evening, Wright stayed home with Wrightsie while Grandma, Feef, Kathy, Beth and I attended the Resurrection. I was delighted for my family when a guest speaker gave an exciting teaching on the power of the Holy Spirit.

And the next morning Feef witnessed that power in action. Beth and Feef were in Wrightsie's room watching the Saturday morning TV cartoons with him. Wright and I were in the kitchen having coffee with Grandma and Kathy when Beth ran in.

"Daddy! Daddy!" she exclaimed. "Wrightsie wants you; his stomach hurts!"

Wright jumped up from the kitchen table and ran to the bedroom. By the time I got there Wrightsie was already relaxed. My dad, sitting on the floor at the foot of the bed, looked on in amazement as Wright asked Jesus for the priceless gift of sleep to be given to his son. In three or four minutes, Wrightsie dropped off into a peaceful, relaxed and pain-free sleep.

Feef walked into the kitchen and said, "I wouldn't believe it, if I hadn't seen it. Amazing!"

Later that morning Wingo Hamilton called on the phone. "Is your dad there?" he asked when I picked up the phone.

"Yes, I'll call him," I answered.

Before Feef got to the phone, Wingo asked, "Are you all still going to that Full Gospel Business Men's meeting in Dallas tonight?"

"Yes," I answered. "Everybody except Wright and Wrightsie."

"Fine. Why don't you drive by our house on the way, then you can follow us over."

"Okay," I agreed. "Here's Feef," I said, handing the phone to dad.

The two "look alikes" talked for a long time that Saturday. When their conversation was over Feef turned to me and said, "I really respect that man. And he makes a great deal of sense to me when he talks, particularly when it comes to this charismatic renewal."

"Well, I'm glad you two could spend some time together," I replied. "And I'm happy for Beth's sake. She really wanted you two to meet. She fell in love with Wingo the first time she met him—because he looks like you."

"By the way," I asked, "does he remember you're leaving tomorrow?"

"Yes," Feef answered. "He'd like us to all sit together at the meeting. Oh, he said to tell you Mike and Marge O'Halloran will be there too. Nan, that's a wonderful group of people you know down here."

"I know," I answered. "I'm sure the Lord sent them our way."

Saturday night we once again heard about the power of the Holy Spirit when we attended the Full Gospel Business Men's meeting in Dallas. The speaker told of the miracles which are occurring in Indonesia—much like those of the first century—and how thousands of people were converting to Christianity.

Then came Sunday, and it was time for Feef to say goodbye. The final farewells were said in Wrightsie's bedroom. Feef looked down at his grandson and said, "Bye, Wrightsie. I'll be praying for you. Oh, how I'll be praying for you."

"Bye, Feef," Wrightsie answered. "I love you."

Feef knelt by the bed and hugged his grandson. Wrightsie reached up and put his left arm around Feef's neck, squeezed tightly and said, "Someday we won't have to say goodbye any more; we'll all be together in heaven—forever."

Feef gave him one last hug, then hurried out of the room, his eyes clouded with tears.

Wrightsie and I stayed home while everybody else rode to Love Field to see Feef off on his flight. No sooner had the car pulled out of the driveway when I heard a weak, "Ma, ma," come from Wrightsie's bedroom.

I hurried into the room; he'd been sick again. "Oh, Wrightsie," I said, my heart breaking for my little boy. He looked so pitiful. "I'm going to run a nice warm bath. You can soak awhile. Then you can wear your cowboy pajamas; I just took them out of the dryer."

After his bath, I tucked him in and fluffed his pillow saying, "And here's Yogi Bear—all fresh and clean. I've changed your bed linen too."

He tried to smile a "thank you," but instead he vomited again.

After freshening him again—another change of pajamas and bed linen—I tucked him back into bed. I was about to pick up the soiled sheets, pillowcases and pajamas which were around the room, when the phone rang.

"Feef just boarded the plane," Wright said in a jovial voice. "We'll start home after his plane takes off."

I couldn't control my fears, my frustrations, my heartache. In tears I blurted out, "Oh, Wright, Wrightsie's been sick ever since you left the house."

"Oh, Nan," Wright answered sympathetically. "We'll leave now. And I'll be praying for you."

At that moment the doorbell rang. "Wait a minute," I said, "someone's at the door."

I put the phone down and hurried for the door. When I saw what appeared to be two children through the opaque glass in the door, I returned to the phone and said, "I've got to go; there are two kids at the door."

I hung up the phone and hurried back to the front door, calling out in a defeated voice, "I'll be right there."

I opened the door and there stood Phyllis and Gordon Bell. The Lord had answered Wright's prayer before he said it.

"Are you all right? How's Wrightsie?" Gordon asked.

"Yes," I said, already feeling better at the sight of my Christian friends.

"I'm sorry it took so long to answer the door. Wright was on the phone," I said smiling an apology, "and I thought you were a couple of kids."

Gordon laughed and said, "Nan, we may be short, but we're not that short."

Then Gordon became serious and asked, "How's Wrightsie?"

"He's just been sick," I explained. "Let me take you back to his room."

Then Gordon explained their visit saying, "We were on the turnpike headed for Fort Worth. When we passed the first Arlington exit, the Lord told me to come over here and see Wrightsie."

Gordon sat down on the side of the bed and Wrightsie gave a little smile at the sight of his earthly guardian angel.

"I'll leave you two alone," I said. "I'm sure you've got a few things to talk over."

I joined Phyllis in the den and began to relate some of the spiritual highlights of my father's visit, when Gordon called, "Nan? Nan!"

I hurried into Wrightsie's room. Gordon was standing over the bed, looking down at his earthly charge and rubbing the small of his own back with his hand.

"What's the matter?" I asked.

"Oh, Nan—" Gordon said, almost as if he'd forgotten he'd called me. "A—a— Never mind," he said in a faraway voice. "Never mind."

Many weeks passed before Gordon was led to tell me what happened in Wrightsie's bedroom that Sunday afternoon.

# 34
## I've Called An Ambulance!

By the time Wright, Beth, Mom and Kathy returned from the airport, the Bells had left to resume their trip to Fort Worth.

Wright noticed the change in my attitude since he'd called from Love Field. "What happened to you?"

"Those two kids at the front door I told you about over the phone were Gordon and Phyllis," I explained.

"Well, how's that for an immediate answer to a prayer?" Wright commented.

Then I told him how Gordon had called me back to Wrightsie's bedroom. "Yes," Wright said. "I've seen Gordon do that before. Sometimes he stops in mid-sentence. At first it bothered me, but now I just figure it's something the Lord doesn't want revealed at the time. We'll find out if we're supposed to know."

"I guess you're right," I agreed.

Later that evening, after supper, Wright said, "Nan, I think I should go back to work tomorrow. I'm using up an awful amount of my leave time. What do you think?"

"Well, Wrightsie seems to be holding his own," I answered. "And I've got plenty of help with mom and Kathy here. Maybe you'd better go back to work."

It was agreed and Wright returned to work Monday. Beth, mom, Kathy and I relaxed around home and looked after Wrightsie. Tuesday night after supper, we watched a Billy Graham TV special. At the end of the service an invitation was extended to the TV audience to accept Jesus as their Savior or to rededicate their lives to Him. My mother was seated on the den couch and suddenly she leaped up.

I thought, "My goodness, I'm twenty-two years younger than she is and I can't move that fast."

"I—I started to get up," she explained with wonderment in her voice, "and a strong force pushed me the rest of the way."

"Maybe the Lord's trying to tell you something," I said with a smile.

"Yes," she agreed thoughtfully. "Maybe He is."

Then she said, "Well, it's late, I think I'll get ready for bed."

Mom walked into the guest room, Kathy and I picked up and Bethy too started to get ready for bed. (We'd said our evening prayers with Wrightsie before the TV show, and he was already in bed.) Then I turned off the TV and said to Kathy, "Want to check Wrightsie with me?"

He was sound asleep and above his gentle breathing I heard his two little turtles scratching around in their small plastic aquarium. "Let's get some canal water for the turtles," I whispered to Kathy.

After we'd filled the aquarium, Kathy suggested, "Why don't we talk a minute with mother before she goes to sleep?"

Kathy walked into the guest room first and said in a low but alarmed voice, "Nan! Nan!"

I hurried into the room. Mom was laying on her back in bed, her eyes were closed and there was a quiet, serene look on her face. I recognized immediately she'd been baptized in the Holy Spirit, for she was speaking softly in her new prayer language.

And then I realized why Kathy was alarmed; I knew my medically-oriented sister probably thought mom had had a stroke. "Don't worry, Kathy," I said. "There's nothing wrong with her—in fact she's never been better in her life."

Mom heard us talking, opened her eyes and, still praying in her new language, got up and knelt beside the bed. Then she motioned for us to leave the room.

"It's all right, mom," I said. "We'll leave, but don't worry; you won't lose it."

A few minutes later she joined Kathy and me in the den. Before I could say a word, she said, "Nan, I feel like I have to pray for Wrightsie. Is it all right to go in his room?"

"Yes," I said.

And she hurried back to pray over her grandson.

Mom was still beaming and smiling the next day. And that evening, while Wright stayed home with Beth and Wrightsie, mom, Kathy and I attended the Arlington Wednesday night prayer meeting at Mike and Marge O'Halloran's home. My mother witnessed to the large group of Christians. I thrilled as she told confidently of her baptism in the Holy Spirit.

After the meeting Lorena and Wingo congratulated my mother on her new Christian maturity. She beamed and said, "I wish dad would get it too."

"Well, I wouldn't be surprised if he does. I talked with Feef a great deal before he left for Connecticut," Wingo said.

Then with a knowing, yet shy grin, my dad's "look alike" continued and said, "You know, maybe it takes a Feef to catch a Feef."

Wingo's play on words delighted us and we all had a hearty, hopeful laugh.

I don't think I'd ever seen my mother more joyful than she was during her last five days with us in Texas. Then all too soon it was time for her and Kathy to leave.

Sunday afternoon we held another farewell ceremony in Wrightsie's bedroom. We presented Mom and Kathy each with a copy of the Bible—one of the newer translations. Then, tearfully, they said their goodbyes to Wrightsie.

He talked very little but when he hugged my sister, he said, "Goodbye, Kaki," using his little boy name for Kathy, "I love you."

Then mom hugged him and said, "I love you, Wrightsie. I'll be praying."

"Goodbye, Gramma," he said. "I love you." Then with great difficulty in forming the words, he said, "Thank you for the flashlight."

Then we left for Dallas and Love Field. I drove while Wright stayed home with his best buddy. There was an hour-and-a-half wait between my mother's flight to New York and my sister's flight to San Francisco. So it was at least four hours before Beth and I returned home.

When we walked into the den, both Wrights greeted us with proud smiles of accomplishment. Wrightsie was propped up with pillows on the den couch. He had a large towel around his neck that served as a bib and Wright had an empty plate in his hand.

"Boy, did we have a great time!" Wright exclaimed.

Wrightsie smiled and nodded his agreement.

"We prayed and ate," Wright explained. "Prayed and ate. Each time he swallowed a bite, we prayed he'd keep it down."

"And look," Wright said, showing us the empty plate. "He finished the chicken Kathy made yesterday and drank a little ginger ale, with nary a hiccup."

"Wonderful!" I said, sharing their enthusiasm.

Suddenly Wrightsie's smile disappeared, he tightened his lips, his little chest heaved, then vomit spilled from his mouth, down the bib and onto his pajamas.

Chagrin, defeat, heartbreak crossed my poor husband's face, adding to the tragedy of the moment.

Beth ran to get a washcloth and I said, "Oh, Wright, I'm so sorry. I'll take care of Wrightsie."

I lifted our son from the couch and cradled him in my arms. "That's all right," I said. "You and daddy did the best you could."

Tears of frustration and disappointment filled his sad eyes. I knew they were as much for his best buddy as they were for himself.

"You can take a long, long shower," I said as I carried him into the master bedroom. I sat him on the carpeted floor and rested his back on the foot of our bed. After I'd adjusted the water flow and temperature, I undressed Wrightsie and sat him in the shower. He leaned back, and the round-down of the side of the shower stall to the floor fit comfortably the lower curve of his spine. I aimed the nozzle at his knees and the gentle stream of water splashed over his body. Wrightsie luxuriated in the warmth.

A steamy, comforting mist drifted up and enclosed him in its gentleness. "Want to be alone a few minutes?" I asked.

His eyes were closed in peace and he barely nodded.

"Okay," I answered. "I'll sit on the carpet just outside the door. If you need me, call."

I closed the shower door, sat down on the shag carpet and rested my back and head against the bathroom door casing. I closed my eyes and relaxed to the sound of the running water and to the thought of how it was comforting my son.

Four or five minutes passed and then I opened the shower door. Wrightsie was half dozing. Millions of tiny water droplets from the warm mist had settled on his new downy hair and it sparkled in the soft overhead light.

"I'm still here," I assured him, and closed the door again.

Every few minutes or so, I'd call and say, "You okay?"

I could barely hear his, "Yes, mom," over the gentle sound of the shower.

Thirty minutes passed before he was ready to leave his heavenly seclusion. I wrapped him in two huge, soft, terry cloth towels, snuggled him in my arms and rubbed his thin, slender body through the towels. "Oh," I thought, "he's lost so much weight and he's grown so tall."

When I carried him into his bedroom, his legs seemed endless and I thought, "My little boy is growing up."

After I tucked him into bed, Beth and Wright came in the room and we said our bedtime prayers.

He slept through the night and woke up the next morning in time to watch his favorite morning TV show—"I Love Lucy." After eating a little dry toast, he had rolled himself on his left side so he faced the wall—almost as if he wanted to shut out the world. Oh, how my heart ached to talk with him, but I could see he wanted to be alone. I left his room saying, "The intercom's on. Call me if you need anything. I'm going to call Dr. Welch."

After I'd talked with the doctor, I planned to give Wrightsie a suppository—he hadn't had a bowel movement in a number of days. But then I decided to wait until after the visit of a friend.

Our family had met Estelle at an art show when we'd first arrived in Arlington, and one of her paintings hung over our fireplace in the den. She'd developed a deep love for Wrightsie—a fact she couldn't explain—even before his illness.

She'd wanted to visit him and Monday provided the first opportunity. When she arrived, she had gifts for Beth and Wrightsie.

Wrightsie managed a slight smile of appreciation with the right side of his lips and then he closed his eyes and drifted off to sleep.

Estelle and I had tea in the kitchen. And after about fifteen minutes I heard a weak, "Ma, ma," over the intercom.

I hurried back to Wrightsie's room. "What is it?" I asked gently, hoping he wanted to talk with me.

But he didn't answer. I'm sure he just wanted to insure I was there.

Estelle excused herself shortly after that and then it was suppository time. He dreaded the experience—we both did.

While I waited for the suppository to work I placed him on his side and put my hand on his abdomen. Then my courageous little boy fought the dreaded battle he'd been through so many times before.

He had terrible cramps and his face contorted in pain. He clenched his little fist in agony but still he battled.

"Oh, Jesus," I prayed to myself, "help him! Help him!"

Finally, it was over. Wrightsie had won. My brave little Christian warrior never shed a tear—never whimpered. But the fight had taken its toll; Wrightsie lay back on his bed exhausted, drained. I wiped his forehead and hands with a cool, damp washcloth, darkened his room and said, "You're a brave, brave boy, Wrightsie. Oh, how I love you."

He didn't respond.

"Try to get some sleep now," I said. "But call me if you want. I'll be waiting."

A few minutes later, I checked him. He didn't look right. Then I gasped, "Oh, my God! Wrightsie!! Wrightsie!!!"—I thought he was dead.

Vomit stained the corner of his mouth. His eyes were open but he wasn't seeing. I ran to the bed, grabbed a bulb syringe from the bedside table and sucked the nauseant from his mouth. Then I worked a wash cloth around the inside of his mouth to get more out.

"Speak to me, Wrightsie! Say something!" I pleaded.

He didn't respond.

Then I took his hand in mine and said, "Squeeze my hand. Oh, Wrightsie, please squeeze my hand!"

A flood of relief swept over me as his little hand tightened on mine.

"Beth! Beth!" I hollered at the top of my lungs.

She heard me through the walls and ran into the house.

"Something's wrong with Wrightsie! Get me your stethoscope."

Beth got her child's—yet functioning—stethoscope and I checked Wrightsie's heart. He had a weak heartbeat and I saw his little chest barely heave with each breath.

"Beth, watch him! I'm going to call Dr. Welch!"

I ran to the master bedroom, grabbed the extension phone, took it into Wrightsie's room and dialed the doctor.

"Watch him for a few minutes; then call me back," Dr. Welch instructed. "Immediately, if necessary."

Then I called Wright at work. "Something's wrong with Wrightsie!" I hollered into the phone.

"I'm on my way!" Wright responded.

Wrightsie was all right for a few minutes, then he looked distressed again.

Again I dialed Dr. Welch, but the receptionist put me on hold while she called him to the phone.

Then I decided to call an ambulance but I didn't want to break the connection.

"Beth! Run to the Foxes'; tell them to call an ambulance!" I ordered.

Moments later, Wright ran into the bedroom. I told him what happened, then Dr. Welch came on the line.

"I've called an ambulance!" I explained.

"I'll meet you at the hospital," he responded.

Then Beth returned and said, "Mrs. Fox wasn't home so I ran to the next house down. They called!"

Within minutes the ambulance pulled in the driveway and around to the back of the house. Wright led the attendants into the bedroom, I explained the situation, and in seconds they'd strapped Wrightsie to the litter.

As they carried Wrightsie out to the ambulance, Evelyn Fox ran up. "What can I do?!" she asked.

"Call Father Smart!" Wright said.

"I'll ride with Wrightsie," I said.

"Okay. Beth, get in front with me," Wright instructed.

When the ambulance pulled out of the driveway, I couldn't help but notice the neighbor who'd placed the call for it. For months that wonderful Christian man had prayed for Wrightsie. And there he stood by our driveway; his face was stricken and tears ran down his cheeks.

The siren wailed and although I prayed for a quick trip, the ambulance seemed to barely move. I kept a constant check on Wrightsie, holding my fingers to the pulse in his wrist.

Then I lost the pulse. His eyes went blank and I shouted to myself, "I can't believe it! He's gone! He's gone!"

Wright was watching us from the front seat. I looked at him and formed the words with my mouth, "He's gone! He's gone!"

Wright hollered through the glass that separated us, "Give him oxygen! Give him oxygen!"

The attendant riding in back grabbed the oxygen mask from its container and turned on the valve, but no oxygen came out. Then he attempted to change to another oxygen bottle.

Wright, seeing the difficulty, hollered again, "Nan! Give him mouth-to-mouth resuscitation!"

I did and the life-saving effort worked. By the time the oxygen was finally flowing and the mask was placed on Wrightsie's face his chest was heaving and I could feel a weak pulse again.

Finally, we arrived at the hospital. The ambulance attendant replaced the mask with a portable Ambu bag resuscitator. Two hospital orderlies threw open the back door to the ambulance, grabbed the litter and rushed Wrightsie into the hospital. The attendant ran alongside the litter, squeezing the Ambu bag.

A sigh of relief and thanksgiving escaped from my lips when I looked up and saw Dr. Welch and Father Smart waiting for us at the entrance to the emergency room.

# 35
## *No Heroics!*

Dr. Welch followed the litter into the hospital and Wrightsie was put into a cubicle. The doctor started emergency procedures on him immediately. The Ambu bag was replaced with a hospital oxygen mask, an i.v. solution was started, and Dr. Welch checked his vital signs: heart, blood pressure, pulse rate.

Wright and I stayed in the cubicle, but then a girl stepped into the room and said, "Mr. Brunson, would you mind filling out the admission form?"

"I'll be right back," Wright said, as he left the cubicle.

Wrightsie's breathing was very irregular and Dr. Welch attended him continuously. I stood by in case he might need me and hoped and prayed.

Finally, Wright reentered the room and said, "I'm sorry it took so long, but I had to answer some questions a policeman had on a form too."

"A policeman?" I asked.

"Yes," Wright answered. "The implication behind the questions was child abuse. I'm glad they check for such things."

Then Wright said, "And I talked with Beth."

"Poor Beth. How is she? I wonder what she's thinking," I said.

"She's doing okay," Wright said. "Father Smart has stayed with her, and now Evelyn Fox is with her too."

"Oh," I said, "I want to see Beth and talk with Father Smart and Evelyn. I'll only be gone for a minute. Call me if there's any change with Wrightsie. Okay?"

"Don't worry; I will," Wright assured me.

I walked out to the small waiting room. Beth spotted me, ran up and hugged me. "Mom, mom, how's Wrightsie?"

"He's holding his own, Beth," I said, giving her a hug. "But he's very critical."

Then Father Smart and Evelyn walked up to us. Father Smart put his arms around Beth and me and I said, "Evelyn, thanks for calling father. I don't know what we'd do without him." Then I told them about Wrightsie's condition.

Next, Evelyn asked, "Would you like Beth to come home with me?"

Beth looked up at me and said, "I'd kinda like to, mom."

"That will really help," I said. "I know I'll be staying overnight with Wrightsie and daddy can pick you up when he goes home."

I hugged them all goodbye, then hurried back to the cubicle. Dr. Welch was still keeping a watchful eye on Wrightsie.

While the doctor maintained his vigil, Wright and I discussed plans in low voices off to one side of the cubicle. "Nan, when Wrightsie's better, I think we should transfer him to Dallas."

"But, Wright," I said. "I don't think Dr. Welch will be able to see him up there."

"I know, but he's been there before, and we know what kind of care he'll receive," Wright said.

"I'm not sure, Wright," I replied. "I don't want to lose Dr. Welch. Let's see what happens."

Wrightsie had been in the emergency room for about three hours when Dr. Welch said, "I'm making arrangements to admit him to the pediatrics ward."

"You don't think he should be in the intensive care unit?" I asked.

"No. He's stable now," Dr. Welch explained. "I'm going to put him in a private room directly across from the nurses' station and I want private duty nurses for him. And you'll be with him, won't you?"

"Yes," I answered.

"Well, if I put him in ICU you wouldn't be able to see much of him," the doctor reminded me.

As Wrightsie was being wheeled towards the pediatric ward, I turned to Wright and asked, "Do you think this is all right?"

"Oh, yes," he said with a positive note. "I think Wrightsie will have the finest intensive care in the world—his mother. You!"

Then Wright put his arm around my waist and said, "Nan, I've never been so proud of you in my life as when I saw you giving mouth-to-mouth resuscitation to our son."

"Wright," I protested, "I don't even remember what I did." Then I added seriously, "It was really the Lord. I mean it."

When Wrightsie was settled in the room, Dr. Welch wrote his orders for the nurses, then he said, "I'll see you in the morning."

Next, Wright left for home to get my pajamas, robe and cosmetics. As soon as he came back to the hospital, I suggested, "Why don't you go home now."

"I guess you're right. I'll pick up Beth at the Foxes'. Let's see," he said, looking at his watch, "it's almost ten o'clock; I'm sure I can't call back here into the room this late. Why don't you call me at home around ten-thirty?"

"Okay," I answered. "Love you."

When I called, I talked with both Wright and Beth then I settled in for the night—rather, I tried to. It was a nightmare.

Even though a private duty nurse was in the room I was up

and down, out of the chair bed, all night long. Whenever she took his blood pressure and pulse, or suctioned out his mouth, I was right there watching her every move. Then, when I tried to sleep, I found myself listening to Wrightsie's breathing, waiting for each and every breath. And after one breath I'd pray for the next one. I was thankful when the first ray of sunshine hit the window; the long night was over.

Wright walked in about 7:00 A.M. when the second private duty nurse arrived on the scene. Then Dr. Welch arrived. He checked Wrightsie's chart at the nurses' station, then examined him. When he'd finished, Wright said in an apologetic voice, "Doctor, we've always planned that if anything like this happened we'd take Wrightsie to Dallas. I hope you—"

"Well, if you'd like," Dr. Welch said, anticipating Wright's next words, "I'll call and arrange a bed for him."

Wright was relieved that Dr. Welch wasn't offended, and he said a grateful, "Thank you."

Dr. Welch left the room to make the arrangements. I said, "Oh, Wright, I'm not sure we're doing the right thing."

"Don't worry," Wright answered.

It took a long time to make the arrangements and they weren't completed yet when Lorena Hamiton walked into the room. Just then Wrightsie took a turn for the worse. His whole body stiffened and his spine arched backwards so far I feared it would snap. Within seconds Dr. Welch, the head nurse and two floor nurses were standing over Wrightsie's bed. And I noticed Wright holding Wrightsie's feet in his hands while he silently prayed.

Then Wright said in a loud voice, "—in Jesus Christ's name, do something!"

Dr. Welch ordered a hypodermic, a nurse hurried out of the room and moments later she returned with the hypo. Dr. Welch injected the medicine and within the minute Wrightsie's contorted, rigid body began to relax.

Next Dr. Welch said, "We'd better not move him for a few days. I'm going to cancel that room in Dallas."

Wright nodded and I thought to myself, "Thank you, Lord. I want Dr. Welch to take care of Wrightsie."

Later, Lorena, Wright and I were talking out in the hallway about Wrightsie's episode. "Wright, things really began to happen when you said, 'Doctor, in Jesus Christ's name, do something,'" Lorena commented.

Wright got an embarrassed look on his face and explained, "That's not what I said, Lorena. You see, I was praying silently yet I knew in my heart I should be praying out loud. You know, 'What would people think?' Then I thought to myself, 'Why you fool! Your son may be dying and you can't even bring yourself to pray out loud!' That's when I spoke up and prayed, 'Holy Father, in Jesus Christ's name, do something.' "

"Well, He did something all right," Lorena said.

"Yes, and I've had time to think things over," I said. "I think this all happened for the best; I like Dr. Welch so much I want to keep Wrightsie here in Arlington."

"You're right," Wright agreed.

"And that reminds me," I said, "I should call the neurologist in Dallas and tell him what's happened.

"I've got to make another call too. Wright, remember a long time ago—before Wrightsie was sick, he said, 'When I die, I want to leave my eyes so someone can see again'?"

"Yes," Wright answered. "Now that you mention it, I do."

"Well, I'm going to find out what we have to do—just in case."

"All right. Lorena and I will sit with Wrightsie while you call," Wright said.

After completing my call to the neurologist in Dallas, I placed four or five more calls trying to find out what paperwork and procedures were needed to provide for Wrightsie's cornea in case the situation arose. I was unsuccessful and returned to the room very frustrated.

Lorena sensed the urgency and my frustration and said, "Nan, I'll get the information for you and any paperwork you need."

"Would you, Lorena?" I said with a sense of relief. "I sure need you."

We hugged each other, then leaving the room, Lorena said, "I'll see you later."

Then Wright asked, "What did the neurologist say?"

"He'll be out as soon as he can get here," I answered. "He sounded upset on the phone, but I think he expected something like this to happen."

I checked Wrightsie and talked with the nurse a few minutes, then I decided to see how Lorena was doing with her phone calls. I stepped out to the nurses' station and that's when I saw Father Ted Nelson walking up the hall towards me. I thought, "He's not his usual vibrant self." His head was lowered and he walked as if his feet were encased in two heavy pots of clay. Without speaking, he gave me a quick hug and then walked into the room. For many minutes he stood over the bed and just stared down at Wrightsie.

Finally he spoke, saying a quiet, yet determined, prayer for Wrightsie. I couldn't miss the heartbreak in his voice.

After his prayer we all stepped into the hall. "I don't understand—I can't explain this—even to myself," he said in a sad, halting voice.

Then, as if to suggest a partial answer for all of us, he said, "But I do know one thing; for a long time I've felt Wrightsie was different—not really one of us. The Lord has a special purpose for him and I don't know how it will end. But I'm not going to give up his healing—I still claim it in the name of the Lord."

Then I heard Father Smart's gentle voice behind me as he said, "Hello, Nan, Wright."

"Hello, Ted," he said to his fellow priest and friend.

"Hello, Dennis," Father Ted answered.

Father Smart hugged me, shook hands with Wright and Father Ted, then we walked into the room.

"Thank you, Lord," I thought as the two officers of the Christian army walked up to the little warrior's bed, one on each side. "I need both of them."

The two priests looked down at Wrightsie for a few minutes then Father Smart said a gentle, humble prayer.

After the prayer Father Ted turned and stared out the window and Father Smart said to Wright and me, with deep concern, "How are you both doing?"

"All right, I guess," Wright answered, looking at me.

"Oh, father," I said, "I want to thank you for looking after Beth yesterday in the emergency room."

"She's a brave girl," he answered.

While we talked on, I couldn't help but notice Father Ted staring out the window. The expression on his face changed constantly. First he'd have a determined, searching look, then his face brightened a bit as if he'd found an answer or solution to a problem. That look was followed by doubt, then rejection and the searching look reappeared.

The two priests were still with us when the neurologist walked in. He hurried over to Wrightsie and examined him. Pain and heartbreak were written all over his face.

After his examination we all walked into the empty room adjoining Wrightsie's. He took my hand and said, "Sorry it took me so long to get here."

I introduced him to the two priests. Then, trying to use a clinical tone of voice, he talked of the possible treatments the doctors could use for a patient in Wrightsie's condition. But, by the tone in his voice, we all knew what he thought the final outcome would be.

It was obvious by the look on Father Ted's face that he was not about to accept that final outcome.

Then the neurologist said a warm goodbye to me. He had come to us as a good friend, as well as a physician, and I knew it hadn't been an easy task. My heart went out to him.

Soon after his departure, Father Smart and Father Ted said their goodbyes. Lorena walked up to us and said, "I reached the eye bank. The forms will be here shortly. I've got to run now. See you tonight."

Wright and I returned to the room, checked Wrightsie, then Wright said, "Well, I guess we'd better call our families."

"Yes," I agreed.

"Nan, I know they'll all want to come down here," Wright said, "but I don't think they should. It won't be easy for any of them. I'm going to ask my family to stand by at home and pray for us. What do you think?"

"You're right," I said. "I'll do the same."

We took turns calling from the phone in the empty room so Wrightsie wouldn't overhear our conversations. Our families all agreed to wait and pray.

Wrightsie remained stable for the next few days. Dr. Welch was pleased and Thursday afternoon he said, "If he keeps this up we can roll that oxygen tent back and out of the way."

Later Wright left the hospital to pick up Beth and bring her back to visit Wrightsie. I was expecting them to return any minute when the private duty nurse started to suction Wrightsie's throat and mouth.

Suddenly she exclaimed with alarm, "He's not breathing right!"

"I'll get the head nurse!" I said, running for the nurses' station.

The head nurse called inhalation therapy and within seconds, two technicians ran into the room. One flooded the tent with oxygen while the other gave Wrightsie an external heart massage as the nurses worked over him.

I stood at the foot of the bed and tears rolled down my cheeks as I thought, "He's going to die before Wright and Beth get here!"

"Why don't they get here!" I said to myself, running to the hall.

Wright and Beth had just entered the hall. He saw my distress and started running, holding on to Beth's hand.

"Mom!" Beth cried. "What's the matter?"

"Wrightsie's having trouble breathing!"

Then one of Dr. Welch's associates hurried past us into the room. Within what seemed hours, but was only a matter of minutes, Wrightsie's breathing was normal and the crisis was over. But Wright, Beth and I were emotionally drained.

Then from the doorway I heard a cheery, "Hello, Brunsons." It was Lee Ann Nelson and close behind her was Father Ted.

"Oh, Father Ted," I said, putting my arms around him.

"What's the matter? What happened?" he asked.

I explained the situation, then he asked, "What time did this all take place?"

"Around 7:00 P.M., I think," I answered.

He looked at Lee Ann, then back to me and said, "We were driving over here at that time and I felt a strong urge to pray. Lee Ann and I prayed together."

"Your prayers were answered," I said with thankful conviction.

"Let's say a prayer of thanks right now," Father Ted insisted.

We all held hands in a circle, including Beth, and thanked the Lord for sparing Wrightsie.

Later, I was talking with Father Ted in the hall and I said, "A few weeks ago when my family was here, there was a beautiful sunset and we all held hands on the patio and prayed for Wrightsie. And as we prayed, I felt the Lord was going to take Wrightsie that night. Later that same night I layed hands on him and gave him up to the Lord and I actually felt the Holy Spirit in his bedroom. But tonight, I wasn't ready for the Lord to take him."

Father Ted gave me a serious, yet understanding, look and said, "Nan, there are many of us who are not willing to give your son up to the Lord."

Father Ted and Lee Ann strengthened me that night, but he looked downhearted himself.

"All we can do is keep him in our prayers," I whispered to Wright as Father Ted and Lee Ann walked down the hall.

Then Wright said, "Well, it's late. I'd better get Beth home."

"Let's say a prayer with Wrightsie," I said.

We gathered around his bed and the private duty nurse joined us as we said, "Now I lay me down to sleep. . . ."

After I hugged and kissed Beth goodnight, Wright said, "Call me later, okay? Night."

I went into the empty room next door and called home about forty-five minutes later. I talked with Beth a few minutes then Wright came on the line.

"Beth sounds tired," I said. "How's she taking all this?"

"She doesn't say much," Wright answered, "but I think she's doing okay. And I told her that Dr. Welch said he'd talk to her anytime she wanted to."

"I wish I had more time with her," I said. "I wanted to shop with her for fall school clothes."

"She understands why you can't spend time with her, Nan. Don't worry about that. And why don't you two plan to go shopping this Saturday. I'll sit with my best buddy."

"All right," I said. "I think one of us should always be with him. Oh, Wright, I was so frightened tonight when he had his problem. I didn't think you would get to the hospital in time; it was horrible."

"Let's pray about that right now," Wright said over the phone.

"Holy Father, we ask you to heal Wrightsie by the power of your Holy Spirit. But if you're going to take him to heaven, please let Nancy and me be together at his bedside. In Jesus' precious name we pray. Amen."

"Amen," I said.

"Now, Nan, I've got to ask you something," Wright said. "It's not very pleasant, but I think we should discuss the subject."

"What is it?" I asked.

"How far do you think they'll go to keep Wrightsie alive? I mean if the Lord's going to take him, I don't want his life prolonged by any machines. Do you?"

"No," I answered. "I want them to give him nutrients and vitamins with his i.v.'s, oxygen if he needs it, external heart massage, even adrenaline directly into his heart if he needs it. But no machines or open heart massage. No heroics!"

"Nan," Wright said, "it may sound dumb at a time like this, but I love you. You're a brave woman, a brave mother."

"Oh, Wright, not really," I answered. "I love Wrightsie—maybe too much, and I don't want the Lord to take him. But I have to trust in Jesus. And I keep remembering that day in the parking lot when Wrightsie said, 'Mom, I love Jesus so much that if He calls me I'm going to go.' "

"I know," Wright answered. "I can't forget that either."

We were both silent for a few seconds, then Wright said over the phone, "Well, I'd better let you get some sleep. I'll see you in the morning. Love you."

"Love you," I answered. "Night, hon."

# 36
## He Looks Like An Angel

The next morning Wright walked into the hospital room about seven-thirty. "I saw Frank leaving the pediatric ward as I walked in," he said, referring to a member of the Arlington Wednesday night prayer group.

"Yes," I answered. "He's stopped by here every morning—on his way to work—ever since he heard Wrightsie was in the hospital."

And later that afternoon, more people from the Arlington prayer group visited Wrightsie and me. Then that evening I was pleasantly surprised when Little Kimmy Henderson's mother, Beverly, and her grandparents, Mr. and Mrs. Lane, walked into the room.

After we exchanged warm greetings, they walked over to the bed, and in silence they looked down at Wrightsie. Then his nurse came up to take Wrightsie's blood pressure and Beverly and the Lanes turned to talk with me.

"How's Kimmy?" I asked.

"She's all right," Beverly answered. "She's not walking yet but she's still trying." Then Mrs. Lane said, "And she's praying for Wrightsie too. But we decided not to tell her that he's in the hospital."

"You're right," I agreed. "She doesn't need to know."

Beverly and the Lanes were the last people to visit us that

evening. When they had left, I made up my chair bed and settled in for the night.

The next morning I received a call from Anne—the woman who'd received a healing, and had started to cry for the first time in her memory when she'd seen Wrightsie praising the Lord at the Resurrection.

"Nan!" she exclaimed in an excited voice, "I have to tell you what happened at the Resurrection last night. Father Ted told the prayer meeting about Wrightsie. I didn't know he'd let himself cry in public, but the tears streamed down his face.

"Then after he'd told the story," Anne continued, "a nurse stood up and said, 'That's why I'm here tonight—because of that boy and his family. I haven't been in a church in years, but when I saw that Brunson family in the hospital and they told me about the Resurrection, I had to get over here and see what was going on.'

"Nan, I mean it," Anne said, "Wrightsie may be in a coma, but he's still ministering for the Lord."

"Thanks, Anne," I answered, feeling a sense of thankfulness over the ways of the Lord. "Thank you for telling me."

Sunday morning Dr. Welch made his rounds and after he'd checked the chart and examined Wrightsie, he said, "I'm going to start him on tube feedings today. I'd like to get him off the i.v. If he remains stable you can take him home in say, ten days or so. It would be good for Beth and for you. And Wrightsie would sense the familiar surroundings.

Wright and I were thrilled with the doctor's plans.

A few minutes later a nurse walked in the room with a Levine tube. She carefully guided the tube into Wrightsie's nostril and down into his stomach. Then he had the first food in his stomach since he'd entered the hospital. The liquid food slowly and carefully poured down the tube containing all the nutrients and vitamins necessary to sustain him.

Wrightsie had no difficulty holding the food down. Dr.

Welch looked on and said, "Fine, fine. If he does all right through the day and night we can remove the i.v. tomorrow."

Sunday afternoon we had a host of visitors, including Father Smart who came to serve us Holy Communion. All the visitors participated. And then Father Smart ended the service saying, "The peace of God, which passeth all understanding, keep your hearts and minds in the knowledge and love of God, and of His Son Jesus Christ our Lord."

Then making the sign of the cross with his hand, father continued, "And the blessing of God Almighty, the Father, the Son, and the Holy Ghost, be amongst you, and remain with you always."

"Amen," everyone said in unison.

In the moment of reflective silence that followed the blessing, everybody heard Wrightsie take a deep breath and issue a long, satisfied, peaceful sigh.

Wrightsie's sigh thrilled Father Smart. And from then on Wrightsie's reaction was the same, every time Father Smart said the blessing.

The visitors began to say their goodbyes and soon only Father Smart remained. And, as he turned to leave, Wright and I followed him into the hall, leaving Beth and the nurse to look after Wrightsie.

"Father," Wright said, "Nan and I need to talk something over with you."

"Yes," Father Smart answered with his usual gentle patience.

"Well, Nan and I talked this over the other night," Wright said, "and we're in agreement. If the Lord wants Wrightsie in heaven, we don't want any heroics performed to keep him here—no open heart massage or machines. Is that all right with the church?"

Father Smart reached out and took my hand, then he took Wright's hand too, and said, "Wrightsie has lived his life in dignity." Then he squeezed my hand and continued, "And I've watched Nan protect that dignity here in the hospital, and if the Lord wants him, he should be allowed to die with dignity."

"Thank you, father," I said and hugged him. "Thank you."

He squeezed my hand again and said, "I love you both. See you in the morning."

After Father Smart left, Wright turned to me and said, "Well, it's been quite a day. I guess I never realized how many people were praying for Wrightsie and for us.

"And I can't get over how many people exclaimed over how much Wrightsie's hair has grown. Did you hear that one woman who said, 'Oh, look at his hair! He looks like an angel.' "

"Well, many people haven't seen him since he was at Saint Alban's back in June," I said. "And they knew one doctor said his hair wouldn't grow back for a year or so. So they are surprised."

"Well, for some reason it's a witness to them," Wright said.

Then I turned to go back in the room and Wright said, "Nan, I've got to ask you something before we go in the room. I think I should go back to work tomorrow."

"Oh, Wright," I said.

"I don't want to, Nan," he said, "but I've used up most of my leave time. I think we should save what's left. I might—well, you know—"

He stopped in mid-sentence but I knew what he meant. "I don't know, Wright. If anything happens I want you here," I said.

"And I want to be here, Nan," he said. "But we've prayed to God about that and I think we should trust in Him."

I knew in my heart that what Wright said was true. "All right," I agreed, "but I'll miss you."

"And I'm going to miss you and my best buddy," Wright said as we walked back into Wrightsie's room.

Beth, a book in her hand, was sitting by the bed as she

watched the nurse take her brother's blood pressure. She looked up and said, "I was reading Wrightsie a story."

I had to fight back a tear.

When the nurse finished checking Wrightsie's vital signs, Beth started reading again. Every once in a while, she'd stop reading and chat with Wrightsie in an easy manner, never phrasing her words such that they required an answer from Wrightsie. And her conversations were worded so there was ample opportunity for her to take his hand and say, "I love you, Wrightsie."

It was all a touching sight.

We had a quiet family evening in the room that Sunday night.

Wrightsie pretty much held his own during the next week. He did have a few periods of irregular breathing but nothing like the episode he'd had on the fourth day in the hospital.

Tuesday or Wednesday of that week, Father Ted rushed in the room unexpectedly, bringing a guest with him. "Nan," he said, in a hurried voice, "I think you remember Anne White; she prayed for you and your family last February in Fort Worth at a healing seminar."

"Yes!" I exclaimed. "I remember."

"Hello again, Nancy," Mrs. White said, taking my hand.

"It's good to see you again, Mrs. White," I said. "I never did get a chance to thank you way back then in Fort Worth."

"Oh, please," she answered, a little embarrassed by my appreciation. "I only hope the Lord has blessed you because of our prayers."

"He did," I assured her. "I couldn't have gotten this far if He hadn't answered those prayers.

"And I've read your book, *Healing Adventure*, since then, Mrs. White, and I've shared it with some friends."

"Nancy," she said seriously, "I've learned a different way to approach these things since I wrote that book. And I'd like to pray for Wrightsie. Would you mind?"

"Oh, no. Please," I said, and I felt a surge of hope.

She walked over to the bed and Father Ted joined her. Then in a firm, positive voice and, in the name of Jesus Christ, she commanded the tumor to leave Wrightsie's body.

Next she prayed, asking for the healing power of the Holy Spirit to restore Wrightsie to perfect health.

My heart went out to Mrs. White as she said her dynamic prayer over Wrightsie. "Oh, Lord, you've sent another one of your people to us," I thought. "Thank you."

I wanted to talk more with Mrs. White after the prayer but Father Ted started to rush her out of the room saying, "I've got to get Anne to her plane."

"Father Ted!" I said, stopping him. "There's a woman here in the hospital that Wrightsie prayed for at the Resurrection one night to receive the baptism in the Holy Spirit. She did and I wonder if you and Mrs. White would go up to her room on the second floor and pray for her?"

"I think we have a few minutes to spare," Father Ted answered, looking at his watch.

I gave Father Ted her room number. Then he and Anne White hurried down the corridor to the elevators.

"Bye," I called after them. "Thanks for coming. Thanks for your prayers."

Anne White turned, smiled and waved a goodbye.

Later that evening I called my friend on the phone and we chatted about Anne White. Then I said, "Say, I've got a book here in the room that she wrote. It's called *Healing Adventure*. Would you like to read it?"

"Yes, please," came the enthusiastic answer.

"Okay," I said. "Wrightsie's had a good day; I can leave him for a few minutes. I'll bring it up to you."

I gave the number of the room to which I was going to the private duty nurse and said, "I'll be gone only a few minutes.

They're going to change Wrightsie's catheter tonight. Would you give me a call if I'm not back when they get here?"

When I found the room on the second floor, I realized I'd given the nurse the wrong number. I handed the book to my friend and explained my mistake. Then I said, "I've got to call Wrightsie's nurse."

When the nurse answered, I said, "I'm sorry I gave you the wrong room number."

"I was just going to call you," she answered. "They're here to change the catheter."

"I'll be right there. Have them wait!" I instructed. I hung up the phone and ran from the room, angry and frustrated with myself over my mistake.

When I rushed into the room, four technicians were standing over Wrightsie. Then I thought, "This looks like a training session and they're using my son as if he's nothing more than part of their equipment."

I looked at the technician who seemed to be in charge and heard myself angrily ask, "And who's the instructor that's—"

I was going to cry and broke off my question in frustration.

The technician in charge said, "Well, I'm going to change the catheter. I was just—"

I didn't hear any more of what he said—I didn't want to hear him. And I desperately did not want to cry. Then I caught sight of two unopened letters that had arrived in the afternoon mail—I hadn't had a chance to open them.

Then, in an effort to gain control of my emotions, I found myself opening the larger of the two envelopes. I pulled a card from the envelope and saw a large ink drawing of Jesus' head and shoulders. Over the drawing in big letters were printed the words: "This is the Now Jesus."

Next I opened the card and read, "He is with you now just like He has been yesterday, today and forever." The card was signed, "Love in Christ, Anne."

My frustrations were overwhelmed by Jesus. I thought with awe and wonderment in my heart, "Jesus used Wrightsie's praising the Lord at the Resurrection to cause Anne to cry, and now He's using her to keep me from crying! Thank you, Jesus."

Before I knew it, Wrightsie's catheter was changed, the technicians had left the room and my peace and calm had returned.

The next few days were more or less uneventful. But then on Sunday I talked with Kimmy Henderson's grandmother on the phone.

"Nancy," she said, "we're worried sick; Kim's started to vomit."

I was shocked but I tried to encourage Mrs. Lane, and I prayed with her before we ended the conversation.

The following Thursday—the last day of August—Mrs. Lane called again and said Kim was getting worse, but they still didn't have any plans to put her back in the hospital.

In contrast, Wrightsie's condition remained more or less stable. Dr. Welch did tell us Wrightsie appeared to be deeper in his coma, and that he probably couldn't hear us any longer. Nevertheless, we continued to talk with him, pray with him and read from the Bible. And he never failed to give the long comforting sigh whenever Father Smart said the blessing. And we also continued hoping and praying for his healing.

Then on the sixth of September, Dr. Welch said, "Well, I think you can take him home in a few days or so. His vital signs are stable, he's tolerating his food—in fact, his face has filled out some. I'm sure he's put on a little weight.

"Let's see how he does over the weekend. Then Monday we'll make a decision. But let's plan on him going home Tuesday."

When Dr. Welch left the room, I called Wright at work and told him the news. "Well, I don't know if I like it," he said.

"I'm worried too," I said. "But Dr. Welch thinks it best. He wants the private duty nurses around the clock and he's given me a list of equipment including emergency oxygen and a suction machine."

"Well, maybe it is the best," Wright said. "Really what difference does it make? Nan, I know the Lord's either going to heal him or take him. And it'll be great to have my best buddy home."

Wright began to convince me and by the time our conversation was ending we had become enthusiastic.

"Read off the list of hospital equipment we'll need at home," Wright said. "I'll start calling the supply outlets right now."

"Wright, I can do that," I said.

"No, no," he answered. "I want to do something."

After I read him the list, Wright asked, "Are you going to call Beth when she gets to the Foxes' after school and tell her the good news?"

"No," I answered. "Lorena Hamilton's going to pick her up at school and take her shopping."

"Oh," Wright answered. "Well, look, I'll stop at the hospital on my way home from work. Then you can call Beth. Okay? Then I'll talk to her and see what her reaction is."

"Fine," I agreed. "See you later. Bye."

About 5:00 P.M. Lorena surprised me when she dropped by. "I just dropped Beth off at the Foxes', and I thought I'd stop by and see you and Wrightsie on my way home," she explained.

"Oh, Lorena," I said, "Dr. Welch is going to let Wrightsie go home next Tuesday!"

"Nan!" she exclaimed. "That's wonderful! Oh, I'm so happy for you."

Then she walked over to Wrightsie's bed and said, "Wrightsie, I'm very happy for you and Beth that you're going home soon. I was shopping with Beth this afternoon. We looked in a pet shop and saw some awfully cute puppies. Now that you're going home, maybe you and Beth might like a little doggie."

She paused a moment, then said, "Wrightsie, if you can hear me and you think Beth and you should have a dog, stick your little tongue out."

Wrightsie's mouth opened slightly and, as Lorena and I watched, he slowly pushed his tongue out of his mouth. Then for good measure he did it again.

Moments later Wright walked into the room. "Oh, Wright," I said, disappointed for him. "Wrightsie just stuck out his tongue for Lorena. You just misssed it.

"Lorena, try it again," I said.

"Wrightsie," Lorena said, "Your dad's here. Can you stick out your tongue for him?"

Wrightsie didn't respond.

"I'm sorry, Wright," I said. "Oh, I wish you'd seen him."

"Nan," Wright said. "Don't be upset; that was for you and Lorena to see."

Then Wright said, "I've made all the arrangements for the hospital equipment to be delivered tomorrow. I thought it was better to have it over the weekend so we can check it out before Wrightsie comes home.

"And I've scheduled the ambulance to pick you up at the hospital Tuesday afternoon at one-thirty," Wright said.

The weekend couldn't pass fast enough for us. Then on Monday morning I eagerly waited for the verdict from Dr. Welch. He looked over and restudied the weekend's charts, examined Wrightsie, looked up and smiled saying, "You can take him home."

I called Wright at work and told him. Then he suggested, "Look, I'll sit with Wrightsie this afternoon and you can go home and check out the equipment."

"Okay, " I agreed.

Monday afternoon, after I'd checked everything, I was about to return to the hospital when I thought, "I'd better call and check on Kimmy."

I dialed the phone and Mrs. Lane, Kimmy's grandmother, answered. "I was going to call you; we admitted Kim to the hospital yesterday afternoon."

"Oh, no," I exclaimed. "And I was calling you to see how Kimmy was and to tell you we're bringing Wrightsie home tomorrow. I'm so sorry for Kimmy."

"Nan, she was so sick," Mrs. Lane said in a sad voice. "She couldn't swallow or even talk. She'd blink her eyes to answer yes to a question.

"I think she was happy to go back in the hospital," Mrs. Lane explained "When I told her about the arrangements and that she'd get better again she blinked her eyes a couple of times."

"Mrs. Lane," I said, "I'll tell Wright. I'm sure he'll want to see Kimmy. I'll try to get up in a couple of days after I have Wrightsie situated at home."

We talked a few minutes longer, then I hung up the phone and hurried back to the hospital. "Aw, who put the Snoopy sheets on Wrightsie's hospital bed at home?" I asked when I entered the room.

"I did," Wright smiled. "But it was Beth's idea."

Then I said, "I'm afraid I've got some bad news. Kimmy's back in the hospital."

Wright's face went blank for a moment. Then he asked in a fearful, low voice, "How bad?"

I shook my head from side to side.

"Well," he said, letting out a sad breath, "I'm going to take an early lunch tomorrow and go up and see her. Then I'll come here about twelve-thirty."

Later that night, as I lay on the chair bed for my last night in the hospital, I began to recall all the wonderful people the Lord had sent to minister to us over the past five weeks.

There had been a ward clerk from another floor who'd brought a different colored carnation each day she was on duty.

Each afternoon she'd say hello to Wrightsie and tell him the color of the flower for the day.

Next, I recalled how Commander Carl Wilgus had called many times from Virginia. He'd prayed with me—and encouraged me. How I'd needed those prayers.

Then I was reminded of the new prayers of praise I'd read about. "I wonder who gave me that book, *Power in Praise*, I thought to myself. The book had appeared in the hospital room at the first of our stay. I read the book and found that the author recommended praising the Lord in prayer, regardless of how difficult the situation might be.

After that, each night before I went to bed, I'd praised the Lord as I took my shower in the tiny shower off our room. At first, it had been nearly impossible to praise God for my situation, but I did. Then I'd cry, praise the Lord again and cry some more.

When I'd cried myself out, I'd finish my shower, get ready for bed and say a prayer with Wrightsie. I'd take his little hand in mine, lay my other hand on his forehead and say, "Now I lay me down to sleep. . . ." Then I'd kiss his cheek and whisper in his ear, "I'm sleeping here right next to you."

Still waiting for sleep to overtake me on that last night, I looked around the room in the dim light. Cut flowers and potted plants of every description were nestled in every available spot. I thought of little Mary Swor when I caught sight of a small boyish vase of assorted plants she'd given Wrightsie. Mary had never forgotten her little friend; she had visited him throughout his entire recovery period.

Then I smiled, recalling that the previous Sunday afternoon Hutch and his family, members of the Church of the Resurrection, had traveled from Dallas to see Wrightsie. He walked in the room carrying a large bouquet of flowers from the altar in one arm, and in the other arm, he held the largest Bible I'd ever seen.

"Oh, Lord, what wonderful people you've sent to us," I thought. So many people had visited us—most I knew, but some I didn't.

Margaret was one I hadn't known before. She apologized when she introduced herself saying, "I don't want to bother you, but I just had to see your son again. You see, the first night I attended the Church of the Resurrection I saw him lay hands on another little baldheaded boy and pray for his healing. I'll never forget that scene as long as I live."

"Nor will I," I thought.

I'd almost dropped off to sleep when the head nurse walked in the room for a moment, made a quick check and departed.

"How sweet the nurses have been," I thought. The hospital nurses along with the private duty nurses had fallen in love with Wrightsie. Without exception they'd given him the most gentle, compassionate care possible. And then there was the Navy doctor who'd looked after Wrightsie at the Naval Air Station. He'd visited a number of times.

"Thank you, Lord," I thought again.

Then I got up from my chair bed to check Wrightsie again. Dr. Welch was right; Wrightsie's cheeks had filled out. His chubby little cheeks were evident again. And he had a full head of hair. He was dressed in a long white hospital gown that covered him to his ankles and lying on a white sheepskin—to prevent bed sores.

"He does look like an angel," I thought, "an angel in heaven, floating on a white cloud."

Lying back down on my chair bed, I easily slipped into a deep, peaceful sleep.

# 37
## We've Got a Big God

I can't remember ever having slept so soundly. And when I woke up the next morning I felt stronger physically, emotionally and spiritually than I'd ever felt in my life.

I started out with my usual morning routine even though it was to be Wrightsie's last day in the hospital. First, I dressed quickly and had a fast cup of coffee with his private duty nurse. Then, I got my Bible from the bookshelf, put it on the bed, laid my hand on Wrightsie's forehead, turned to the Book of Ephesians, and read chapter six, verses eleven through eighteen. Having put on the whole armor of God, I once again claimed Wrightsie's healing and thanked the Lord for it.

Next, the nurse gave Wrightsie his bed bath. Then it was time for his breakfast. The nurse prepared the liquid food, we said grace, then she slowly poured the food into the tube.

After his breakfast, I started to pack my suitcase for our afternoon departure. I was in the midst of that chore when Wright called on the phone.

"Nan," he cried, "Kimmy's dead!"

"Oh, Wright! When? How'd you find out?"

"I called to tell Beverly I'd be up to see Kimmy later in the morning," Wright explained, trying unsuccessfully to hold back his tears. "Some stranger answered the phone in her room, so I called the admissions office. They told me. She died about 9:00 A.M.

"Poor Kimmy. I wanted to see her. I—loved her. I wanted to pray for her—and—" Wright broke down and sobbed.

"Wright, she's in heaven now," I whispered in the phone so Wrightsie wouldn't hear. I was amazed at my own strength and faith as I tried to comfort my husband.

"Her pain is over. She's healed. She's walking with Jesus. Oh, Wright, just think; she's finally walking!"

Wright was silent for a moment, then he said quietly, "You're right, Nan, she's in heaven."

"Let me pray, hon," I said. "Dear Jesus, we lift up Kimmy's soul to you. Take care of her and tell her how much we love her—how much Wright loves her.

"And we lift up Kimmy's family to you, Lord. Let your Holy Spirit comfort them and give them the peace that passes all understanding.

"Jesus, I ask you to comfort Wright and strengthen him. In your precious name I pray. Amen."

"Amen," Wright said.

"Thank you, Nan."

Then Wright said, "I'm going to call her family."

"Why don't you let me?" I suggested. And I explained the great strength I'd had ever since I'd awakened that morning.

"All right," he agreed. "I'll be up to the hospital at 12:30 P.M. as we planned."

"Fine," I answered. "You all right now?"

"Yes."

"I love you," I said, feeling a great sense of compassion for my husband. "Bye."

I talked with Beverly Henderson for a long time. Then she ended our conversation saying, "Thank you for calling, Nan. I'll let you know about the funeral arrangements."

"We love you, Beverly," I said. "You're in our prayers. God

bless you."

"Thank you, Nan. We love you too. Goodbye."

Wright walked into Wrightsie's room at twelve-thirty sharp. He took one look at Wrightsie, rushed over to the bed and said, "He doesn't look right!" And he started to suction Wrightsie's throat.

I couldn't believe it! I'd checked him only moments before and so had the private duty nurse.

She hurried over to help Wright, and I ran for the head nurse. Within seconds the room filled with nurses who all worked over Wrightsie. Then Dr. Welch rushed into the room.

Within a few minutes, Wrightsie—an oxygen mask strapped to his face—was breathing normally again. Dr. Welch stepped back from the bed, looked down and said, "I don't know, Wrightsie. Every time I try to get you out of this hospital, you do this.

"Wrightsie, I think you're trying to tell me something."

The only reply to the doctor's question was the quiet hiss of oxygen flowing into the mask on Wrightsie's face.

"Well, I'll have to keep you here awhile longer," Dr. Welch said in a resigned voice.

Next, he turned to me and said, "I'll cancel the ambulance."

We watched Wrightsie very closely and then I remembered Lorena Hamilton was going to meet us at the house.

"I've got to call Lorena," I said to Wright. "If she gets to the house and we're not there she'll worry herself sick."

I explained the situation to Lorena on the phone and she said, "I'm coming to the hospital."

"That's all right," I said. "Everything's normal now."

"No. I'm coming up," she insisted. "I've got to pray for you."

She arrived within minutes and we all prayed around Wrightsie's bed.

He began to have difficulty again about 2:45 P.M. as the three-to-eleven nursing shift was coming on duty.

For the second time the room filled with nurses and Dr. Welch ran into the room. As they worked over Wrightsie, I held the mask firmly to his face to insure no oxygen would escape.

His breathing became more labored and sporadic.

"He's going to die," I thought, surprised by my calm acceptance of the fact.

I looked at Wright. He was standing at the foot of the bed, holding our son's feet in his hands and praying in a low voice.

I looked back at Wrightsie. Then I said, "Our Father, who art in heaven, hallowed be thy name. . . ."

Wright, Lorena, Dr. Welch and the nurses joined me in the Lord's Prayer.

Then I took Wrightsie's hand in mine and said, "I love you. Beth and daddy love you. Jesus loves you."

The battle was over. Wrightsie had fought the good fight and I said, "Now I lay me down to sleep. . . ."

Wright joined me and we finished our family bedtime prayer.

Wrightsie's words, "Mom, I love Jesus so much that if He calls me I'm going to go," echoed in my ear.

Everything possible had been done. And around 3:00 P.M. on September 12, 1972, Jesus called my courageous little warrior to heaven.

I looked at Wright standing at the foot of the bed and we gave each other a sad, sad smile.

I noticed Dr. Welch standing beside Wright. Two large tears slowly rolled down his cheeks. "Wrightsie," he said, "now I know what you were trying to tell me; you were really going home."

Then Dr. Welch turned and left the room. The nurses followed him—except for Wrightsie's three-to-eleven private duty nurse. She walked over to the bedside table, picked up Wrightsie's little comb and tenderly combed his hair the way he always wore it.

"I just had to do that one more time for him," she said in a soft, tearful voice. Then she too left the room, closing the door behind her.

Wright turned to me and said in a quiet, serious voice, "Nan, I'm going to ask Jesus to give Wrightsie back to us. Jesus did it. It's happened before."

Wright and I walked to the head of the hospital bed—one of us on each side, and as Lorena looked on, we quietly, respectfully, reverently asked Jesus to restore Wrightsie to our keeping.

I suppose fifteen minutes had passed, when Father Ted Nelson walked in the room. Wright stopped praying and looked over at Father Ted. And I waited to see if he would join us in our prayer request. After a few moments I knew he would not.

"Nan," Wright said tearfully, "Jesus wants to keep our son."

Then he reached over the bed, I gave him my hand and we repeated the Lord's Prayer again.

Next, Father Ted said a prayer, then he, Lorena, Wright and I left the room and walked up to the nurses' station where Dr. Welch was standing.

Wright said, "Beth! Oh, I've got to call Beth. She'll be home from school now and wondering why Wrightsie isn't home."

"I'll get her," Lorena volunteered.

"Oh, don't let her know what's happened," I pleaded.

"Lorena, I'll just tell Beth you'll be picking her up," Wright said.

I stood by Wright while he called from the phone at the nurses' station.

"Beth," he said, trying desperately to control his voice, "Mrs. Hamilton is going to bring you to the hospital."

Wright paused, then he answered, "Oh, he's all right. It's just that Dr. Welch wants to wait a few more days.

"See you in a few minutes," Wright said, ending the conversation.

As he hung up the phone, he said, "I've got to call the eye bank."

Wright had a great deal of difficulty getting an outside line. Then the eye bank number was busy.

Then I had a thought and said to Wright, "Beth may want to see Wrightsie. What should we do?"

Dr. Welch overheard my question and said, "I don't think there's any need for Beth to see her brother. Does she know he wanted to donate his cornea?"

"Well, yes," I answered, wondering at the doctor's question. "In fact both Beth and Wrightsie had talked about donating their cornea if anything ever happened to them."

Then Dr. Welch explained, "If Beth should ask to see him you can just say, 'He's on a special mission.' Then if necessary, you can explain the cornea donation later."

"Thank you, doctor," I said, with a sense of relief.

Then Wright said, "Let's go out to the reception desk and meet Lorena and Beth before they walk into pediatrics.

Father Ted, Wright and I hurried down the corridor and left the pediatric ward just as Lorena and Beth rounded the corner into the crowded lobby.

Beth took one look at me and then she knew what had happened. She started to cry uncontrollably.

I looked at her stricken face and thought, "We've done so well accepting her brother's death, but how can we cope with her grief?"

We hurried towards Beth and Wright tried to hold her. All we could do was stand there and watch as she wailed over and over, "Wrightsie, Wrightsie, Wrightsie!"

How my heart broke for my daughter. "She's lost the dearest friend she's ever had," I said to myself. "We've moved over half the world and when they had no one else to turn to they clung to each other. She's loved her little brother, she's taught him, she's protected him, soothed his hurts, nursed him and prayed for him. And now she's lost him.

"Oh, God, help her," I prayed.

I looked around the lobby, hoping we could find some privacy. A sensitive hospital volunteer saw our dilemma and said, "There's a chapel downstairs when you can be alone. I'll take you."

She led us from the lobby, down a back stairway and into the chapel.

When we entered the chapel, Lorena whispered, "I'll go back to pediatrics; Father Smart should be here any minute. I'll tell him you're down here."

"Good," Father Ted agreed.

We let Beth cry and slowly she regained some composure. Then Wright asked, "Beth, do you want to say a prayer with us?"

"No!" she answered. "I hate God. He took Wrightsie."

With that she began to cry again. Then, after a few minutes, she looked up at me through tearful eyes and asked, "Mom, can I call Kathy Fox?"

"Oh, yes," I answered.

As Beth dialed the phone I explained to Father Ted, "Kathy lives next door, and she's really helped Beth during Wrightsie's coma."

Then Wright said, "Nan, we'd better go back upstairs."

Father Ted said, "Go ahead. I'll stay—she's going to be all right."

Beth was talking with Kathy Fox when we left the chapel.

We returned to the pediatric nurses' station and once again Wright tried to call the eye bank.

As I waited for Wright, I noticed the head nurse for the seven-to-three shift was still there. "It's late and you're still here?" I asked.

"Mrs. Brunson," she explained, "I just had to take the last walk with your son. I'm waiting to escort him down the hall."

"Thank you. Thank you," I said, as I recalled the meaningful tradition I'd first seen during my early nursing days.

Wright was finally successful in calling the eye bank and just as he hung up the phone Father Smart walked up. He hugged Wright and me, then asked, "Does Beth know yet?"

"Yes," I answered. "She's down in the chapel with Father Ted."

"Are you all right?" he asked Wright and me, searching our faces.

"Yes," I answered.

"Yes," Wright answered. "But maybe Father Ted could use some help; Beth hates God right now."

"Don't you?" Father Smart asked.

"No," Wright answered thoughtfully, as if he were searching his mind. "No, I can't."

"Well, don't worry about Beth," Father Smart said. "We've got a big God. He understands. He knows how Beth hurts."

Then Father Smart said, "I'll go down to the chapel."

"Why don't you and Wright go with him," Lorena suggested. "I'll take care of everything here."

"You're right," I answered. "Thank you, Lorena. I'll see you later."

When we walked into the chapel I could see Beth was doing well, considering the circumstances.

We lingered with the two priests for fifteen to twenty minutes. Then Wright said, "I think we should go home now."

After a warm, prayerful goodbye with the two priests, Wright, Beth and I drove home.

Evelyn Fox was right there to meet us. "Can I do anything, Nan?" she asked.

"Thank you, Evelyn," I answered. "I don't think so; we've got to call our families now."

"Why don't you let Beth come home with me?" she suggested. "Kathy's waiting for her."

"Please, mom," Beth said, "I want to talk with Kathy some more."

"Yes, Bethy," I answered. "You going to be all right?"

Beth nodded a sad yes and left with Evelyn.

Before we called our families I said, "Wright, I'm worried about my mother; I don't know if she'll be able to take this."

"I know," Wright answered. "Let's say a prayer for all our families right now before we call."

We held hands, said a short prayer for guidance and asked the Lord to protect our families from the shock.

First, we called my brother Tom on Long Island. He and his wife Hilda were stunned. Then Tom began to talk over plans with us. He ended the conversation saying, "After you're through talking with mom and dad, I'll call them, then get back to you."

"Thank you, Tom," I answered.

"I love you, Nan," he said.

"Take care of her, Wright. Bye."

Then I dialed Grandma and Feef in Danbury, Connecticut. They picked up the phones almost at the same time. "Mom, dad," I said simply, quietly, "Wrightsie's in heaven."

After a moment of silence they both chorused, "Oh, no," in surprisingly calm voices.

"We've almost expected this," Feef said. "Your mother's been upset all day; she had this dream—Marie, why don't you tell them your dream?"

In a quiet, reverent tone of voice mom said, "Nan, Wright, early this morning I had a dream—it was so real, I woke up when it was over. I was in your house, walking down the hallway towards Wrightsie's room. Only instead of coming from the den to his room, I was coming from the other direction—sort of through the closet—only there was no

308

closet. As I approached Wrightsie's room, I heard him singing in the most beautiful voice imaginable."

Mom's voice took on a thrill as she relived her dream. "Oh, I can't find the words to describe his singing. It was so beautiful—the only thing I can say is that it was golden.

"Then I thought, 'If he can sing like that he must be healed. He must be perfect. Oh, I want to see him.'

"But when I got to his door, it was closed," mom said. "And I knew I couldn't go into his room. Then I heard another voice—just as beautiful—singing with Wrightsie. At first I thought it was you, Nan, but then I realized it was a young voice—a little girl's voice. Next I thought it was Beth, but it wasn't her either. Oh, how beautifully Wrightsie and the little girl sang together."

"Mom!" I exclaimed, as chills ran up my spine when I realized the meaning of my mother's dream. "Mom, that other voice had to be little Kimmy Henderson; she went to heaven six hours before Wrightsie.

"And that wasn't Wrightsie's bedroom; it was heaven. That's why you couldn't go in. They were singing in heaven. And you're right; he is perfect and so is Kimmy. They're healed. They're with Jesus!

"And I'm sure the Lord gave you the dream to prepare you because of your heart condition. Mom, what a wonderful loving God we have."

"Nan," mom said, "you're right. You're right. I know Wrightsie's in heaven."

Then Feef said, "We'll call Tom and try to get down to Texas as soon as possible—tomorrow."

"Feef, Nan and I have talked this over," Wright said. "We think it's a long way for you to travel to attend the funeral services. You see, the burial's not going to be here. We haven't made all the arrangements yet, but it will be in Arlington National Cemetery outside of Washington, D.C. We plan to fly up there right after the funeral service down here."

"But, Nan, Wright," mom said, "you'll need our help."

"Yes," Feef said. "We can take the trip."

"Well, why don't you call Tom and talk it over with him?" Wright suggested.

"We've already talked with Tom," I explained. "I was so worried about you, we called him first."

"And he's going to call you as soon as we hang up," Wright said.

"And we're going to call my family next," Wright continued. "I'm going to ask all of them to meet us in Washington."

"Well, we'll talk it over with Tom," Feef said.

"Nan, what about flowers?" mom asked.

"We're asking everyone not to send flowers, mom," I explained. "Instead, we'd like them to send a donation to the Franc B. Ingraham Fund at Boston's Children's Hospital Medical Center or to the Wright Abel Brunson the Third Cub Scout Memorial Fund here in Texas."

"Oh, Nan," mom said. "That's wonderful."

"Well, mom, you know our little guy would want it that way. The fund at Children's in Boston is used for brain tumor research in children. And we'll use the Cub Scout fund to buy uniforms and pay dues for boys whose parents can't otherwise afford it."

Then Feef asked, "How's Beth?"

"She's taking it pretty rough," Wright answered.

"She's over next door talking to Evelyn Fox's oldest daughter right now," I explained. "Kathy has really helped her."

We talked a few minutes longer. Mom and dad sounded like they were doing all right so we said our goodbyes.

"Take care of each other," I said. "As soon as we hang up, say a prayer together—for each other. And remember Wrightsie's in heaven."

"We will," they both answered.

"We love you. Bye." I said.

Next, we placed calls to Grandma Flossy, Wright's mother in upstate New York, and to my sister, Kathy, in San Francisco.

After we'd completed our calls, my brother Tom called back. "Mom and dad will meet us in Washington," he said. "So will Hilda and the kids. And I'll be down there as soon as I can get things squared away up here."

After saying goodbye to Tom I said to Wright, "I'm going to call Kimmy's grandmother and tell her what's happened."

Mrs. Lane answered the phone. "Oh, Nancy," she said, "you've called me to tell me Wrightsie's home."

"Yes, Mrs. Lane," I answered. "But not *here* at home. He's home with Kimmy and Jesus—about three o'clock this afternoon."

"Oh, Nancy—oh—" Then after a few moments of silence she said, "I can't believe it."

"Yes, they went home together," I said.

In a voice filled with awe and wonder, Mrs. Lane ended our conversation saying, "I can't believe He took them to heaven on the same day."

Soon after our calls were completed, Father Smart and his assistant, the young priest who'd fished with Wrightsie, arrived at the house. After a cup of coffee we began to talk about the funeral arrangements.

The poor young priest was broken-hearted. He'd served Communion to Wrightsie many times before Father Smart became rector of Saint Alban's. I knew he would miss his little fishing companion; it was written all over his face.

When we started to make our plans, Wright said, "Father Smart, I don't know quite how to say this but we'd like Wrightsie's funeral to be at Saint Alban's.

"Now, I know it's a great deal of work," Wright hurried on, "but—"

"Wait, wait," Father Smart said in a gentle voice. "Wright,

that's what the church is for."

Wright looked a little embarrassed and said, "Oh, I didn't know. I thought it would take too much time—I—well, too much time from your work."

"Wright, Nan," Father Smart said seriously, "this is my work. This is why I joined the priesthood. This is the body of Christ helping each other, comforting each other, loving each other.

"Yes, we'll have Wrightsie's funeral in the church."

"Thank you, father. Thank you," Wright said.

Then the telephone rang and Wright answered it, "Oh, hello, Marge. Yes, he's here. Just a minute."

Wright covered up the phone with his hand and said, "Father Smart, it's Marge O'Halloran. They've called a prayer meeting at their house tonight. She sounds pretty low. I think they need you over there."

"I'll talk with her," Father Smart said, getting up from the kitchen table.

While he talked with Marge, Wright and I spoke with the young priest.

Then Father Smart said, "One of us will be over in a few minutes. Goodbye."

"You're right," he said, hanging up the phone. "They are having a tough time. One of us should go over there," he said to the young priest.

"Oh, father, maybe they need both of you," I suggested. "We're fine and it sounds like they really need your help."

"I think Nan's right," Wright said. "I've never heard Marge so low as when she called.

"Well, all right," Father Smart answered. "But let's say a prayer together."

Just then Beth came home from the Foxes'. Both priests gave her a warm greeting; we talked a few minutes longer and Father Smart led us in prayer.

We saw them to the door and Father Smart said, "Remember, we'll meet at the funeral home at 2:00 P.M. tomorrow to finish the arrangements."

"We'll be there," I said.

"Please tell all the people at the O'Hallorans' that we're fine, that we love them and we can feel their prayers."

"I will. God bless you," Father Smart answered. "Good night."

Then Wright, Beth and I faced the long loneliness of the first night without Wrightsie. The worldly realization of our great loss began to slowly creep into our hearts and souls.

When we were ready for bed, I made a last check of the house, then suggested, "Let's say prayers in Beth's room."

"I don't want to say prayers," Beth answered in an angry voice. Then she started to cry.

I looked at Wright with a hopeless, questioning look.

"We'll let the prayers go for tonight," Wright answered. "But can we tuck you into bed?"

Beth nodded through her tears.

After a long goodnight in her room, we tucked her into bed and retired to our room.

Wright and I turned out our bedside lights, lay back in the dark and talked with each other. We talked and talked—and talked some more.

I suppose an hour passed, then Wright got up, turned his bedside light on and said, "I'm going to check on Beth."

He stayed with her a few minutes and I heard them talking but couldn't make out what was said.

When Wright returned, I asked, "How is she?"

"She can't sleep so I asked her to pray with me," Wright said. "But she wouldn't. She's still angry with God.

"Then I told her the same thing Father Smart said this afternoon," Wright explained. "I said, 'That's all right, Beth. We've got a big God. He understands how you feel.'"

# 38
## Grieve Not for Wrightsie

I don't think Wright, Beth or I slept much that Tuesday night. I couldn't turn my mind off. Wakeful thoughts merged with dreams and vice versa until I couldn't tell which were which.

And about daybreak Wednesday morning—in thought or dream—Mary Lou Muery came to my mind. Then I said to myself, "She'd know how I feel; she's lost her son, Johnny Ben."

Then I heard a knock on the den door. I opened the drapes and there stood Evelyn Fox holding a fresh pot of coffee. I slid back the glass door and she said, "Nan, I'm going to put this in the kitchen and do what I can around here."

"Thank you," I said, following her into the kitchen.

She took a cup from the cupboard and filled it with coffee. "Here," she said gently. "Now you just go ahead with whatever you're doing."

"Hello, Wright," she said as he walked into the kitchen.

I took the coffee and turned to go back to the bedroom. And as I walked through the den my eye caught sight of two pastel portraits hanging on the wall: one of Beth, the other of Wrightsie. I turned my head away quickly and hurried to the bedroom. I just couldn't bear to look at his little face in the portrait. When I reached my room, I started to cry.

Then I heard the phone ring several times. The ringing

stopped and I knew Wright had taken the call on the kitchen phone. I remember thinking, "I'm glad he's taking the calls; I really don't feel like talking to anyone—except for Mary Lou Muery. She'd understand how I feel."

A few minutes later, the phone rang again. Then Wright called back to the bedroom, "Nan, Nan? It's for you."

"Nan," Wright said in a softened voice, "it's long distance from North Carolina; it's Mary Lou Muery."

I picked up the phone in the bedroom and said, "Oh, Mary Lou. I can't believe it's you. I've been thinking of you all morning."

"Nan, my daughter called me last night from Arlington and told me about Wrightsie."

Then we talked for a long, long time. As she poured out her love and understanding, I felt myself being comforted.

Towards the end of our conversation she said, "My husband and I were out driving yesterday afternoon and around four o'clock our time I said, 'Louis, I know something's happened to Wrightsie. I just feel it.'

"So, although I was shocked by my daughter's call last night," Mary Lou said, "I halfway expected it."

I knew the Lord had arranged everything. And He had used Mary Lou to dry my tears. There were to be many more of His divine and loving interventions to the extent it seemed He was almost apologizing for taking Wrightsie to heaven.

Shortly after I'd finished talking with Mary Lou, the Lord sent a second blessing to us. The doorbell rang and when I answered it, I was greatly surprised to see Joy Jeffrey standing at the door. Poor Joy, with all the problems, fears and heartache about her Air Force husband, still a prisoner of war in far off Hanoi, North Vietnam, yet she still had time to minister to us.

"For you," she said, handing me one of three beautiful yellow roses she held in her hand.

"Joy, thank you," I answered. And we hugged each other.

"You all right?" she asked.

"Yes," I replied. "I didn't get much sleep—none of us did. But we're all right."

"How's Beth?" she asked next.

"She's taking it pretty hard," I explained. "She's still in her room."

"Let me take these roses to her," Joy said.

"Joy, you're so thoughtful," I said. "Go ahead. I'll pour you a cup of coffee in the kitchen."

In a few minutes Joy walked in the kitchen with her arm around Beth and said, "If it's okay with you and Wright, I thought I'd take Beth off for the day—to Dallas."

I could tell by Beth's face she wanted to go. I looked at Wright, he nodded and I said, "Sure."

Beth was ready within minutes.

"Don't worry about us," Joy said as they went out the door. "We'll browse in the stores, look in the pet shops and I know a great place for lunch. We'll do anything that strikes our fancy. And anytime she wants to come home, I'll bring her."

Wright and I waved goodbye to them as they drove off.

Turning to Wright, I said, "I can't believe how the Lord works. First, Mary Lou's phone call and then Joy taking care of Beth—and look at this yellow rose."

Shortly after that, Lorena Hamilton arrived on the scene. She was followed by some ladies from the Women of Saint Alban's who immediately started working in the kitchen. Then the food started to arrive.

Later that morning, a thoughtful neighborhood wife and her mother lovingly washed and ironed Wrightsie's Cub Scout neckerchief and shirt; we were taking them to the funeral home that afternoon.

Then around noon, I heard a familiar voice say, "Hello, Nancy."

"Oh, Tom!" I exclaimed and ran to my brother.

He hugged me and said, "Hi, Nan."

"We didn't expect you so early," Wright said. "I thought you'd have to get your flight schedule rearranged."

"Well, a strange thing happened!" Tom explained. "I didn't have any more flights scheduled this month. You see, I was scheduled to start refresher training last Monday in Denver, but at the last minute the school was canceled. So here I am, and I'm free for the rest of the month."

"The Lord works in wonderful ways," I thought to myself.

I introduced Tom to our many friends and before I knew it he'd more or less taken charge.

The doorbell rang and Lorena answered it. I heard her say, "Oh, hello, Mr. and Mrs. Lane," followed by, "and you must be Beverly, Kimmy's mother. Come in; Nancy and Wright are in the den."

I hurried to the door to meet them, we hugged and Beverly said, "We've just come from the funeral home."

"I'm sorry," I said. "We're going down there this afternoon to make the arrangements."

We talked a few minutes about our two children in heaven. Then Beverly, her eyes moist with tears said, "Kim's funeral will be at 2:00 P.M. tomorrow."

I took her hand and said, "Wright and I will be there."

We hugged each other and shortly after that, Beverly and the Lanes said goodbye.

Tom walked up and said, "Nan, I want you and Wright to eat something. I already have it set up in the guest room."

We followed Tom into the small, cozy guest room, sat down on the hide-a-bed sofa and started to eat the lunch from wooden trays on the coffee table.

After we'd finished our lunch, Tom handed me a small picture frame and said, "Hilda made this for you."

Inside the frame two beautifully hand-drawn angels were

blowing their long slender trumpets in heaven. And underneath that scene, Hilda had written the prayer, "Now I Lay Me Down to Sleep," in her exquisite, precise longhand.

"She worked on it 'til late last night so I could bring it down here with me," Tom explained.

"It's beautiful—just beautiful," I said. Then I noticed several tear smudges on her labor of love.

We talked a few minutes longer in the guest room, then it was time for Wright and me to keep our appointment at the funeral home.

On the way, I said, "Wright, I'm going to dread picking out the casket."

"I know, hon," Wright sympathized. "But it should only take a minute or so."

We drove on in silence a few blocks, then Wright said, "I wish there were some way Father Ted could participate in the funeral service."

"So do I," I said. "But since we're members of Saint Alban's I guess that's not possible."

"No, I suppose not," Wright answered.

Father Smart and the young priest met us at the funeral home. Our funeral director was a neighbor from across the street. And when we entered the office he greeted us graciously, "Hello, Nancy—Wright."

"Hello, Don," I answered.

Then Wright introduced him to the two priests. And Don introduced us to an associate who would also help with the funeral.

First we discussed the date for the funeral. It was decided that it would be held on Friday at Saint Alban's Episcopal Church.

Then Wright said, "And the burial will be Monday at Arlington National Cemetery; I've already made the arrangements with the Army at the National Cemetery."

Once that was settled, we next discussed the order for the service at Saint Alban's. When Father Smart began to discuss the hymns, Wright asked, "Can we have, 'Amazing Grace' and 'How Great Thou Art'?"

Patiently, gently, the two priests explained the tradition in the Episcopal Church of singing the glorious and joyful great hymns of Easter at a Christian's funeral. The young priest named a number of appropriate hymns from which Wright and I chose, "Jesus Christ is Risen Today."

Then Wright said, "Father, the Navy—all the services—meant a great deal to Wrightsie. Could we have the hymn, 'Eternal Father Strong to Save'?"

"I'm sure that's all right," Father Smart answered.

After we'd decided on the service, I asked, "Father Smart, Wright and I have talked it over and we don't want the casket opened at any time—before or after the service. Is that all right?"

"Oh, yes," he answered.

"Wrightsie's no longer imprisoned in an earthly body. He's with the heavenly hosts. I agree with your decision."

"Thank you, father," I answered, relieved that we were doing the right thing.

Next, Father Smart said, "I would like to have a Requiem Mass Thursday night at six-thirty for Wrightsie."

Wright and I looked at each other in surprise. I turned to Father Smart and said, "We hadn't even thought about a Requiem Mass."

Then Wright said in an awed, yet embarrassed, voice, "Father, I thought funerals in the church and Requiem Masses were only for—well, you know—for important people—I mean, well-known people."

"Wright, Nan," father said seriously, "every Christian that goes to heaven is important, and well known to God."

Then Father Smart said, "I thought I'd ask Father Ted

319

Nelson to assist me at the funeral service on Friday."

Wright took my hand, and we looked at each other through joyful tears of gratitude.

"Thank you, father," Wright said. "You don't know how much we appreciate that."

Next Father Smart asked, "Have you a priest to officiate at the burial service in Arlington National Cemetery?"

"Well, we'd planned to ask Father Eby, rector of the Church of the Good Shepherd in Virginia. We attended his church when we lived in Fairfax," I explained. "But we haven't called him yet."

"If you like, I'll call him," Father Smart offered. "I'll tell him what we've arranged here and I'm sure he'll take care of things up there.

"Now, is there anything else I can do?" Father Smart asked. "Reservations in Washington, plane tickets?"

"Thank you, father," I answered, "but my brother, Tom, is taking care of that.

"Please give Father Eby our love and tell him we'll call him first thing Saturday morning from our hotel."

Once the arrangements were made, Father Smart and the young priest excused themselves and we continued our discussion with Don and his associate. "Would you like to pick out the casket?" he said as gently as possible.

I shuddered inwardly. And Wright said, "Yes, Don. Please."

We walked down a long corridor and Don opened the door. He and Wright walked in the display room first and I'd barely entered when Wright said, "Nan, I think that's the one." And he pointed to a simply designed, rich looking, dark oak casket, immediately to the left of the door.

I nodded and on the way back to Don's office, Wright said, "I'll get the things from the car."

When he returned to Don's office he set the things down on the desk. First, there was the cowboy sleeping bag-comforter.

On top of that was the blue Cub Scout uniform, yellow neckerchief and blue cap. All of this pile was topped by Snoopy. Next to the pile Wright placed the rough leather, cord-soled shoes that had traveled all the way to Boston's Children's Hospital and back again.

We completed our discussion with Don and his associate and left for home.

On the way, Wright said, "I couldn't believe it when Father Smart said he wanted Father Ted to help him."

I answered, "The Lord seems to be with us all the way. Oh, I dreaded walking into that display room, and then the casket was just inside the doorway.

"And what about the arrangements with the Army at Arlington National? How did that happen?"

"That was all the Lord too," Wright answered. "He gave me the strength. About a week or so ago—soon after Wrightsie had one of those breathing episodes, I called Don and ordered that oak casket. Then I called Arlington National Cemetery and found out what paperwork was needed for a burial there. I drafted the letter and the captain signed it. Then Tuesday, I called Wacil, the captain's secretary, she mailed the letter, called Arlington National and told them the letter was on the way and they set Monday as the date."

"You could have told me about it; I'd have understood," I said.

"No," Wright answered. "I didn't want to burden you. As Wrightsie would have said, 'It's a man's job.'

"But it was rough," Wright admitted. "You know, many people have said, 'You've got to have faith or your son won't be healed.' I don't agree with that, but it still bothered me when I thought about making the arrangements—just in case the Lord was going to take Wrightsie to heaven. But I prayed about it and realized I had to trust God. He gave me the strength," Wright said.

"I love you for what you did," I answered.

Tom met us at the door when we returned home. "Let's go into your bedroom," he suggested since there were many friends in the house. "I want to tell you the plans."

We sat down on the bed in the cool stillness of our room and Tom began, "I've made hotel reservations for everyone, including your family, Wright. And I've ordered the plane tickets for mom and dad, Kathy, Hilda and the kids. When you all leave Dallas for Washington Friday afternoon, I'll go home, then we'll all fly down to Washington Sunday afternoon and meet you at the hotel."

"Good," Wright said. "My family's planned to arrive in Washington on Sunday afternoon too."

"Oh, Tom," I said gratefully, "what would we do without you."

"That's what big brothers are for," Tom answered.

We then joined our friends in the den. When Beth returned home later that afternoon, I could see she'd had an enjoyable time with Joy Jeffrey and she was exhausted.

Our loving friends and neighbors slowly drifted away and we were all tired. I knew we would sleep that night and it was so comforting to have Tom with us.

That night, as Beth got ready for bed, my heart went out to her as she cried in the shower, "Wrightsie, Wrightsie, Wrightsie." But some of the hurt was gone from her voice.

Wright, Tom and I tucked her into bed but we made no mention of prayer.

After we left Beth's room we talked in the kitchen awhile, then Wright said, "I'm going to check Beth."

He returned in five or ten minutes. I asked, "Is she asleep?"

"Just about," he answered. "She said a prayer with me."

"Oh?" I asked.

"Well, when I first asked her," Wright said, "she answered, 'I'm not going to pray to that mean old God.'

"I answered, 'Okay, Beth, let's pray to Jesus. You know, He thought the Father had forsaken Him too. He knows how you feel.'

"So we prayed to Jesus," Wright said. "Then I asked Him to give her His priceless gift of sleep. Now I know one reason why we have the Trinity," Wright said.

Then I turned to Tom and said, "Wright and I were planning to go down to the funeral home tonight. Would you mind staying with Beth?"

"No, no," Tom replied. "Go right ahead."

When we arrived at the funeral home, I placed a bouquet I'd made up from the yellow rose Joy Jeffrey gave me, a red rose from a bouquet Wright's commanding officer's wife had given us and a periwinkle from a plant Wrightsie had given Beth. When we walked up to the closed casket, I noticed two flower arrangements—one at the head of the casket, the other at the foot.

"I wonder who sent the flowers?" I said in a low voice.

Wright handed me the cards from the arrangements and I said, "How thoughtful. One's from Denise, Father Smart's daughter, and the second's from Mary Bingaman and her family."

Wright and I placed our little bouquet on the casket and said a prayer together. We then left for home.

We all slept soundly Wednesday night.

The next morning loving friends again filled our home. The Women of Saint Alban's worked in the kitchen. They kept the coffeepot full, stored the food away, and prepared our meals at the appropriate times.

Around noon Tom led us into our formal dining room, shut the doors and the women graciously served us lunch.

Near the end of our meal Tom said, "Beth and I have talked it over, and we'll stay here while you go to little Kimmy's funeral in Dallas."

Wright and I agreed and we arrived at the chapel about 1:45 P.M. Many people were already seated, so we sat towards the back and waited for the service to begin. Then Wright turned to me, and said with tears in his eyes, "Listen."

The organist was playing, "Amazing Grace." I squeezed Wright's hand, knowing the Lord had arranged it all.

A few minutes later Wright whispered, "Nan, look at the front of the casket. Do you see what I see?"

I strained my eyes. Silhouetted against the pink lining of the casket I saw a white muzzle topped by a little black nose.

"Wright, it's the Snoopy Wrightsie gave Kimmy!"

Wright and I held hands and had a nostalgic cry for ourselves.

The Lord had another touching accolade for us. At the end of the service the organist played, "How Great Thou Art." Tears streamed down Wright's face as he said, "Oh, Nan, the Lord knows what He's doing. I don't think I could have taken, 'Amazing Grace' and 'How Great Thou Art' at Wrightsie's service. So he had them played at Kimmy's."

If a funeral service can be beautiful—and for Christians it can be—Kim's was. Everything spoke of God's love for Kimmy and her sweet Christian femininity. The whites, soft reds, and gentle pinks of the flowers; the hymns; the minister's eulogy and the service were the perfect earthly tribute to a faithful, loving girl who had said, ". . . if Jesus wants to use me this way, it's all right with me."

On the drive back to Arlington after the funeral service I said, "Wright, after the Requiem Mass tonight I think we should take Beth down to the funeral home. Since she's never been to a funeral before or seen a real casket it could be rough for her tomorrow unless she's prepared."

"You're right," he answered. "And it will help to have Tom along too."

The Requiem Mass was stirring that night. Before Holy

Communion, Father Smart stepped down from the altar, stood beside the pew where Tom, Wright, Beth and I were seated and said a few words about Wrightsie. He mentioned Wrightsie's Christian courage, Christian faithfulness and his Christian ministry.

He concluded the eulogy saying, "It is difficult to understand why the Lord takes a child to heaven, or why children are afflicted with such serious illnesses.

"But when we get to heaven we will be amazed by the number of souls who have been saved as a result of these situations. Yes, we will find the Lord used Wrightsie to save souls. Nothing could be more important."

Then since many people of different denominations were present at the Mass, Father Smart explained the meaning of the service.

"Tonight," he said, "we will honor the Lord's commandment to dine at His table. And when we partake of the Body and Blood of our Lord and Savior Jesus Christ, all the saints in heaven will join us in the celebration."

Then Father Smart looked down at us, and said, "Wrightsie will be dining with us tonight at the altar rail of the Lord."

Next, turning to the congregation he issued the invitation saying, "Anyone here tonight who calls Jesus 'Lord' is invited to His table."

The Holy Communion that night was the most meaningful one in my life.

After the service, Tom drove Wright, Beth and me to the funeral home. When we entered the foyer, I said, "Beth, would you go in and say a prayer with us?"

Beth stopped, looked up at me, then to Wright and said, "Oh, I can't. I can't."

Wright put his hand on her back and tried to coax her along saying, "Bethy, it'll only take a minute."

But Beth wouldn't budge.

"Beth," I said, "the funeral's tomorrow and it would be easier for you if you prayed with us tonight."

"Oh, mom," Beth cried, "I can't."

Then Tom put his arm around Beth and said, "I haven't been in yet either, Beth. Maybe we could go in together and help each other."

Wright and I walked off a few feet as Beth and her Uncle Tom spoke in whispers.

Soon, with Tom supporting her, Beth walked into the room. Wright and I followed as we slowly walked up to the closed casket. We said a short prayer together, then left the room.

As we were about to leave, the associate who'd assisted our neighbor with the arrangements walked up and said, "You're welcome to come here any time at all. We do close at midnight, but if you or your family should want to visit after that just give a call—someone's always here."

"Thank you," I answered.

Beth had sat down in a chair across the foyer out of hearing range, and I asked Tom, "Did you want to see Wrightsie?"

"Oh, no," Tom said gently. "I want to remember him as he was."

"Wright?" I questioned.

"No, Nan," Wright said.

Then he took my hand and said, "But if you want to, go ahead. It's all right."

"I do, but I don't," I answered. "I'd love to tuck in the cowboy sleeping bag one more time—for the last time."

Then understanding the dilemma in my heart, the funeral home associate, with perfect tact and appropriateness for the moment, said, "Mrs. Brunson, he doesn't look like he's ever been sick. He's a handsome young Cub Scout in his uniform, with his cap on."

"Thank you," I answered. "But I think I won't. Thank you anyway."

Tom and Beth were in the car when Wright and I walked slowly out of the funeral home.

"Wright," I said, "I would like to see him one more time. What should I do?"

With painful sympathy, Wright said, "Nan, I don't want to. It just doesn't seem right for me. But that's for me alone. You do whatever seems right for you."

I thought for a moment and said, "No, I won't. I'll remember him when I put on his armor of God Tuesday morning.

"But there is one thing," I continued as we reached the car. "Would you go back and ask them to take off his hat—Wrightsie was so proud of the hair he'd prayed for."

"Oh, yes," Wright answered softly.

"And one more thing, Wright," I said. "Oh, they'll think I've lost my mind; but I brought along a bottle of after shave lotion. I always put it on his chubby little cheeks before church. Would you ask them to put some on?"

"Nan," Wright answered. "That's perfect."

I handed him the after shave lotion and he hurried back into the funeral home.

When we arrived at home it was filled with many loving friends who'd attended the Requiem Mass. Mike and Marge O'Halloran who hosted the Arlington Wednesday prayer meeting were among the people.

However, they left earlier than most of our friends. But, after perhaps an hour, I was surprised when they hurried back in the door. Marge O'Halloran fairly ran up to us and said, "Nan, Wright, I've got to tell you what the Lord told me tonight when I was kneeling at the altar rail waiting for Communion."

But first she explained why she hadn't mentioned the event when she was at the house earlier in the evening. "Well," she said, "I didn't know if this word of knowledge was from the Lord or from Marge O'Halloran. But when Mike and I were getting ready for bed I asked, 'Mike, what's a lyre?'

" 'Well, I suppose you mean a type of small harp. Is that what you mean?' Mike asked.

" 'Come on," I said. 'We're going back to the Brunsons'. I didn't even know what a lyre was. That message had to come from the Lord.' "

Then Marge said, "Here's what the Lord told me: 'My children, grieve not for Wrightsie: for when the veil is lifted he will be there with a flute and lyre, to greet his loved ones and those he's ministered to.' "

# 39
## *Prayer Answered!*

By ten o'clock that Thursday night all our friends had left. Tom, Wright, Beth and I quickly prepared for bed and then slept soundly through the night.

Around nine o'clock the next morning the doorbell rang. It was Father Smart. "I just came by to see you for a minute," he said when I answered the door. "How are things going?"

"Fine," I answered. "Come in and have a cup of coffee with us. Please."

As we sat around the kitchen table Beth came in the room. She walked up to Father Smart and put a little tissue-wrapped gift in his hand. Father hugged her and Beth said, "Wrightsie would want you to have this."

Father Smart carefully opened the tissue paper and then held up a small red, white and blue lapel pin with the words "I CARE" imprinted on it.

"It's a prisoner-of-war pin," Beth explained. "Wrightsie always wore it on the lapel of his little blue blazer."

"Oh, thank you, Beth," Father Smart said, "I'm going to put it on right now."

Father Smart left our house a few minutes later, but not until he said a prayer asking the Lord to comfort and strengthen us during the funeral service.

About ten forty-five the doorbell rang again. Wright walked to the door saying, "It must be Don."

The funeral director said, "I've got the family car here."

When we walked out the door, I couldn't help but notice the car was not the traditional black vehicle that had always generated a sense of hopelessness and morbidity within me. Instead it was painted a rich subdued silver grey with a black vinyl roof.

"The Lord has provided for every detail," I thought as Wright helped Beth and me into the back seat.

Tom sat in front with Don and we started on our way to Saint Alban's Episcopal Church behind a motorcycle escort.

On the way Wright took Beth's hand and mine and prayed, "Jesus, we thank you for taking Wrightsie to heaven. Now please give us the strength during the funeral service we need to be a witness to your love and glory. Amen."

As we drove to the church, I smiled inwardly when I thought, "Oh, Wrightsie would be so impressed with the motorcycle escort."

When we drove up to Saint Alban's I noticed the hearse—in the same decor as the family car—had already arrived. Next I caught sight of the six bearers. Tears filled my eyes as I saw those loving men and recalled their devotion to Wrightsie. Then I dried my eyes and Wright helped me from the car and Tom helped Beth.

The six pallbearers carried the casket into the church. They so well represented the meaningful things in Wrightsie's life. There was Wingo Hamilton, who Wrightsie had prayed with when he received the baptism in the Holy Spirit.

Mike O'Halloran who with Marge hosted the Arlington prayer group. And Frank, a member of that prayer group, who'd visited Wrightsie each morning in the hospital.

Then there was Nick Fox, Evelyn's husband, who represented our loving neighbors. And Wrightsie's Cub Scout den mother's husband was also a bearer. And the sixth man was Wright's commanding officer, wearing his gleaming white Navy uniform.

Once in the church, two women of the Saint Alban's Altar Guild quickly and lovingly covered the casket with a beautiful pall. The design on the pall included a large cross. Once again I was reminded of eternal life in Christ.

Next, I heard Wright say, "There's Chuck."

Wright walked over to his cousin and said, "Please sit with us, Chuck."

Chuck shook his head sadly. I noticed his eyes were moist and red. Then I realized it would be too difficult for him to join us.

The funeral service became a triumphant Christian victory celebration. The head acolyte, Jerry, serving as the crucifer, led the way carrying the cross—he was escorted by two altar boys, torch bearers, each carrying a candle.

The pallbearers guided the casket down the aisle and they were followed by Father Smart, Father Ted Nelson and the young priest.

Tom, Wright, Beth and I followed the priests.

As the procession moved Father Smart's voice boomed as he said, "I am the resurrection and the life, saith the Lord: he that believeth in me, though he were dead, yet shall he live: and whosoever liveth and believeth in me, shall never die.

"I know that my redeemer liveth, and that He shall stand at the latter day upon the earth: and though this body be destroyed, yet shall I see God: whom I shall see for myself, and mine eyes shall behold, and not as a stranger.

"We brought nothing into this world, and it is certain we can carry nothing out. The Lord gave, and the Lord hath taken away; blessed be the name of the Lord."

From the moment Father Smart had said, "I am the resurrection and the life, saith the Lord," my spirit thrilled and

I felt as if I were marching to heaven.

"Oh, Wrightsie," I thought, "I hope the Lord is letting you see this victory."

The casket was brought to a halt in the front of the church between two rows of candles mounted on six stands and the sacrament continued. Father Ted Nelson was radiant and his voice was strong and confident as he read the twenty-third Psalm. The hymns were glorious and the words of Scripture were filled with hope and the blessed assurance of everlasting life in Jesus Christ.

When the service came to a close we again proceeded back up the aisle and Father Smart spoke the beautiful and comforting, "Lord, now lettest thou thy servant depart in peace, according to thy word. For mine eyes have seen thy salvation, which thou hast prepared before the face of all people; to be a light to lighten the Gentiles, and to be the glory of thy people Israel."

The crucifer preceded the pallbearers as they carried the casket to the hearse. He stood at rigid attention, cross held high, until the casket was lovingly placed inside the hearse. Then the door was closed and the hearse slowly disappeared from sight on its drive to Dallas and Love Field.

After the funeral service the priests and many friends came to the house to give us a word of comfort and to say goodbye. Finally it was time for us to leave for Love Field.

Cousin Chuck came to the airport to say goodbye. He and Tom—who was leaving for home on a later flight—stayed with us until we boarded our plane.

On the flight to Washington, D.C., Wright, Beth and I read some of the mail we hadn't had time to open during the past three or four days. Then we talked over some of our plans for the future.

When we neared Washington's National Airport I began to feel a little down and I turned to Wright and said, "Please don't get me wrong, and I'm happy the Lord gave Marge O'Halloran a message that we should not grieve for Wrightsie, but I wish He'd give me something—I was Wrightsie's mother."

Wright took my hand and said, "Oh, Nan. I know how you must feel. He will give you something—I'm sure."

When we landed we were met by two couples we'd known earlier in Wright's Navy career. After Wright checked out a rental car, we drove to the home of one of the couples where we spent a few hours. Then we drove to our hotel and registered.

As Beth was taking her shower, I said with a heavy heart, "It hurts a little being back in Washington without Wrightsie. I hope I can get through these next few days."

"Why don't you read the Bible for a few minutes," Wright answered, handing me the Gideon Bible that was in the room. "Maybe you'll find something just for you."

With a great deal less than hope in my heart, I opened the Bible at random. My eyes fell on the middle of a page in the Book of Psalms, and I read: "O give thanks unto the Lord; for he is good: because his mercy endureth forever" (Ps. 118:1).

I read the next three verses of Psalm 118 and each verse ended with: "his mercy endureth forever."

Suddenly, the significance of Psalm 118 came to me.

"Wright! Wright!" I exclaimed in a loud voice.

He dropped the book he was reading, and said, "What is it! What's the matter!"

"Remember the night I received the baptism in the Holy Spirit and the next day I told you how as I prayed in my new prayer language the Lord put a thought in my mind?"

"Yes, Yes!" Wright answered. "He told you, 'His mercy endureth forever.'"

"Exactly! Oh, Wright, the Lord is speaking to me! Listen." And I reread Psalm 118, verse one, 'O give thanks unto the Lord for he is good: because his mercy endureth forever.'

"And the next three verses end the same way: 'his mercy

endureth forever.'

"Listen to this! Oh, Wright, here's another answer!" I exclaimed again. "Remember when I saw Dr. Shaw the first time in Boston and I said, 'You've just got to be the answer to my prayers.'?"

Wright nodded.

"Here's the Lord's answer," I said. "Verses eight and nine read: 'It is better to trust in the Lord than to put confidence in man'; and: 'It is better to trust in the Lord than to put confidence in princes.'

"And listen to the last verse—here it is again: 'O give thanks unto the Lord; for he is good: for his mercy endureth forever.'

"Oh, Wright, I almost feel guilty for complaining when we flew up here that the Lord hadn't given me anything."

"Don't feel guilty," Wright advised. "I think the Lord can look at a complaint as a prayer."

"Oh, what a blessing. What a blessing," I said.

And in the following days the Lord continued to shower us with his love and assurance. Everywhere we turned there seemed to be a reminder that Wrightsie was in heaven. The next afternoon we were eating lunch in a downtown Washington, D.C. restaurant and when I glanced at the menu cover I saw two cherubs.

"Look, Wright, Beth," I said. "Do you suppose they represent Wrightsie and Kimmy in heaven?"

"Yes," they joyously agreed.

After lunch we drove to our old neighborhood in Fairfax, Virginia, to visit with friends. We talked the longest with a couple who lived just down the street from our old house on Glennrose Street. Their son, Scott, had been one of Wrightsie's closest friends.

When we drove away from their house that afternoon, Beth said, "Mom, dad, remember how Wrightsie and Scott used to call each other 'best buddy'?"

"Yes," Wright answered. "I'd forgotten that. I guess it was after we'd left Virginia for Texas that Wrightsie started calling me best buddy."

Then I asked, "Wright, do we have time to see Wrightsie's school?"

"Sure," Wright answered and turned right onto Braddock Road.

We wound our way through the Virginia countryside and pulled into the driveway of Fairfax Christian School. "Let's get out and walk," Wright suggested.

Our stroll finally took us up a little hill in back of the school. Wright looked over the empty campus, tree-shaded in the late Saturday afternoon sun, and said, "How wonderful it is to think it is probably right here that Wrightsie first learned to love Jesus."

Then Wright smiled and I said, "And maybe he learned to like mathematics here too."

"Nan, do you think the Lord has forgiven me for the time I said, 'Wrightsie, I wish you'd spend more time on math and less time on the Bible,' that day he brought his first report card home?"

"I'm sure He has," I assured Wright with a smile.

Then, pointing down to the empty playground—off to our left—I said, "You know, I can almost see Wrightsie, dressed in his gray flannel short pants, knee socks and blue blazer—remember the blazer had the school emblem sewn on the breast pocket?—running for that swing set over there."

Wright nodded and I saw tears in his eyes.

"Oh, Wright," I apologized. "I didn't mean to—"

"I'm not crying with sorrow, Nan," Wright explained. "It's thankfulness; I'm thankful for you and the way you've taken care of Beth and Wrightsie—the way you dressed them, the places you took them while I worked, the things you did together.

"I love you," Wright said. "Wrightsie was a lucky little boy to have you for his mother."

"Oh, Wright," I answered.

Then Beth said, "Mom, do you remember when we moved from Virginia and I helped you pack Wrightsie's clothes?"

"Yes," I answered.

"Well, when we put his short pants and knee socks in the suitcase I remember saying, 'Oh, I wish Wrightsie would always be a little boy.'

"And now he always will be a little boy," Beth said.

Next she said, "You know the day Wrightsie was supposed to come home from the hospital, I was so disappointed he wasn't there when I came in from school. Then I thought, "He's probably had trouble breathing again." So I prayed, 'Lord, please heal Wrightsie. But if you're not going to, please take him to heaven.' "

Then she continued saying, "And, mom, dad, I've been thinking about what the Lord told Mrs. O'Halloran at Communion. Did you know Wrightsie always wanted to play a little flute?"

"No!" I exclaimed. "I didn't. When did he tell you that?"

"When we lived here in Virginia," Beth answered. "Lots of times."

We stood on the hill in silence for a few minutes longer, each of us recalling our favorite memories.

Then Wright ended the nostalgia saying, "We'd better head back to Washington."

That night after our evening prayers, I was in bed waiting for sleep to overtake me when I added a silent prayer: "Lord, I hope Wrightsie saw his victorious funeral service at Saint Alban's and please let him see his burial service next Monday. Amen."

Sunday morning we drove back to Fairfax and attended services at our old parish church, the Church of the Good

Shepherd. Father Eby had a warm greeting and he was surprised and pleased by the long, firm hug Beth gave him. We had coffee after church, then Father Eby invited us into his office to discuss Monday's burial service.

He explained the service he would use and agreed to modify the closing prayer to meet a special request I had. Then it was time to say goodbye.

"Thank you so much, father, for helping us," I said.

"Please, don't thank me," he replied. "I want to do everything I can to help you."

Then almost speaking to himself, he said a little sadly, "In all my years as a priest, this is the first child I've ever buried."

On our way back to Washington, we stopped to see the Navy couple that had moved from Arlington, Texas, to Fairfax a few months before. Wright and I had recommended they look for a house near our old neighborhood and they had found one.

Louise welcomed us at the door. "Come in. Come in," she said. "Oh, it's good to see you. I hope you can stay for brunch."

"Hi, Louise," I answered as we hugged each other. "Yes, we can stay for a while. Our families will be coming in around three o'clock or three thirty. We've plenty of time."

We talked during the delicious meal with Lousie, her husband and two children. And later over coffee we told them how the Lord was blessing and strengthening us. Louise and her family had kept us all in their prayers for many months and it helped them to know that the Lord was providing for us.

Then Louise said, "Nan, I've got to tell you about a dream I had. I suppose I had it only a week to ten days before Wrightsie died. It bothered me greatly, but now I see the Lord was trying to tell me something.

"I dreamed that Wrightsie and I were sitting in a big car—well, it was more a—well, a long car than just big. We were parked next to the curb on this road, and we were watching a funeral procession," Louise continued. "We watched in silence a few minutes, then I looked down at Wrightsie, sitting beside me, and said, 'I wonder whose funeral it is?' Wrightsie looked up at me and said one word, 'Mine.'"

"Oh, Louise!" I exclaimed, as tears came to my eyes. "That's an answer to my prayers! Last night I prayed hoping that the Lord had let Wrightsie watch his triumphant funeral service at Saint Alban's and that he'd see his burial service Monday.

"And the Lord gave you the answer. Oh, how wonderful!"

We talked awhile longer with Louise and her family, then it was time to head back for Washington.

When we returned to our hotel, we immediately joined our families. They'd checked in only moments before we arrived. Later we met in two suites—side by side—and talked until supper time.

That night, after bedtime prayers with Wright and Beth, I wrote the day's events in my diary. The final incident I recorded was Louise's dream. And the last entry in my diary for that date reads: "Prayer Answered!"

When we woke up Monday morning I pulled the drapes back to check the weather. "Oh, Wright," I said in a disappointed voice, "it's been raining. And from the looks of those dark gray clouds we're going to get more."

Wright took my hand, and said, "Let's pray."

Beth joined us as Wright pray d, "Dear Lord, you've been so good to us and we don't want to ask for too much. But would you take care of the weath     so it doesn't rain during Wrightsie's burial service? Ame    "

Next, I called a nearby florist shop and asked them to deliver a bouquet of three red long-stem roses and a small cluster of white daisies to be wrapped with a plain white ribbon and bow. "They're to be from us," I said to Wright as I hung up the phone.

About 10:00 A.M. we all met in the hotel lobby. I picked up the bouquet at the desk and Beth, Wright and I walked to the

Navy sedan parked at the curb. Wright squeezed my hand as he looked up to the sky and saw the first rays of sunshine breaking through the overcast sky.

Our families followed the Navy sedan as the driver made his way to the chapel at Arlington National Cemetery. At the chapel the Navy driver fell in behind the hearse and the procession wound its way through beautifully kept grounds.

For some reason I noticed the US ARMY printed on the license plate of the Army hearse. I mentioned it to Wright and Beth. Then, in the distance, I saw the six young Navy enlisted men who would serve as the pallbearers for the service. They were standing at attention under a sky that had turned blue within thirty minutes. Their fresh starched white dress uniforms gleamed in the bright sunlight.

When Wright saw the Navy men, he took my hand and said, "Nan, the services meant so much to Wrightsie, I wish there were someone here in a Marine uniform."

At first I wasn't sure why Wright had such a wish, then I realized why. All the services had been represented in the last year of Wrightsie's life. He'd flown in an Air Force hospital plane, the hearse ahead of us was an Army vehicle, and there—at that moment—stood the six Navy men. But there was no Marine in sight.

The hearse stopped and the Navy men, with perfect precision and great distinction, removed the casket from the hearse and carried it to the grave site.

Wright helped Beth and me from the sedan and held our hands as we walked to our places and sat down in chairs provided for the service.

Then Wright handed our bouquet to the funeral director who placed it on the casket. And when Wright returned to his chair, Father Eby began the Episcopal burial service. Then he ended that rite with my special request.

"We will close the service," he said, "with the Brunson

family's favorite bedtime prayer: Now I lay me down to sleep
. . . If I should die—" Father Eby's voice broke for a moment,
"—before I wake, I pray the Lord my soul to take. Amen."

How comforting it was to know that the Lord had taken
Wrightsie's soul and at that moment he was watching his own
burial service from heaven on high.

# 40
## Be Not Regretful

After the burial service, Wright helped Beth and me back into the Navy sedan. When he closed the door he started to walk around to the other side of the car. I turned my head and watched my mother and father and Wright's mother as they walked sadly towards the cars parked behind us. My heart went out to Wrightsie's grandparents.

A few moments passed and, about the time I turned my head back to see why Wright hadn't gotten in the car yet, he opened the door and said, "Nan! Did you see that?"

"No, hon. What?" I asked.

"That Marine!" Wright answered, his eyes glistening with tears.

"I did, daddy," Beth said. "I did."

"Nan, after I helped you and Beth in the car, I looked up the road—there, beyond the grave site," he said pointing, "and I saw this Marine private walking towards me. When he got beside the grave, he stopped, faced the casket and saluted. Then he came on towards me.

"He probably thinks I've lost my mind. I walked out to meet him," Wright continued, "we exchanged salutes, then I shook his hand and said, 'You don't know what you just did! Thank you! Thank you!' "

"Oh, Wright," I said, thrilled for my husband, "the Lord answered your prayer."

"I know! I know!" Wright exclaimed. "And it wasn't even a prayer—it was just a wish. I'd forgotten all about it 'til I saw him.

"I tell you," Wright said, "if ever I should doubt the existence of the living God, I'll remind myself of what happened here today. Thank you, Lord."

"Oh, daddy," Beth said, "maybe the Marine was really an angel."

"Maybe so," Wright answered thoughtfully. "Maybe you're right, Beth."

The Navy driver took us back to the chapel where Wright had made arrangements with the funeral director for coffee to be served in a reception area. We'd wanted our families to meet all our Navy friends, Virginia neighbors and Father Eby.

Commander Carl Wilgus, his wife Jean, and their three daughters were some of the first people to meet us.

"Carl," I said, taking his hand, "thank you for everything; for your prayers, your phone calls, your love. I praise the Lord for you, Carl."

"We love you, Nan," Carl replied. "You had hundreds of people praying up here for Wrightsie, and you, and Beth and Wright. You know, there's a prayer group that meets in the Pentagon; they were praying too."

Then a man in a civilian suit walked up and Carl introduced him as a major in the Marine Corps. "He was a member of that prayer group at the Pentagon," Carl said. "And he fasted many days for Wrightsie."

Wright and I tried to thank the major for his prayers but he wouldn't have it. He gave all the credit for everything to the Lord.

"What a Christian," Wright said in admiration when the major joined another group in the reception room.

Then Father Eby walked up to say farewell. "Will you be in the area long?" he asked.

"No, we're leaving this afternoon for my brother's home on Long Island," I explained. "We plan to spend a few days there, then stay the weekend with my folks in Connecticut. Then we're going to visit Wright's family in upstate New York and finally back to Texas."

"That's fine," he said. "Should give you a chance to pull things together."

Then he put his arm around Beth and said, "And I know Beth will help you. She's a lovely girl."

He looked down at Beth. "I'll remember that hug you gave me," he said with a warm smile.

"Father, I'll never be able to thank you enough for your help," I said. "I'll drop you a line when we get back to Texas."

"Goodbye," he said. "I'll keep you in my prayers. God bless you."

Then the Reverend Thoburn, headmaster of Fairfax Christian School, talked with Wright and me for a while. He thrilled us when he said, "I'd like to do something in memory of your son at the school. I was thinking of maybe a Bible memory contest for each grade, with awards to be presented to the winners at the end of the school year."

"That would be wonderful," I said.

"Well, let's get in touch with each other when you get back home. We can finalize the arrangements then."

"Good," Wright and I agreed.

The headmaster said goodbye. And after lingering awhile longer to talk with our close friends, we too left the chapel reception area and returned to the hotel.

We gathered together for a late lunch. We were a large group, with Wright's mother, three sisters and their husbands; and my mother, dad, sister and brother with his wife and their three children.

After lunch, Beth, Wright and I returned to our room and packed for the late afternoon shuttle flight to New York. When I'd finished packing my suitcase, I looked around the room to see if I'd forgotten anything. And once again my heart was warmed by the sight of flowers friends had had sent to our room. There were bouquets from the Wilgus family, Father Ted and Lee Ann Nelson, and Wingo and Lorena Hamilton.

"Wright, I'd like to take all these flowers over to the grave. Look at them—they're beautiful."

"Sure," Wright said, "we'll stop on our way to the airport."

We all checked out of the hotel together. Wright hugged Grandma Flossy and said, "We'll see you in a week or so. I'll call when we have a definite date."

Flossy nodded her head a little sadly.

"Oh, mom," Wright said, putting his arm around his mother's shoulders. "Remember Wrightsie's in heaven with the one grandfather he'd never met. Just think, mom—Wright Abel, Senior and Wright Abel the Third together in heaven—I guess they don't get confused over names up there."

Flossy with tear-filled eyes tried to give a little smile in answer to Wright's encouragement.

"I love you, mom," Wright said.

"Goodbye," Flossy answered. "Goodbye, Nan, Beth. Be careful."

When we left the parking lot my mother, father and sister Kathy rode with us while Tom, Hilda and their three children followed in their car as we drove back to Arlington National Cemetery.

Wright parked the car near the grave site and when we walked up to it, I noticed a little basket of flowers on the grave. "Look at the daisies and little wildflowers."

Wright reached down and handed me the card from the basket.

"Listen to this," I said as tears of gratitude filled my eyes.

"From your buddy, Scott."

Then Hilda walked up and showed me a bouquet of yellow brown-eyed Susans. "Nan," she said, "we spotted these along the highway in New York on our way to La Guardia for the flight down here. I thought maybe each one of us could put a wildflower on Wrightsie's grave."

"Oh, Hilda," I exclaimed. "You're so wonderful—I love you."

Then each one of us in turn placed a brown-eyed Susan on the grave and said a short, silent prayer.

Next, I looked around the cemetery and realized for the first time that the grave site was in a perfect setting. "Wright, how did you know where to tell them you wanted the grave?" I asked.

"I didn't," Wright answered. "I left that up to the Lord."

"It's just perfect," I said.

Wright pointed off in the distance towards Washington, D.C., and said, "You can see the top of the Washington Monument over the trees there."

I looked in the direction Wright was pointing, then I spotted an airplane and followed it as it made its approach to National Airport.

"Looks like an Air Force hospital plane," I commented.

"Same model," Wright answered. "But it's a civilian airliner."

Then Tom said, "I don't want to rush you, but we should get to the airport."

I took one more look at around the grave site and said to myself, "Thank you, Lord."

On the way to the airport Wright said, "It's going to rain again; look at that sky."

"The Lord gave us the weather we prayed for this morning. Remember?" I said.

"That's right," he answered as he recalled his prayer. "I'd

forgotten."

When we boarded the shuttle plane for New York, Wright said, "Nan, why don't you take the window seat? You may be able to see Arlington National right after we take off."

I sat down in my seat, buckled my seat belt and looked out the window. The first rain drops had begun to streak the glass. As we taxied out to the runway, a great sense of peace and joy came over me.

I turned to Wright and said, "I wouldn't mind if the Lord raptured us all to heaven right now."

"I know what you mean, Nan," he answered. "But I'm afraid he's got some more work for His Christians to do."

The pilot started his takeoff run and when the wheels left the runway Wright leaned over in front of me and peered out the window. "There it is," he said.

I looked down through the light rain and saw the beautifully sculptured landscape of Arlington National Cemetery.

"It's right there in the corner of the cemetery closest to us," Wright explained.

I recognized the area he was talking about. When it passed from view I took Wright's hand and said, "The Lord couldn't have found a more perfect spot."

"He's been good to us," Wright said.

We stayed at my brother's home in Huntington Bay on Long Island until the end of the week. Tom and Hilda took wonderful care of Wright and me. And Beth needed and enjoyed the companionship of her cousins—Susan, Tommy and David.

Late one afternoon Tom suggested we all take a walk along the north shore. Tom and Hilda stayed with the kids as they played at the water's edge while Wright and I walked up the beach.

The light fall breeze was cool but comfortable and the trees were beginning to change color from their summer green. We came to a small boat that had been pulled up on the sand and overturned. Wright and I leaned against the weather-beaten hull and talked.

I began, "Sometimes it's so hard to believe all these things have happened to us—the good and the bad. And I can't believe I won't see Wrightsie again for a long, long time."

"We've got to believe he's with us," Wright said, taking my hand. "He is, you know. And we've got to trust in the Lord. Remember, when Peter said to Jesus, 'You're all we have, Lord.' Well, Nan, He's all we have, all we need."

"Well, I know I couldn't have gotten through this without Him," I said. "How do other people do it—those who don't know Jesus?"

"I'm sure He helps those who don't know Him," Wright answered. "He gave us our house in Texas and I didn't know Him as my Savior then."

"You're right," I said. "And remember the time when we lived in Virginia—and that trailer broke loose from that truck and headed towards us? It's a miracle we weren't all killed."

"Yes," Wright answered. "In fact, I think Jesus has a special love for those people who don't know Him yet."

"But what about the miracles He provided for us—my mother's dream, the word of knowledge He gave to Marge O'Halloran, '. . .grieve not for Wrightsie,' Louise's dream about Wrightsie seeing his own funeral, Psalm 118 in the hotel room, the Marine at the cemetery? Why has He been so good to us?"

"I think He's helped us so much because we gave ourselves to Him so completely," Wright answered. "We knew we couldn't help ourselves so we got off the throne and let Jesus become our King. Then we really asked Him for miracles and believed He'd give 'em to us."

"And maybe He gave the miracles to us because He knew my faith was weak," I suggested with a smile.

"Yes, and that too," Wright said, also smiling.

"Well, I hope He stays with us," I said.

"He will," Wright answered. "If we stay with Him."

"Let's pray, Wright," I said.

Wright took my hand, we lowered our heads and I said, "Thank you, Jesus. Thank you for the strength, thank you for the love, thank you for the miracles. And thank you for your enduring mercy and for taking Wrightsie to heaven. Keep us in your will. Amen."

"Nan!" Wright said, looking up with tears in his eyes. "You are a miracle—to think that you can sit here and thank Jesus for taking your son to heaven. That's the greatest miracle of all!"

"One more thing," I said, lowering my head again. "Jesus, please tell Wrightsie I love him."

Then we walked down the beach and joined Beth, Tom, Hilda and their kids.

Friday, we left Long Island and drove to my parents' home in Danbury, Connecticut. While we were there my folks had a coffee where we met all the loving friends who had prayed for us, and sent so many cards, notes and gifts to Wrightsie.

Saturday afternoon Wright, Beth and I visited with a large family—seven children—whose children were great friends of Beth and Wrightsie. One of the boys in the family was mentally retarded, and he had a special place in the heart of every family member. Many times during Wrightsie's illness I'd thought of his brave mother. The deep love she had for her little retarded son was a great strengthening witness for me.

During our visit we talked about Wrightsie. And I admitted that although Wrightsie was in heaven I would miss him. When we started walking up Seeley Street on our way home, Beth must have remembered this, for she came running up to Wright and me, took our hands and said, "Mom, dad, please don't worry about missing Wrightsie. I'm going to be your daughter and your son; you can call me your 'dauson.' "

"Oh, Bethy," I said as tears flooded my eyes.

Wright hugged Beth and then seriously he said, "Beth, you're the sweetest, most lovable daughter in the world. And that's exactly the way your mom and I want it to be. Our son, your brother, is in heaven and you, our daughter, are here with us. We want you as our daughter."

As we turned the corner onto Deer Hill Avenue and walked to my folks' home on that sunny fall afternoon, we were a close, joyous family.

A few days later my folks drove us to White Plains, New York, to catch a plane for Grandma Flossy's home. During the drive, my mother said with a twinkle in her eye, "Nan, dad and I have been talking and we've decided to join a Pentecostal church in Danbury."

"Wonderful! Wonderful!" I exclaimed.

Then Wright started to laugh. "Isn't that just like the Holy Spirit?"

"What do you mean?" I asked.

"Well, I had it all figured out that Feef would go back to the Roman Catholic Church, your mom would join the Roman Catholic Church and they'd live happily ever after. Then I thought, 'No, maybe Feef will join the Lutheran Church with your mom and they'll live happily ever after. But now they're going to both join a Pentecostal church.

"Thank you, Lord," Wright said. "I hope I've learned something."

We laughed with Wright, then I said, "Mom, dad, if I know Wrightsie, he's tugging at Jesus' hand right now saying, "See, Jesus? What'd I tell you about Gramma and Feef?' "

We spent a restful three days at Grandma Flossy's home in Sinclairville, New York. During our stay we visited Wright Senior's grave in the little cemetery on the outskirts of town.

We said a prayer over the grave then Wright said, "I'll never forget the last time we came here. Remember, Nan, we were reading some of the old tombstone inscriptions down there," and he pointed down the hill. "And we turned around to look at Beth and Wrightsie and they were praying over my dad's grave."

I remembered all right.

When we left Sinclairville, Flossy rode to the airport in Buffalo with us. Before we boarded the plane I said goodbye to Flossy. "Thanks for helping us when Wrightsie came home from Boston. You gave us a lot of extra time to be with him."

Then Flossy said, "Nan, thank you for being so brave."

When we returned home to Arlington, there were tons of mail—wonderful friends had sent notes of sympathy. Many notes pointed up the fact that God can use all situations for the good of His people.

"Wright, listen to this letter," I said, "it's dated September 14, 1972."

"Commander and Mrs. Brunson, To say thank you may seem just a little strange to you at a time of your loss. I only had a few opportunities to meet Wrightsie and it was a real inspiration to observe him during the Cub Scout parade in February. In talking with Wrightsie's cubmaster of Pack 535, I began to realize just how great an influence Wrightsie had on others. It would have been much easier, and certainly socially acceptable, for you and Wrightsie to have stayed home and not participated in scouting; but because you didn't, many Cub Scouts were privileged to witness true bravery in action which will help them throughout life. Unfortunately, we cannot bring Wrightsie back; however, he will be with us in the memory of those who knew him and a challenge to anyone who might be tempted to feel sorry for himself or to give up too easily.

"I think we can truly say Wrightsie lived up to the Cub Scout promise and the law of the pack for he certainly helped make the pack go and the pack to help other scouts to grow. So I just want to say thank you for sharing Wrightsie with us.

"May God continue to bless you."

I read Wright the signature, "Walt Richey—he's the commissioner for the Crosstimbers District, Boy Scouts of America."

We were thrilled with the letter. Then Wright said, "Nan, I think I know that man; he's an engineer with the company where my office is located. When I go back to work I'm going to look him up."

Wright returned to work the next day and when he came home that first evening he said, "Nan, you won't believe what Mr. Richey told me—something more important than he had in his letter."

"What is it?" I asked.

"Well, when he saw Wrightsie riding in Old Ironsides that day during the scout parade, the Lord put an idea into his mind.

"He's going to start a special Boy Scout troop for mentally retarded boys. Isn't that tremendous!"

"Oh, Wright," I exclaimed, "the Lord is still showing us how he used Wrightsie. I've got chills running up and down my spine."

A few days later, Gordon Bell called me. "Nan," he said, "I know the Lord won't mind if I tell you what happened in Wrightsie's bedroom when I prayed for him that Sunday afternoon. Remember I called you back there but then I said, 'Never mind. Never mind'?"

"Yes," I answered.

"Well," Gordon explained, "I was sitting on the bed praying when the Lord said, 'Commit his spirit to me.'

"I jumped up from the bed and called, 'Nan? Nan!' and that's when I felt and heard a loud pop in the small of my back.

"By the time you came to the bedroom, I realized what the Lord had told me was for me alone. So that's why I didn't have anything to say to you.

"And as for my back—I'd had back problems for years but I don't any longer."

Then Gordon said apologetically, "I probably shouldn't be telling you this now—my back is nothing compared to Wrightsie. I wish—I prayed that the Lord would take me instead."

"Oh, I know, I know, Gordon," I said. "Many wonderful people like you prayed that the Lord would take them instead of Wrightsie, but that's not what He wanted. No, Wrightsie got an early reward."

The second week we were home in Texas, Wright and I attended the Arlington Wednesday night prayer meeting at Mike and Marge O'Halloran's home. We both witnessed to the miracles that had occurred, but when we drove home that night I felt very down.

Wright drove the car into the garage and I said, "Well, it's over. Who wants to hear about a dead boy? And besides we probably won't hear from the Lord for twenty more years."

I had trouble getting to sleep that night, yet I was in a deep sleep when the phone startled me awake at seven o'clock the next morning.

As I groped for the phone I heard the bathroom shower running and realized Wright was getting ready for work.

I found the phone on my night stand and said, "Hello."

"Mrs. Brunson?" a woman's voice asked, apologetically. "Yes?"

"Mrs. Brunson," she continued in a relieved, yet hurried, tone of voice, "Please forgive me for calling so early, but I've been waiting since about three this morning to talk with you; the Lord woke me up at three and gave me a message to give to you."

Then she paused a moment, and said, "Maybe I'd better introduce myself first."

She gave me her name and explained, "You probably don't remember me, but Marge O'Halloran introduced us last night at the prayer meeting.

"I hope you don't think I'm some sort of a religious fanatic," she apologized, "because I know this message came from the Lord. You see, He used me once this way before. And just like this morning He woke me up about three and He told me to give a message to a woman I barely knew. I didn't know the meaning behind the message and I reluctantly called the woman and explained the circumstances. Then I gave her the message, 'Don't grieve over Robert; he's with me.'

"Later, I found out that her son, Robert, had been killed in a plane crash some eight weeks earlier."

Then the caller continued, saying, "Mrs. Brunson, like I said before—I barely knew the woman, I didn't know about her son and I didn't know about the plane crash and I didn't know what the Lord's message meant.

"Now, I know about your son but I don't know the meaning of the message He gave me for you, but here it is—I wrote it down: 'Be not regretful, for where your heart is there you may be also.' "

My heart quickened and I felt a definite sense of awe mixed with a twinge of guilt—guilt over my thoughts and comment of the night before. I knew exactly what the Lord meant. His message was a loving, yet firm, and unmistakable warning.

I thanked the woman, hung up the phone, got down on my knees beside the bed and prayed, "Thank you, Jesus. Thank you."

Confessed, "Forgive me, Lord."

And promised, "I won't forget. Amen."

For free information on how to receive
the international magazine

**LOGOS JOURNAL**

with NATIONAL COURIER update
also Book Catalog

Write: Information - LOGOS JOURNAL CATALOG
Box 191
Plainfield, NJ 07061